Water Resources Management

Realities and Challenges

Water Resources Management

Realities and Challenges

Edited by

Professor K. Nageswara Rao
Vice-President
The Indian Economic Association

New Century Publications
New Delhi, India

NEW CENTURY PUBLICATIONS
4800/24, Bharat Ram Road,
Ansari Road, Daryaganj,
New Delhi - 110 002
Tel.: 23247798, 55396605
Telefax: 011-41017798
E-mail: indiatax@vsnl.com
www.newcenturypublications.com

Editorial office:
34, Gujranwala Town, Part-2,
Delhi - 110 009
Tel.: 27247805, 27464774

First Published 2006

ISBN: 81-7708-106-3

Published by New Century Publications and printed at Singhal Print Media, New Delhi -110 005

PRINTED IN INDIA

About the Book

Water is a prime natural resource, a basic human need and a precious national asset. Planning, development and management of water resources need to be governed by national perspectives. Ecological concern is not merely an environmental concern but also calls for prudent use of water resources.

Planning and implementation of water resources projects involve a number of socio-economic aspects and issues such as environmental sustainability, appropriate resettlement and rehabilitation of project-affected people and livestock, public health concerns of water impoundment, dam safety etc.

Economic development has posed certain challenges for the planners and administrators, associated with the allocation and distribution of water resources.

This book presents views and opinions of experts regarding conservation and effective utilization of water resources that are fast becoming scarce in their availability. The gravity of the problem, the realities and consequences on the present and future generations is a well-recognized fact which calls for rational utilization of water resources. Watershed management through extensive soil conservation, catchment-area treatment, preservation of forests and increasing the forest cover and the construction of check-dams should be promoted. The contributors in the book include experts in drought studies, environmental studies, public utility studies, agriculture and watershed management areas. The articles discuss elaborately the realities in the utilisation and challenges for effective allocation of water resources. The suggestions based on the micro level studies are of immense relevance and would be useful for policy formulation and practical implementation of the programmes.

The book would prove useful for researchers, policy makers, academicians, environmentalists and students.

Editor's Profile

Professor K. Nageswara Rao obtained his Ph.D degree in economics from Sri Krishnadevaraya University, Anantapur, Andhra Pradesh and has twenty seven years of teaching and research experience at the University level. His areas of specialisation include public economics and Indian economic development. He has carried out six research projects and submitted reports to UGC, ICSSR and Government of Andhra Pradesh in different areas.

Professor Rao has published one book and edited thirteen books including three text books for under-graduate students. He has forty six published research papers to his credit. He was also the recipient of Andhra Pradesh Government Award for University Teachers in 2002.

Professor Rao served as Head, Department of Economics, Chairman, Board of studies and is currently the Co-ordinator, UGC Special Assistance Programme and Dean, Faculty of Social Sciences, Sri Krishnadevaraya University, Anantapur, Andhra Pradesh. He served as the sub-editor of Indian Economic Journal and was the executive member of Indian Economic Association from Andhra Pradesh for six years. Presently, Professor Rao is Vice-President, Indian Economic Association.

FOREWORD

Disaster preparedness was in the past viewed only in terms of relief and rehabilitation after the event took place. Current thinking realizes that there is much more to disaster management, especially strategies which need to be in place and measures taken before the event to mitigate the effects of disasters.

In the words of Brandt Commission, sustainable development is that which "meets the needs of the present without compromising the ability of future generations." Water is a must for the existence of mankind or for that matter any living being. As a matter of fact, agricultural development was originally confined to irrigated areas only. Gradually, it has spread to other areas also. Rain-fed agriculture accounts for 70 per cent of the total cultivable land and contributes 40 per cent to total agricultural production in India.

Apart from agriculture, water is required for drinking and other purposes. Linking of rivers is one of the alternatives to meet these needs of the people. The rainfall, which is the primary source of fresh water in the country, is confined to 90-100 days of monsoon season. The country is supposed to receive about 4,000 bcm of water as precipitation annually. The rainfall varies from 10 cms. in the western parts of Rajasthan to over 1000 cms. in Cherapunji in Meghalaya and with varying degrees in other parts of the country. India is often affected by drought-flood-drought syndrome.

Macro and micro studies relating to various facets of irrigation have been carried out not only in the country as a whole, but also in various States of South India. Watershed as an approach to development was adopted in the U.S. in Tennessee Valley for reducing soil erosion in the Valley areas during early 1920s. The history of watershed management in India started in 1880 with the Report of the Famine Commission and then with the Report of the Royal Commission in 1928.

In this volume there are 31 papers dealing with not only Water Resources Management, but also covering environmental impact, interlinking of rivers, drought prone areas, watershed development, role of women in water management etc. All of them are not only exhaustive but informative too. The credit for organizing such a Herculean task on a very important and topical subject goes to Dr. K. Nageswara Rao. I wholeheartedly congratulate him for this and hope many more studies of this nature will be undertaken in future also.

Professor B. Satyanaryan,
Chairman, Third State Finance Commission
Andhra Pradesh, Hyderabad

Editor's Note on the Book

Climate, culture and natural resources were once thought to be the keys to economic development. Later on, thinking on development shifted repeatedly during the last forty years and it has been realised that economic progress must look beyond growth in per capita income — towards reduction in poverty and promoting greater equity, towards progress in education, health and nutrition and towards protection of environment, including water resources. Hence, development of an economy has become a challenge for the planners and administrators associated with the allocation and distribution of water resources for furthering improvement in the quality of life.

The World Commission on Environment noted, "The heaviest burden in international economic adjustment has been carried by the world's poorest population. The consequence has been the considerable increase in human distress and over exploitation of land and water resources to ensure survival in the short term.. Further, our desire to solve all social and human problems at one stroke has influenced the pace of development. Its reaction is visible in the atmosphere and in our natural, physical and social environment. Awareness regarding the consequences of this event has developed into a consensus referred to as 'ecological concern'.

Ecological concern is not merely an environmental concern but also calls for an effective use of water resources. In view of the vital importance of water for human and animal life, for maintaining ecological balance and for economic and developmental activities of all kinds, and considering its increasing scarcity, the planning and management of this resource and its optimal, economical and equitable use has become a matter of utmost urgency. Concerns of the community need to be taken into account for water resources development and management. The success of the National Water Policy will depend entirely on evolving and maintaining a national consensus and commitment to its underlying principles and objectives.

However, the solution to our long-run socio-economic problems should not ignore water resource depletion and ecological balance. Further, Government intervention to protect the ground water is necessary for sustainable development.

Conjunctive use of water resources may change the acceptable size and dimensions of irrigation, specifically in the drought prone areas. From an ecological point of view, this may lend a new significance and status to irrigation requirements.

It is estimated that one-sixth of the population in India, with 40 per cent of the cultivated area, lives in drought prone areas. These areas miss the priorities of planned development and experience the problems of environmental imbalance. Recurring droughts have left devastating impact on these areas in the form of depletion of water resources and deprivation of the dependent people on ground water. In view of this, there is the need to create awareness among the public about efficient management of available water resources.

Water resource development projects should, as far as possible, be planned and developed as multi-purpose projects. Provision for drinking water should be a primary consideration.

Professor K. Nageswara Rao
Anantapur, Andhra Pradesh

Contributors

A. Muralidhar Rao
Department of Economics,
University College for Women,
Koti,
Hyderabad

A. Ranga Reddy,
Department of Economics,
Sri Venkateswara University,
Tirupati

B. Sambasiva Rao,
Department of Economics,
Acharya Nagarjuna University,
Guntur

B. Saranga Pani,
Lecturer in Economics,
The Hindu College,
Machlipatnam

C. Basavaiah,
Department of Economics,
S. V. U. P.G. Centre,
Kavali

C. Bhupathi,
Lecturer in Commerce,
Thigarajar College,
M.K.University,
Madurai

D. Chenna Reddy,
Department of Rural Development,
Sri Krishnadevaraya University,
Anantapur

Dhulasi Birundha Varadarajan,
Department of Economics,
M. K. University,
Madurai

D. Kailasa Rao,
Department of Economics,
Acharya Nagarjuna University,
Nagarjuna Nagar,
Guntur

D. Krishnamoorthy,
Department of Economics,
Sri Venkateswara University,
Tirupati

D. Sreenivasa Rao,
Department of Economics,
Sri Krishnadevaraya University,
Anantapur

G.B. Franklin,
Department of Economics,
Acharya Nagarjuna University,
Nagarjuna Nagar,
Guntur

G. Chandrasekar Rao,
Department of Economics,
Sri Venkateswara University,
Tirupati

G. Mallikarjun,
Department of Economics,
Kakatiya University,
Warangal

G. Jaya Raju,
Department of Economics,
Sri Krishnadevaraya University,
Anantapur

G. Satyanarayana,
Department of Economics,
Sri Krishnadevaraya University,
Anantapur

G. Sivaiah,
Department of Economics,
Sri Krishnadevaraya University,
Anantapur

G. Sreedhar,
Department of Rural Development,
Sri Krishnadevaraya University,
Anantapur

G. Venkata Naidu,
Department of Economics,
Sri Krishnadevaraya University,
Anantapur

K. Dasaratha Ramaiah,
Department of Economics,
Sri Krishnadevaraya University,
Anantapur

K. Nagendra Reddy,
Department of Rural Development,
Sri Krishnadevaraya University,
Anantapur

K. Nageswara Rao,
Department of Economics,
Sri Krishnadevaraya University,
Anantapur

Manu Mahesh
Department of Economics,
Mysore University P.G.Centre,
Mandya,
Karnataka

M.D. Umesh,
Department of Economics,
Mysore University P.G.Centre,
Mandya,
Karnataka

M.G. Basava Raja,
Department of Economics,
Mysore University P.G.Centre,
Mandya
Karnataka

M. Krishna Naidu,
Department of Economics,
Sri Krishnadevaraya University,
Anantapur

M. Lakshmi Narasaiah,
Department of Economics,
S.K.U.P.G.Centre,
Kurnool

Mohd. Iqbal Ali,
Mr. G. Mallikarjun,
Department of Economics,
Kakatiya University,
Warangal

M. Rajaduraj,
Department of Economics,
M. K. University,
Madurai

M. Ramanjaneyulu,
Department of Economics,
Bangalore University,
Bangalore

M. Ramesh,
Department of Economics,
A.N.U.P.G.Centre,
Etcherla,
Srikakulam

M. Reddi Ramu,
Department of Economics,
Sri Krishnadevaraya University,
Anantapur

M. Sambasiva Rao,
Department of Geography,
Sri Krishnadevaraya University,
Anantapur

M. Sankara Reddi,
Department of Economics,
A.N.U.P.G.Centre,
Etcherla,
Srikakulam

M.S. Kallur,
Department of Economics,
Gulbarga University,
Gulbarga

M. Syamala,
Department of Economics,
Acharya Nagarjuna University,
Guntur

M. Sundara Rao,
Department of Economics,
A.N.U.P.G.Centre,
Etcherla,
Srikakulam

M. Thyagaraju,
Research Scholar,
Department of Management,
Sri Krishnadevaraya University,
Anantapur

M.V. Narasimha Sarma,
Department of Economics,
Acharya Nagarjuna University,
Nagarjuna Nagar,
Guntur

M.V. Raghavulu,
Department of Economics,
Sri Krishnadevaraya University,
Anantapur

N. Ravindra Babu,
Department of Rural Development,
Sri Krishnadevaraya University,
Anantapur

N. Saraswathy,
Department of Economics,
M. K. University,
Madurai

N. Sreedhar,
Department of Economics,
S.K.U.P.G.Centre,
Kurnool

P. Dhavamani,
Department of Economics,
V.H.N.S.N. College,
Virudhunagar

P. Ramappa,
Department of Economics,
Sri Krishnadevaraya University,
Anantapur

P. Regina Devi,
Department of Economics,
M. K. University,
Madurai

R. Kuruppa Swamy,
Lecturer in Commerce,
Thigarajar College,
M.K.University,
Madurai

R. Ramudu,
Department of Economics,
S.K.U.P.G.Centre,
Kurnool

S. Lakshmi Narayana,
Department of Geography,
Sri Krishnadevaraya University,
Anantapur

S. Mani Kandan,
Department of Economics,
M. K. University,
Madurai

T. Narayana Reddy,
Department of Economics,
Sri Krishnadevaraya University,
Anantapur

T. Ramesh
Department of Economics,
Mysore University P.G.Centre,
Mandya,
Karnataka

T. Vijaya Kumar,
Department of Economics,
V.H.N.S.N. College,
Virudhunagar

T.V. Seshaiah,
Department of Economics,
S.K.U.P.G.Centre,
Kurnool

U. Sankara,
Department of Economics,
Sri Krishnadevaraya University,
Anantapur

Contents

1

Interlinking of Rivers in India

G. Satyanarayana, M.V. Raghavulu and M.Reddi Ramu

The idea of the 'linking of rivers', dormant for a long time, has acquired new prominence now, particularly in the context of the acute form that the Cauvery dispute has taken, as well as the prevailing drought in several parts of the country. In response to a public interest litigation (PIL), the Supreme Court has decreed that the rivers of India shall be linked within ten years, and has directed that a Task Force should be set up for working out the modalities.

Three questions arise: first, whether the Supreme Court was right in issuing this direction: secondly, why the Government responded with such alacrity and enthusiasm; and thirdly, whether the idea of 'linking of rivers' is a sound one on merits. There are many different ways in which the future drinking water needs of the people can be met, and the linking of rivers is only one of the ideas mooted in this context. Moreover, it is by no means clear that there is a direct link between the right to water and the linking of rivers.

The 'human right' to water is invoked in the context of water as life-support, i.e., drinking water. Drinking water is only a small part of total water needs. The really large demands for water usually arise in the context of irrigation which accounts for upwards of 80 per cent of our usable water resources. It is for meeting those huge demands that big project—large dams, long – distance water transfers, the linking of rivers etc. was mooted. Thus, the link with human rights that justifies judicial activism cannot be invoked in aid of a direction for the linking or rivers. The Supreme Court seems to have assumed that the linking of rivers was an accepted idea that has been languishing for decades for want of attention and action.

The linking of rivers did not figure in the Ninth plan, and so far as one know, the Tenth plan document now awaiting release does not mention it; a reference may of course be added now. The Report of the National Commission for Integrated Water Resources Development Plan (NCIWRDP) 1999 did not make any major recommendations in this regard; we shall return to this. The Prime Minister's address to the National Water Resources Council (NWRC) commending the National Water Policy (NWP) 2002 for adoption did not refer to it. Thus, it is clear that the Government did not have any river- linking project on the anvil. The idea is doubtless and old one, but there have always been doubts about its soundness and practicability.

Rationale for Interlinking of Rivers

India is facing the problem of water both in quantity and quality. The rainfall, which is the primary source of fresh water in the country, is confined to 90-100 days of monsoon season. The country receives about 4000 bcm of water as precipitation annually, a large part of which in the Himalayan catchments of the Ganga-Brahmaputra-Meghana-Basin. The rainfall varies from 10 cm in the western parts of Rajasthan to over 1000 cm at Cherapunji in Meghalaya as well as in the western ghats of Southern India. The spatial and temporal variations in the precipitation over India often lead to immense human sufferings through floods, drought, scarcity of water etc, and the country in affected by drought- flood –drought syndrome. Nearly one-third area of the country is droughts prone where water is not available even for drinking purpose during the summer season. The rationale behind the interlinking of rivers is based on the view that the transfer of water from water surplus river basins to deficit-water river basins would provide a permanent solution to the problem of floods, drought and water scarcity.

Proposed Rivers for Interlinking in India

The Himalayan component envisages a number of links that need not be detailed here. The general idea is to transfer water form the Brahmaputra and Ganga systems westwards to southern Uttar Pradesh, Haryana, Punjab and Rajasthan, and perhaps eventually southwards to the peninsular component. As data relating to difficult to study these proposals

Kosi- Mechi, Kosi-Ghagra, Gandak-Ganga, Ghagra-Yamuna, Sarda-Yamuna, Yamuna-Rajasthan, Rajasthan-Sabarmati, chimer-Sone Barrage, Sone Dam—Southern Tributaries of Ganga, Brahmaputra—Ganga, Farakka—Sunderbans, Ganga—Damodar—Subamarekha, Subamarekha—Mahanadi.

The peninsular rivers component involves a number of links of which the most important would be those connecting Mahanadi, Godavari, Krishna, Pennar and Cauvery. The details are given in Table 1.1.

Need for Interlinking of River

The National Water Commission has estimated the total water requirements of the country in the year 2050 would be about 973 bcm on the lower side and 1180 bcm on the upper side depending upon the actual population growth. However the Union Ministry of Water resources on the basis of other studies has estimated the 'countries' water requirement to be around 1093 bcm for the year 2025 and about 1447 bcm for the year 2050.

According to the latest world Development Report (2004) of the World Bank, Delhi and Chennai on the average get barely two hours of water supply daily while cities like Beijing. Hong Kong and Bangkok have nearly 24 hours of water supply.

The present utilization from surface and ground water is about 63 percent and 37 percent respectively of the total utilized water resources. The present extent and pattern of water utilization for various purposes is as under (Table 1.2).

Table 1.1

S.No.	Name of Link	From River	To River	Annual volume of Transfer (mm3)
1.	Manibhadra to Dowleswaram	Mahandadi	Godavari	11,176 (6,500)
2.	Inchampalli to Nagarjunasagar	Godavari	Krishna	16,426 (14,2000)
3.	Inchampalli to pulichintala	Godavari	Krishna	4,371
4.	Polavaram to Vijayawada	Godavari	Krishna	4,903 (3,305)
5.	Almatti to pennar	Krishna	Pennar	1,980
6.	Srisailam to pennar	Krishna	Pennar	2,310 2,095
7.	Nagarjunasagar to Somasila	Krishna	Pennar	12,146 (8,648)
8.	Srisailam to Grand Anicut	Pennar	Cauvery	8,565 (3,855)
9.	Kattalai regulator to Vaigi to Gundar	Cauvery	Vaigai	2,252

Source: NCIWRDP's Report, September 1996.

Since the total water requirement of the country would barely match or may even exceeds the present utilizable water resources there is need for both water conservation of what is available and further augmentation of usable water resources.

The tentative assessment for the future water requirement for various sectors as assessed is presented in Table 1.3.

Table 1.2: Purpose-wise Utilization of Water Resources

Purpose	**Present utilizations (bcm)**
Irrigation	501
Domestic	30
Industrial	20
Energy	20
Others	34
	605

Source: National Water Development Agency.

Table 1.3: Future Demand of Water

Purpose	Year 2010 (bcm)	Year 2025 (bcm)
Irrigation	688	910
Domestic	56	73
Industrial	12	23
Energy	5	15
Others	52	72
Total	813	1093

Source: National Water Development Agency.

Beyond 2025 augmentation of the resources would be imperative through means that are presently conventional.

Since irrigation for agricultural purpose claims major part of available water (around 68 per cent for the country as a whole). There has to be greater efforts in economy and efficiency of water used in the sector. Nearly 51 per cent of irrigation is based on ground water. The present irrigation efficiency in the country is estimated to between 30 to 40 per cent and can improve to around 65 to 70 per cent with better practices.

The cultivable areas of the country are estimated to be about 186 mha out of which about 142 mha is under cultivation. The production of food grains, which was just about 51 million tones (mt) in 1950-51, has increase to more than 210 million tones at present. This has resulted in the country becoming self-sufficient in food production in the country. With the rise in population and industrialization mounting of more pressure on land is expected that cultivation areas will stabilize at 140-45 mha which requires water in sufficient quantity. To meet the water requirement of their cultivable land inter linking of river is necessary.

The safe drinking water is essential for sustenance of life. By March 2000, about 92 per cent of urban population has been covered by safe drinking water. Drinking water requirement of most of mega cities are met form reservoir of irrigation of multipurpose schemes existing nearby or even by long distance transfers.

Only 77 of the 299 class-one cities have 100 per cent water supply coverage. 203 of the 345 class-two towns have low per capita supply of less the 100 litre per capita per day.

Nearly 97 per cent of the total rural habitations have been provided access to the save drinking from nearly 3 million hand pumps and stand-post and about 0.11 million and regional piped water supply schemes. More than 85 per cent of rural water supply is ground water based.

Benefits from the Interlinking of Rivers

The project of interlinking of rivers (ILR) in India is expected to provide multidimensional benefits. The expected benefits from ILR are augmentation of irrigation facilities, potable water supply for rural and urban area, industrial water supply, more generation of hydropower inland navigation, ecological up gradation due to minimum flow guarantee in rivers, sizeable employment generation, flood and drought mitigation, increased tree farming and many other indirect benefits. It is a programme for greening

India, for providing much needed hydropower, for navigation along water ways, for arresting desertification, for water for our parched land, for food, growth, employment and prosperity. Following benefits are expected to accrue during the implementation and after the completion of the projects:

1. Control of Floods: The country is experiencing severe floods in some pacts while severe drought in some areas due to variations in rainfall over time and space. The Brahmaputra and the Ganga rivers carry about 60 per cent of total water resources of the country. The fury of flood causes heavy losses in the entire region of these river valleys and the annual average financial loss approximates Rs. 1343 crores. The interlinking project will prove effective in reducing the severity of floods besides causing recharging of ground and underground water with the help of canals.

2. Mitigation of Drought: Transfer of surplus water, which runs waste in to the sea, from flood prone areas to drought prone areas-especially in Rajasthan and Gujarat, will help to mitigate the severity of drought. An area of about 25 lakh hectare in most of the big states is likely to reap the benefits of drought reduction. The project will also reduce the inequalities in the distribution of renewable water resources and thus reduce the regional imbalance in the availability of water in different river basins of India.

3. Boost to Agri-Business Activities: The inter-linking project will help boost the Agri-Business activities such as fisheries, bee keeping, horticulture etc. Of late these activities are attracting the attention of planner's in the wake of globalisation. Most of the link canals will be 50 to 100 mt wide and more then 6 mt deep. The reservoir, filled with fresh water would boost the practice of Pisciculture and Aquaculture.

4. Expansion of Irrigation Facilities: The ILR will provide additional irrigation facilities to 35 million hectare-25 million (ha) from surface water and 10 million (ha) by increased use of ground water apart from the benefits of flood control, drought mitigation, navigation, salinity and pollution control etc. This 35 million ha of irrigation will be in addition to the ultimate irrigation potential of 140 million ha.

5. Increase in Hydro Power Generation Capacity: The storage dams proposed for interlinking of rivers would also generate huge hydropower to the tune of 3400 MW (Installed capacity).

6. Increase in Domestic and Industrial Water Supply: The interlinking project also proposes to augment domestic and industrial water supply to the metropolitan cities and several other towns and villages enroute of the link canals. This will also facilitate inland navigation from the north to the south as most of the link canal would be 100 m wide and 6 m deep.

7. Encouragement to Allied Agricultural Activities: The ILR scheme by providing additional irrigation 'facilities to agriculture will not only help increase agricultural production but also enable farmers to raise diversified crops and to undertake allied activities such as dairying, fishing, etc. Irrigated agriculture would also lead to the establishment of agro-industries and some other activities such as transport, marketing, storage, banking, insurance etc. would also be promoted.

8. Increase in Employment Opportunities: Construction of canals, storage dams, long canal, tunnels, cross drainage structures etc. under ILR Programme would require huge manpower. Increased demand for construction materials, machinery, equipment etc, will lead to massive industrialization. All these will result in enormous employment opportunities. Besides, implementation of ILR programme will increase intensive agricultural activities with higher crop intensity providing engagement people engaged in agriculture throughout the year.

9. Help in Solving the Problem of Water Scarcity: India is faced with the regime of stress as the per capita availability of water has declined from about 5177 bcm in 1951 to 1869 bcm in 2001. And given the rise in population by 2025, the per capita availability is likely to drop below 1000 bcm and this situation will be treated as that of water scarcity. ILR proposal would help in solving this vital problem of water scarcity.

10. Augmentation of Utilizable Water: India receives and annual precipitation of 4000 bcm out of which 1869 bcm appears as run off in various river basins.

Against this, the utilizable water resources haves been estimated at 1132 bcm. Hence it is necessary to find our ways for augmentation of utilizable water and one important option is the implementation of ILR Programme.

Conclusion

Prosperity of the Indian Agriculture lies in the speedy measures taken to interlinking rivers in India. Interlinking of rivers is a social emotional, Economic environmental and Engineering issue.

Politicians in India belonging to different states and parties must rise above the narrow politics feeling and have to show true statesmanship by way of supporting the implementation of the Supreme Court's direction of interlinking rivers in India by 2010, thereby satisfying the water requirements for all the stated purposes to improve the quality of life in the country.

References

1. Ramaswamy R. Iyer, "Water: Perspectives, Issues, Concerns" (2000), Sage Publications India Pvt. Ltd., New Delhi.

2. Chauhan, B.R., "Settlement of International and Inter-State Water Disputes in India", under the auspices of the Indian Law Institute, N.M.Tripathi Pvt..Ltd., Bombay, 1992.

3. Petrella, Ricardo, "The Water Manifesto", (2001), Zed Books, London.

4. Planning Commission, "Report of the Committee on the Pricing of Irrigation Water", New Delhi, 1992.

5. Sir Cyril S .Fox, "Water", The Technical Press Ltd., London.

6. Thomas Dunne and Luna B. Leopold, "Water in Environmental Planning", W.H. Freeman and Company, San Francisco.

7. Ruddar Dutt, and K.P.M. Sundharam, "Indian Economy", S. Chand & Company Limited, New Delhi, 2004.

2

Participation of People in Watershed Management

B. Sambasiva Rao and M. Syamala

Water is the main source and substance of life. It is very essential for realizing the full potential of the agricultural sector and country's development.

During the recent years, water has become a matter of important subject for the National level planning and plan formulation, which led to the establishment of National Water Resources Council as a national apex body. In a country like India, the best way through which a society can progress are by increasing the productivity of the economic activities. Raising the productivity of irrigated and rainfed agriculture combined with soil and water conservation techniques is essential for faster development. India being an agrarian country depends a great deal on natural resources for production of food and economic development of the rural areas. In several parts of India a number of initiatives have been taken by local communities regarding water harvesting and watershed development.

Watershed, a natural entity in itself, combines forest management, land use management and water management. It is hydrologic and physiographic unit that offers a very good base for planning and implementing soil conservation, water harvesting, afforestation and environmental protection programs. Watershed is defined as a natural hydrological entity that covers a specific area expansion of land surface with in boundaries the entire rainfall-run off ultimately passes through a specifically defined stream. From the scientific perspective, a watershed is defined as the drainage areas of a stream. Water development and management should be based on a participatory approach, involving users, planners and policy makers at all levels. It means that the decision taken at the lowest appropriate levels, with full public consultation and involvement of users in the planning and implementation of water projects. Women play a central part in the provision management and safeguarding of water.

In the post Green-Revolution period the thrust of Indian Agriculture is on enhancement of agricultural productivity through sustainable practices. To achieve this end, one of the major initiatives undertaken by the Government of India was the implementation of a national level project/program for the development of rainfed areas through the watershed approach. The watershed Approach aimed at augmentation and stabilization of production and productivity, minimizing ecological degradation, reduction in regional disparity, opening up of greater opportunities for employment of rural poor in the rainfed areas. A similar approach has been adopted for developing the more resource areas-drought prone, desert and wastelands-and to provide sustainable means of livelihood to the rural poor in these areas.

A 25-Years perspective plan for holistic and integrated development of rainfed areas, prepared by the planning Commission, envisages treatment of about 63 million hectares of land involving an estimated outlay of Rs.76,000 crore through various watershed development projects/programs. These include the watershed development projects of the three Central Ministries (Agriculture, Rural Development, Environment and Forest) as well as several externally aided projects. For some time now the need has been felt to bring about convergence and harmonization in the implementation of various watershed development projects. However, this has not been possible so far as the aims and objectives of these projects are different and the watershed approach-because it is holistic, scientific and sustainable has been adopted under these projects to achieve their varied objectives.

The latter include development of degraded arable rainfed areas, desert and drought prone areas, wastelands, catchments of

River Valley Projects and Flood prone Rivers, reclamation of alkaline soils and ravine lands, shifting cultivation areas etc. While some of these projects had a very specialized focus resulting in special norms as well as delivery mechanisms geared to meet those needs, the six major projects/programs, namely National Watershed Development project for Rainfed Areas (NWDPRA), Watershed Development in Shifting Cultivation Areas (WDSCA), Drought Prone Areas Program (DPAP), Desert Development program (DDP), Integrated Wasteland Development project (IWDP), Employment Assurance Scheme (EAS) had elements of convergence and a considerable common geographical area of operation.

The following specific steps may be considered while promoting equity under the watershed program:

a) Focus on development of poor quality and marginal lands owned by resource poor families.
b) Preferential allocation of usufruct rights over produce from the developed common land to landless households / women groups.
c) Equitable right to all households in any new water resource developed under the project.
d) Construction of new water harvesting structures near the land/ recharged wells including drinking water wells owned by resource poor.
e) Groundwater to be treated as a common property resource.
f) Equal employment opportunities and wage rates for implementation of watershed works.
g) Due emphasis on livelihood support systems for landless households.
h) Utilizing the services of the landless poor and women in the post-project management of common property resources.

Objectives of water shed management programs:

- To promote the economic development of the village community, which directly or indirectly depends on the watershed.

- To encourage restoration of ecological balance in the villages through sustained community action for the operation and maintenance of assets created and further development of the potential of natural resources in this area which promotes easy and affordable technological solutions and institutional arrangements that make use of the available knowledge.
- Special emphasis on improving the economic and social conditions of the poor and the disadvantaged sections of the community concerned.
- More equitable distribution of the benefits of land and water resources development and the consequent biomass production.
- Greater access income generating opportunities and focus on their human resources development.
- Employment generation and development of other human resources in the villages in order to promote savings and other income generation activities.

Watershed as a scientific unit has been accepted the world over for area development because of following advantages:

1. Water resource utilization, which is mot crucial in DPAP & DDP areas, is best optimized through basin-wide management.
2. As the water resource component is analogous to the blood systems in animal bodies, it provides the best method to diagnose the state of natural resources in a given watershed.
3. Fluctuation in water regime is mot widely inter-related to the other objectives of area based development.

If the degradation of the resource base is more or less similar in more than one micro watershed, the following criteria may be used in selecting the priority watershed.

-Scarcity of drinking water

-Larger population of SCs/STs.

-Preponderance of common lands

-Watersheds where actual wages are significantly lower than the minimum wages.

For watershed program to be successful people's participation is very important. The participatory watershed Development projects focus on regeneration of the catchments basin if a stream or river system. Treatments comprised developing forests, pasture lands, raising soil conservation measures and building water-harvesting structures along watercourses. The participatory watershed Development program is the conversation and regeneration of an entire catchment area of a drainage line through different physical and vegetation measures. These programs may also result in a doubling of the annual yields as well as in adopting improved technologies, diversified land use pattern and other economic activities like dairy development programs.

Growing recognition of the need for a more holistic perspective for water resource Underlies increasing calls for adopting watershed approaches. Watershed development is attracting considerable attention because it is central to any strategy to develop rain fed agriculture or improve natural resource management. The National watershed Development programme for Rainfed Agriculture was initiated largely to extend the benefits of green revolution to the rainfed areas. The government is also under the consideration to improve the performance of watershed development programmes. Lack of participation of people is very poor, which is a primary reason for the poor outcome of watershed development in India. Community participation is defined here as people acting in-groups to influence the direction and outcome of development programmes that affect them.

The total geographical area of our country is 3290.00 lakh hectares. While at one end 50% of our lands are degraded, at the other, nearly 40% of our people are poor or below poverty line. With proper planning, scientific approach and efficient management it is possible to increase the productivity of the degraded lands, while creating huge employment opportunities for the poor. It is now firmly believed that the development of degraded lands is an important input required for eradication of poverty. In order to combat the frequent recurrence of drought in states, Drought prone Area programme (DPAP) was introduced during the year 1975, as a Centrally Sponsored Scheme (CSS) with matching state share of 50:50. Integrated Wasteland Development Programme (IWDP) was introduced during the year 1991 with 100% central assistance. The wasteland development programmes taken up before April 1995 had not performed well, mainly because they had been planned and implemented on departmental basis by government officials and in isolated patches, without any regard for the complete micro-watershed principle or with people's participation.

Traditionally, India depends on agriculture and the Indian farmers themselves maintained the watershed like ponds, tanks and other irrigation systems for centuries. The importance of micro watershed development was recognized and is being practiced in the country since 1973 due to the recommendations of the task force in Integrated Development or Drought prone Areas. The farmers and villages themselves undertook the program through direct participation. Watershed Development program is also described as a program that holds the key to solve problems of employment, economy, ecology, export and equity. Water shed Development program in India, at this stage of around 50 years of development, appears both fantastic and also frightening.

Watershed Management in Andhra Pradesh

Andhra Pradesh is the fifth largest state if India, both in terms of area and population. The program of dry land development in Andhra Pradesh have undergone a major change from 1995-96 with the introduction of new watershed guidelines, based on the recommendations of Dr. Hanumantha Rao's Committee Report. The main principle adopted in the guidelines lays special emphasis on the active mobilization and participation of the stakeholders in the program including planning, implementation and subsequent management. A great opportunity exists for improving the productivity, profitability and sustainability of dry farming areas through social mobilization. Rainfed agriculture to become productive should be based on watershed as the unit of development. Watershed is not a technology but a concept, which integrates conservation, management and budgeting of rain water through simple but discreet hydrological units. Simultaneously, a watershed supports a holistic framework which means the combined application of technologies on soil and water conservation with improved crop varieties, farming systems and agronomic management, taking in to account both arable and non-farm land. Water resource development, management, harvesting and equity in sharing, forms the nucleus of watershed development. With assured availability of water, farmers are motivated to accept more profitable, sustainable and innovative farming systems. Water availability has also catalyzed the adoption and spread of value-added activities in the entire area of the watershed, such as horticulture. Cropping systems need to be tailored to suit different rainfall-cum-soil zones. Watershed development is the only solution to ensure drought proofing and to mitigate the distress caused by frequent droughts.

A massive programme for development of all the degraded lands in Andhra Pradesh in ten years period was launched during 1997. The ten year action plan for development includes wastelands, degraded lands (i.e. dry lands which are being cultivated under rain-fed conditions) and degraded reserve forests. It is envisaged to develop 100.00 lakh hectares of degraded and wastelands (17.25 lakh ha. By Forest department, 4.55 lakh ha. By Agriculture Department and 78.20 lakh ha. By Rural Development Department), with an outlay of about Rs.4000.00 crores from 1997-2007 at the rate of 10.00 lakh hectares every year by the Department of Rural Development, Forest and Agriculture. About 38.19 lakh hectares every year by the Department of Rural Development, Forest and Agriculture. About 38.19 lakh hectares have been covered through 8618 watersheds, which is the largest number in the whole country. NABARD has sanctioned 1234 RIDF projects covering treatment of an area of 2.63 lakh hectares with Rs. 133.99 Crores to 22 districts during 2000-2001.

The Government of Andhra Pradesh has released an amount of Rs. 95.58 crores up to November 2003. An amount of Rs. 97.82 crores has been utilised up to November 2003. NABARD has sanctioned 290 SMC projects under RIDF VIII, soil and moisture conservation projects during 2002-03 for Rs. 35.33 Crores to Rural Development and other sector to 17 districts and subsequently project cost is revised to Rs. 35.55 crores. So far Rs. 35.33 crores have been utilized out of Rs. 28.54 Crores released. (Up to October 2003) to wards cash component. NABARD has sanctioned 262 SMC projects under RIDF VIII phase-II (RD & Others sectors) for Rs. 53.65 crores to 19 districts with during 2002-03. The GOAP have released an amount of Rs. 23.63 lakhs for implementation. So far an amount of Rs. 29.59 crores utilised up to November 2003. The RIDF-VIII phase-II (RD & Other sector) project will he completed in all respects by March-2004.

To conclude, much work has been done in managing the water in efficient manner but the attempts are not really in deed very successful. Many projects and sanctions are been taken up which are in the process of developing the water use in better. Though we are not in the position of using each drop in efficient manner still the efforts we are making the water is appreciable.

3

Agriculture, Irrigation and Canal Water Resources

Mohd. Iqbal Ali and G. Mallikarjun

Irrigation is a harbinger of prosperity in many countries, more so in developing countries like India. The impact of irrigation is pervading as it leads to change in cropping pattern, increases yield rates and labour utilization and in the ultimate analysis brings prosperity to the area. Hence it is regarded as a catalyst for socio-economic change that sets in motion the productive forces in the productive forces in the agricultural sector.

The area under irrigation in most of the developing countries forms a lesser percentage of the total cultivated area and the provision of irrigation facilities had to be accorded a priority in the strategy of agricultural development. The impetus to agricultural development that could be witnessed in the seventies as mainly due to Green Revolution, which depended more on use of water-seed-fertilizer technology. In this new package programme water became a crucial factor and irrigation of all types-canal, tank, well and underground had been tapped for increasing agricultural productivity. Of all these types of irrigation, canal irrigation is perennial in nature and plans were drawn up in independent India to increase acreage under canal irrigation. Thus a majority of the irrigation projects had been initiated in the second five-year plan as a part of the heavy strategy adopted for rapid development of the country. But serious snags had developed in the implementation process that resulted in either not realizing the full potential of the project or not utilizing property even the potential created.

In developing countries like India, irrigation often leads to modernization of agriculture as highlighted by Colin Clark and others and it also contributes to multiplier effect in the generation of income and employment as stressed by Ishikawa and others. As irrigation projects use scarce resources, economic considerations like removal of rural poverty, settling landless farmers and creating more employment opportunities play an important role in the choice of project. Investment in irrigation in the public sector encourages overall private investment on land. Irrigation also helps for agricultural development in three stages, where initially double cropping leads to investing in bullocks, tractors and later investment in fertilizer gains an importance and finally labour supply plays a crucial role when it becomes scarce resource. However, substituting capital for labour leads to agrarian tensions as reported in some of the areas undergoing green revolution. Thus in the period of revolution, irrigation is supposed to ensure the degree of control that Government can exercise over farmers cropping decisions through extension services and possibly the government may resort to agricultural taxation.

Irrigation also furthers balanced regional development often one of the aims of the government, for a proper redistribution of income among different areas of a country. Therefore, the goals emphasized in public policy can be realized by executing irrigation projects and as such economic considerations of the irrigation projects would involve considerations like the cost-benefit ratio in bringing about the changes that would lead to transformation of the production possibilities and income redistribution.

The creation of irrigation potential and its utilization, thus have crucial role to play in changing the relative shares of different farming groups in the countryside. In India, a large proportion of irrigation potential crated in the country through major and medium irrigation projects had either remained unutilized or underutilized and a number of studies had highlighted snags at different levels in the execution of irrigation projects. Further more, the inefficiency of the current projects partly stems from engineering or technical inefficiency in terms of the current projects partly stems from engineering or technical inefficiency in terms of unreliability of canal system and partly from poor on –farm use of water. Thus actual experience had shown that normally the last one third portion of each canal had inadequate, unreliable or no water supplies and total area as planned would not get adequate water for the crops which are aggravated by indiscipline over irrigation and wastage in early stages. Operation of irrigation main system for equitable water distribution and productive management and reduction of top enders supplies requires a high level political support, legal backing, prompt and impartial prosecution.

Modernization of agriculture due to the impetus given by irrigation facilities is usually hypothesis to evoke response from big farmers alone. But contrary to the above view, the response to modernization is almost uniform by all farmers. The study by B.Sen buttresses the view that small farmer also performed well as the proportion of the area under HYV seeds and its performance were highest due to the availability or irrigation facilities. Even the cropping intensity for the small medium and large farmers in irrigated areas was uniformly higher than the cropping intensity of farmers of the respective groups in dry land areas. Further, it was also observed that intensification of irrigation facilities in Asian Agriculture would lead to higher labour input per crop per hectare, even in the cases where the water for irrigation is supplied from canals.

One of the most important methods for labour absorption is the irrigation-seed-fertilizer innovation which is normally considered land-augmenting and labour-using capable of generating large increase in employment and also distribute these increases more evenly over the years leading to a reduction in the seasonal under-employment and reduction of poverty of the landless and landless and land poor. But tractorisation, as it was highlighted by billings and Singh and Hanumantha Rao on the basis of Punjab experience, may lead to labour displacement leading to underemployment. Therefore, irrigation can generate more employment opportunities as ling as modern agriculture keeps away mechanization. Hence, the distribution of gains also has to be viewed from this angle.

The differential gains to different inputs have been stressed in various studies. Hanumantha Rao, C.H., states that although HYV and fertilizers are size neutral, they are not resource neutral. Since large farmers have better command over resources and their risk-bearing have capacity is greater and so they adopt capital intensive techniques more. Rao V.K.R.V., also states that new technology is not neutral to scale and that some of the inputs are indivisible and are beyond small farmer's capacity. Waheeduddin Khan and Tripathy, R.N., have studied the impact of modernization of agriculture in West Godavari District (Andhra Pradesh) for the period of 1964-70 from two different agricultural zones-the upland and the delta. Production function of the Cobb-Doubles type was used to examine the efficiency of resources use and they found constant returns to scale in upland cultivation while increasing returns to scale in delta farms were in operation. They also opined that the adoption lever is higher for upper size classes of farmers. Parthasarathy, G., had also studied an IADP district of Andhra Pradesh (West Godavari) in the year 1968-69. He states that the share of labour in the benefits of news technology is low and that of land and capital owners is high resulting in an increase in the inequalities between the two. According to him, even PEO and Agro-Economic Center's studies show that the rates of participation of small cultivators in HYV paddy were low compared to big cultivators. Thus the increase in productivity is purely technological phenomenon with the institutional framework remaining constant.

Speaking on the Green Revolution in Punjab, Ladojinsky W. estimated that the real sharing in the progress is restricted to relatively few, perhaps 10 and surely not more than 20 percent of the farm households of Punjab. Srinath Singh has made a study of the transformation of agriculture in Dobhi block of Jaunpur district in Eastern Utter Pradesh. In this study per acre use of fertilizer, HYV of seeds was more in modernized farms than traditional farms. Sengupta and Ghosh have studied the implementation of the HYU programme in IADP (Birbhum District of West Bengal) and found that area under HYV paddy of the total cultivated area in the district was 14.43 percent. Average yield of HYV of paddy was found to be more on participant farms and less by non-participant farms.

And thus in a competitive situation, this may lead to pauperization of certain sections of the peasantry who either belong to marginal farmer category or small farmers category. Ranjit Sau had the opinion about that recent upsurge of capitalist farming may accelerated largely by the arrival of the new agricultural technology. Pranab Bardhan stated that the new Agricultural Strategy followed by the Government is effectively subsidizing and promoting agrarian capitalism in India. And Utsa Patnaik, who under took a study of big farmers in five stages, held that a new class of capitalist farmers is emerging in every operation with varying intensity. Thus, agrarian relations in India have been under going some changes due to certain policy measures initiated by state. Capitalist agriculture, while increasing labour in the water-seed-fertilizer technology lead to an increase in markets, where laborers would exert their influence for wage increases reducing house of work and work-load, etc.

Higher irrigated area raises the demand for labour since the increasing cropping intensity absorbs more labour force, which in turns leads to an increase in the level of wages. Thus demand curve for labour shifts to the right in higher irrigated areas and it can be hypothesized that irrigated area will be positively associated with the wage rates, as the demand for labour will increases with the irrigation. But this might not be true if the land concentration ratio is high, the big farmers having large holdings are expected to be quite sizeable in number and they would be in position to exert monopolistic pressure on them as wage rate, house of work. Work-load and pattern of work would be determined by big farmers only. This might be because of many reasons such as lack of employment opportunities for the above hypothesis could be nullified as wage rate need not be high as these would depend on other extra genius factors. Further inflationary trend arising from the large investments have eroded the read value of the little earnings by the weaker sections in the rural areas. Thus, there is a sharp decline in the economic conditions of this group and in such situations the widening gap between the two groups has become more conscious and could not escape the attention of the weaker sections.

The role of irrigation in raising agricultural production, absorption of labour force and showing unemployment and under-employment in rural India is, though widely recognize, the new dispensation. As most of the laborers depend on agriculture for their subsistence capitalists agriculture may lead to pauperization of the peasantry which may further lead to shift in the supply curve of the labour, while demand for labour is increasing, the supply is also increasing, leaving unemployment unsolved. Two classes of agriculture sector are thus, in antagonistic contradiction in this static agrarian structure.

Therefore, that the impact of irrigation need not be uniform in the localized areas and even within the localized area where certain homogeneity exists as regards availability of canal water, the benefits are not diffused in an equitable manner to all categories of farmers. The gap between upper-reach areas and tail-end-areas which arises mainly due to defective water system and management is wide and unless proper measures are initiated, the gap may be widened and consequently the impact of irrigation may be uneven in nature rather than being uniform and this may lead to inequitable resource use and gains.

References

1) Ian Carruthers & Colin Clark, "The Economics of Irrigation", Liverpool University Press, London, 1970, p.1.
2) Sen, Bandudas, "The Green Revolution India", Wiley Eastern Private Ltd., New Delhi, 1974, p.44.
3) Hanumantha Rao C.H., "Technological Change and Distribution of Gains in Indian Agriculture", Asia Publishing House, New Delhi, 1979, p.52.

4) Rao, V.K.R.V., "Agricultural Development and Social Justice", *Co-operative New Digest*, August 1978, p.45.
5) Khan Waheeduddin and Tripathy, R.N., "Intensive Agriculture and Modern Inputs, NICD, Hyderabad, 1972.
6) Parthasarthy, G., "Green Revolution and Weaker Sections", Thacker and Co., Ltd., Bombay, 1971.
7) Ladejinsky, Wolf, "Green Revolution in Punjab - A Field Trip", *Economic and Political Weekly*, June 28, 1969, p.5.
8) Singh, Srinath, "Modernisation of Agriculture", Heritage Publishers, New Delhi, 1976.
9) Sengupta and Ghosh, "HYVP for Rice Performance in a Bengal District", *Economic and Political Weekly*, October 1968, p.43.
10) Sau Ranjit, "Can Capitalism Develop in Indian Agriculture", *Economic and Political Weekly*, December 25, 1976.
11) Bardhan Pranab, "Trends in Land Relations", *Economic and Political Weekly*, Annual No. 1970.
12) Mishra, V.N., and Gupta, G.B.C., "Productivity, Wages and its Determination in Gujarat Agriculture – An Inter-District Analysis", *Indian Journal of Agricultural Economics*, July-September, 1974, p.30.

4

Irrigation Management

M. Lakshmi Narasaiah, G. Venkata Naidu, G. Jaya Raju and T.V. Seshaiah

---

Irrigated agriculture is up against an enormous challenge. India's population continues to grow at a tremendous rate. Over the next 10 Years, there will be more extra mouths to feed. Water is becoming increasingly scarce for agriculture, with conflicting demands being made on limited supplies by the domestic and industrial sectors. The most attractive irrigation sites have already been exploited. Yet, irrigated agriculture will have to deliver average output increases of at least 3.5 percent per year if future food demands are to be met in India.

Fifty years ago in the 1950s and 1960s, India has worried about its capacity to produce sufficient food to feed its growing population. Episodes of food scarcity were not uncommon. It was dreaded that millions would die of hunger. Then, dawned the miracle of the "green revolution". Cereal production increased by leaps and bounds boosted by expanded irrigation, increased fertilizer application and modern crop varieties. The vigorous response in mobilizing financing towards boosting agricultural production paid off.

Given the importance of irrigation to the India's food supply and the vast resources already expanded on irrigation development, it is tragic that the actual performance of irrigation systems is so disappointingly low. In the post-green revolution era, it has become increasingly evident that the performance of irrigation systems, especially large-scale systems, is sub optimal whether measured in terms of achieving planned area targets or in terms of production created by the physical works.

In many irrigation systems, the actual area irrigated is much less than the command area. Sharp inequities in water supplies between farmers in the head reaches of irrigation systems and those located downstream is another manifestation of poor performance. Investigation in the Tungabhadra Irrigation Scheme reveal that the tail-end of a major distributory commanding 25% of the total area, received approximately 20-40% of the targeted discharge while the upper reaches got more than their share.

Lack of maintenance has caused many systems to fall into disrepair, further inhibiting performance. Overtime, distribution canals have become silted up, increasing the likelihood of breaching, damage to outlets and leading to salt build-up in the soil.

Successful Farmer-managed Irrigation Systems

Farmers have long demonstrated their potential capability to manage irrigation systems efficiently. Farmer-managed irrigation systems, (FMIS) also known as traditional, indigenous, communal or peoples' systems, are often classified "minor" or "small-scale" irrigation systems, although they may be found in command areas of 15,000-20,000 hectares.

Many successful farmer-managed irrigated systems, which have been functioning effectively for hundreds of years, represent a valuable, accumulated investment. They are also reservoirs of largely untapped irrigation management experience.

Research has revealed that FMIS contribute to the production of a significant portion of the subsistence food supply. Ground-water irrigation systems, often found in areas affected by drought, play a strategic role in promoting food security. In India ground-water development which is increasing in importance is predominantly farmer-managed, in this country an estimated 20 millions hectares are already under ground-water irrigation. When mismanaged though, ground-water irrigation could impact negatively on the environment.

In addition to the hectarage under farmer-managed ground-water irrigation, farmer-managed tank irrigation systems cover about 8.5 million hectares in this country. Farmer-managed irrigation systems have also allowed intensification of agriculture to partially meet the food needs of rapidly growing populations.

Yet, despite the widespread interest in irrigation management turnover throughout India there is very little documentation about the process used and the results obtained from irrigation management turnover. Many policy-makers do not know how to turn over management of their irrigation institutions in an effective way. They typically have very little, if any, awareness of the range of organizational options which may be suitable under different conditions. There is an urgent need, therefore, for a systematic, comparative assessment of the range of approaches being used, constraints to implementation and the impacts on performance of transferring management to non-governmental or farmer's organizations.

Successful irrigation in the future will be that which supports much higher levels of agricultural productivity, enhances responsiveness to more diversified and dynamic crop markets, stimulates more profitable irrigated agriculture for wide numbers of rural poor, substantially improves water use efficiency and supports the sustainable use of scarce land, biomass and water resources.

In the coming Years the irrigation sector will be in ferment, with decision makers, agency managers and farmers needing better information and strategic processes to make intelligent choices in the management of irrigated agriculture.

5

Fresh Water: A Precious Resource

M. Lakshmi Narasaiah, N. Sreedhar and
R. Ramudu

Fresh water is scarce commodity. Since it's impossible to increase supply, demand and waste must be reduced. But how?

Water is bond between human beings and nature. It is ever-present in our daily lives and in our imaginations. Since the beginning of time, it has shaped extraordinary social institutions, and access to it has provoked many conflicts.

But most of the world's people, who have never gone short of water, take its availability for granted. Industrialists, farmers and ordinary consumers blithely go on wasting it. These days, though, supplies are diminishing while demand is soaring. Everyone knows that the time has come for attitudes to change.

Few people are aware of the true extent of fresh water scarcity. Many are fooled by the huge expanses of blue that feature on maps of the world. They do not know that 97.5 percent of the planer's water is salty-and that most of the world's fresh water-the remaining 2.5% is cent is unusable: 70% of it is frozen in the icecaps of Antarctica and Greenland and almost all the rest exists in the form of soil humidity or in water tables which are too deep to be tapped. In all, barely one percent of fresh water-0.007% of all the water in the world is easily accessible.

Over the past century, population growth and human activity have caused this precious resource to dwindle. Between 1900 and 1995, world demand for water increased more than six fold-compared with a threefold increase in world population seems to show that in overall terms there is enough water to go round. But in the most vulnerable regions, an estimated 460 million people (8 percent of the world's population) are short of water, and another quarter of the planer's inhabitants are heading for the same fate. Experts say that if nothing is done, two-thirds of humanity will suffer from a moderate to severe lack of water by the year 2025.

Inequalities in the availability of water-sometimes even within a single country-are reflected in huge differences in consumption levels.

Scarcity is just one part of the problem. Water quality is also declining alarmingly. In some areas, contamination levels are so high that water can no longer be used even for industrial purposes. There are many reasons for this untreated sewage, chemical waste, fuel leakages, dumped garbage, and contamination of soil by chemicals used by farmers. The worldwide extent of such pollution is hard to assess because data are lacking for several countries. But some figures give an idea of the problem. It is thought for example that 90% of waste water in developing countries is released without any kind of treatment.

Things are especially bad in cities, where water demand is exploding. For the first time in human history, there will soon be more people living in cities than in the countryside and so water consumption will continue to increase. Soaring urbanization will sharpen the rivalry between the different kinds of water users.

Curbing the Explosion in Demand

Today, farming uses 69 percent of the water consumed in the world, industry 23 percent and house holds 8 percent. In developing countries, agriculture uses as much as 80 percent. The needs of city-dwellers, industry and tourists are expected to increase rapidly, at least as much as the need to produce more farm products to feed the planet. The problem of increasing water supply has long been seen as a technical one, calling for technical solutions such as building more dams and desalination plants. Wild ideas towing chunks of icebergs from the poles have even been mooted.

But today, technical solutions are reaching their limits, Economic and socio-ecological arguments are leveled against building new dams, for example: dams are costing more and more because the best sites have already been used, and they take millions of people out of their environment and upset ecosystems. As a result, twice as many dams were built on average between 1951 and 1977 than during the past decade.

Hydrologists and engineers have less and less room for man oeuvre, but a new consensus with new actors is taking shape. Since supply can no longer be expanded or only at prohibitive cost for many countries the explosion in demand must be curbed along with wasteful practices. An estimated 60 percent of the water used in irrigation is lost through inefficient systems, for example.

Economists have plunged into the debate on water and made quite a few waves. To obtain "rational use" of water, i.e. avoiding waste and maintaining quality, they say consumers must be made to pay for it. Out of the question, reply those in favour of free water, which some cultures regard as " a gift from heaven". And what about the poor ask the champions of human rights and the right to water? Other important and prickly questions being asked by decision-makers are how to calculate the "real price" of water and who should organize its sale.

The State as Mediator

The principle of free water is being challenged. For many people, water has become a commodity to be bought and sold. But management of this shared resource cannot be left exclusively to market forces. Many elements of civil society-NGOs, researchers, community groups are campaigning for the cultural and social aspects of water management to be taken into account.

Even the World Bank, the main advocate of water privatization, is cautious on this point. It recognizes the value of the partnerships between the public and private sectors, which have sprung up in recent years. Only the state seems to be in a position to ensure that practices are fair and to mediate between the parties involved-consumer groups, private firms and public bodies. At any rate, water regulation and management systems need to be based on other than purely financial criteria. If they aren't hundreds of millions of people will have on access to it.

6

Water Use in Drought Areas

K. Nageswara Rao and G. Sivaiah

Water resources are to be used rationally and reasonably, particularly in drought prone areas, as it is one of the most vital resources for life and an important component of economic development. Man uses water for a variety of purposes and water determines the mode and levels of living of man. However, most natural waters are not suitable for human consumption and in course of time they are becoming scare and unsafe for human consumption. It is estimated that only 0.10 percent of total water resources available on the globe are fit for drinking purposes. Hence, man must cease to regard water resources as an inexhaustible gift of nature. Further, they are to be used with greatest care and proper attention is to be paid for their conservation.

Supply of clean and pure water is essential for the health of the people. Hence, the demand for water is for "clean" and "safe" water and it is to be supplied by treating and purifying it. In other words, man has to make some efforts individually and collectively to supply and use water at the required place in required quantity. Thus, public water supplies and water management assume greater importance and provision of drinking water particularly in the villages of drought prone areas, has been the concern of the Government planners and people in the country.

The central government has been assisting the rural water supply schemes through the Public Health Engineering Department and the Union Home ministry is concerned with the provision of drinking water supply to the areas where scheduled castes and scheduled tribes live. To enquire into the problem of providing water supply systems in millions of the villages a Special Investigation Division is started in each state.

Drinking Water Systems in Rural Areas of Andhra Pradesh

The Government of Andhra Pradesh, following the National policy on rural water supply 1937-38. Launched a five-year programme in 1947-48 and provided water supply to 5 of the 393 panchayats in the state. Panchayats Raj Department has been placed in charge of rural water supply schemes in the state to design, execute and maintain the water supply systems in villages. The outlays earmarked to rural water supply system and the villages covered during the five-year plan periods in Andhra Pradesh are shown in Table: I. Government of Andhra Pradesh made a modest beginning to provide drinking water supply, during the period of First Year Plan period, by sinking 7,145 wells and providing water supply to 20 villages in the state.

Efforts were continued during the Second Five Year plan and 786 villages were covered by water supply schemes with an expenditure of Rs. 1.18 crores. However, the supply of drinking water to the villages in the state was nominal during the first ten years of the planning era and the Third Five Year plan conceived that 84.00 percent of the villages were found to be 'no source' villages and the rest having inadequate supply. Assigning greater importance to rural water supply Government of Andhra Pradesh ordered for survey of all villages during the Third Five Year plan.

The survey revealed that 31,873 villages and hamlets were experiencing acute water scarcity. Another survey revealed that only 16.00 percent of the villages had satisfactory sources of water while 54,145 villages continued to experience inadequate water supply. Immediately, an amount of Rs.6.55 crores was provided for providing water supply in some these villages.

The Fourth Five Year plan provided the long awaited and much needed impetus to the rural water supply schemes in the state. Institutional finance particularly from life Insurance corporation was made available to execute village water supply schemes and the rigs supplied by UNICEF were used to sink bore wells in drought affected areas. Further, Accelerated Rural Water Supply scheme, a centrally sponsored scheme was launched in 1972-73 to deal with difficult villages in the state. By the end of the Fourth Five Year plan period 4,178 bore wells were sunk benefiting 42.88 lakh people. On the whole, 31,966 villages and hamlets were provided with water supply at a cost of Rs.7.54 crores during this plan period.

The Fifth Year plan showed much keener insight into the provision of drinking water supply; it stressed "the need to provide drinking water facilities on a priority basis to the rural areas suffering from scarcity, health hazards or special problems such as iron and fluorides etc." At the beginning of the Fifth Five Year plan 21,742 habitations comprising 5,280 difficult and problem villages, 6,156 harijan wadas, 1,500 harijan colonies and 8,806 other villages and hamlets in soft areas were found to be without drinking water supply.

To provide drinking water for all these habitations, it was estimated that it would be necessary to drill 24,550 bore wells of 4"diameter, 5,280 bore wells of 6 inch diameter and 4,000 simple wells in soft areas. The total cost of this programme was estimated at Rs.56.18 crores and the State Government proposed that this outlay should be provided by the Center under "the Minimum Needs Programmes". At last the planning commission allocated only Rs.25.0 crores for the rural water supply schemes. On the whole, during the Fifth Five Year plan period out of 12,269 villages 4,063 villages (nearly on third of total) were provided with water supply facilities.

The congenial atmosphere created by the efforts made by the Government during the earlier plans period provision of rural water supply arrangements were sustained during the Sixth Five Year plan and it was proposed to cover 8,206 uncovered problem villages with an expenditure of Rs.168.40 crores. However, the expenditure was revised to Rs.123.00 crores, including the component of Life Insurance Corporation on rural water supply, to cover 7,019 problem villages. This objective was realized to a large extent by the end of this plan period.

During the Sixth Five Year plan an amount of Rs.90.04 crores was released to Zilla Parishads under the state plan to provide water supply to 7,019 problem villages. Further, an amount of Rs.32.23 crores received from the Government of India under the Centrally Sponsored Accelerated Rural Water Supply programmes was expended to cover 1,187 problem villages. Thus, by the end of the Sixth plan period almost all identified problem villages were tackled and drinking water was made available either fully or partially with an expenditure of Rs.119.60 crores. However, the rural water supply arrangements in many villages were found inadequate and unsatisfactory.

At the beginning of the Seventh Five Year plan period (1980-85) there were 15,834 problem villages in the state. These are the villages that needed one spot source for every 300 persons at average rate of 40-70 liters per capita per day. These villages are identified as problem villages on the basis of a) Villages not having a drinking water source within a radius of 1.6 k.m or depth of 1.5 meters b) Villages endemic to cholera c) Villages with drinking water sources infected with Guinea worm d) Villages with drinking water sources with access to chemicals like carbides, fluoride.

A Master plan pertaining to the supply of safe drinking water to all people in rural areas was prepared during the Seventh Five Year plan period. According to this plan all the identified problem villages (12,269 villages) are to be covered under rural water supply. The plan claims that the protected water supply schemes should be restricted to villages identified as 'health hazard' areas. Besides, it was attempted to cover the 'problem' villages in drought prone areas where drinking water is a serious problem.

The Seventh Five Year Plan envisaged to providing safe drinking water facility to all these villages. With an outlay of Rs.360.00 crores it was attempted to cover 14,400 villages with a population of 260.0 lakhs. The plan claims that to a larger extent the problem villages were covered under water supply. However, a close look at the achievements of the Seventh Five Year Plan reveals that there is short fall of 30.00 percent coverage in respect of problem villages. Further, it should be noted that there is under achievement from the point of view of population coverage under rural water supply. Infact, by the end of the Seventh Five Year Plan 10,290 problem villages were provided with drinking water supply fully or partially with a total expenditure of Rs.260.44 crores. This includes an amount of Rs.152.05 crores released to Zilla Parishads under state plan and Rs.108.39 crores received from the Central Government under Accelerated Rural water supply programmes.

During the two Annual Plans period 1990-91 and 1991-92 a total of Rs.62.37 crores was spent to provide drinking water supply to 2114 villages. An amount of Rs.33.00 crores was provided to cover 105 problem villages in 1990-91 and Rs.29.37 crores was released to cover 100 problem villages in 1991-92. Further another 1909 villages were supplied with drinking water supply under the Centrally Sponsored Accelerated Rural Water Supply programme.

The Eighth Five Year plan provided drinking water facilities to the left over 3424 problem villages. Emphasis was also placed on the provision of clean water in areas with fluorides, salinity and villages prone to diseases. Major Panchayats towns and drought prone areas were also covered with protected water supply. An expenditure of Rs.168.45 crores was incurred to proved water supply facilities to 3424 villages. The Government of India released another Rs.170.00 crores under rural water supply programme.

The outlays earmarked for rural water supply in Andhra Pradesh and the villages covered with protected water supply during the Five Year Plans are shown in Table 6.1. It is noted that the expenditure on rural water supply was very limited and the coverage of villages was also small. This indicates that village water supply schemes were not given priority and smaller outlays were allotted to these schemes till the end of the Fourth Five Year Plan. Only 86,141 villages were supply by the end of the Fourth Five Year Plan period.

Table 6.1: Outlays on Rural Water Supply Schemes during the Five Year Plans in Andhra Pradesh

Plan Period	Outlay (in Rs. Crores)	Villages Covered
First Plan, 1951-56	N.A.	20
Second Plan, 1956-61	1.18	786
Third Plan, 1961-66	6.55	54,145
Fourth Plan, 1969-74	7.54	31,996
Fifth Plan, 1974-78	25.00	4,063
Sixth Plan, 1980-85	119.60	4,370
Seventh Plan, 1985-90	200.00	10,290
Eighth Plan, 1992-97	357.47	3,424

Source: Finance and Planning Department, Government of Andhra Pradesh, *Five Year Plans of Andhra Pradesh.*

Rural water supply programmes were executed on a large scale from the Fifth Five Year Plan period and all identified problem villages were proposed to be covered during the Sixth Five Year plan. However, the famine and drought conditions in several part of the state remained problematic and hence 10290 villages were covered during the Seventh Five Year plan. The left over 3424 villages were proposed to be covered fully of partially during the Eighth Five Year Plan period. This cherished objective of the Government of Andhra Pradesh could not be realized for a variety of reasons including diversified commitment of the Government.

As a result, 69,732 rural habitations in the State population of 534.35 lakhs were left uncovered. Out of which, 34327 habitations were fully covered by March 2000. The balance of 38943 habitations were proposed to be covered in phased manner 21,583 habitations were proposed to be covered partially. Still there are 13,822 no safe source villages that are to be covered. During 2000-2001 it is proposed to cover 4705 habitations at a proposed outlay of Rs.383.41 crores. The Department maintains 246 CPWS schemes and 2.5 lakh hand pumps whereas Gram Panchayats maintains 25387 individual PWS schemes.

To evaluate the functioning of the rural water supply systems in Andhra Pradesh, to identify the problems confronting of the coverage of villages a research survey was conducted in October 2004 and the results of the survey are presented hereunder.

The field survey revealed that rural water supply schemes were not executed in a determined priority. These schemes were not designed according to a determined policy of the Government or the village needs. Many schemes are smaller in their size to meet the requirements of village population and there are abnormal delays in their completion. Hence, the size and cost of the schemes have no relation to the size and requirements of village population. The depth of source wells varied from 80to 200feet.

Less than one fourth of the houses have tap connections and hence house taps in villages in rural areas serves not more than 3.0 percent of the people. This is contrast to the percentage (more than one quarter) of population served by house service connections in urban areas. It is found that in many villages the house tap holders are big farmers. Larger proportion of the villagers depends upon public taps for their water requirements. On an average, nearly 300 people depend upon each public tap, which is expected to cater to the needs of 200 people, indicating excess pressure.

The local self Governments' financial position is not permitting them to meet at least a part of the total cost of the schemes. Further, the indifference of local bodies is retarding the expansion of water supply systems and their functioning. Nearly one half of the villages covered under rural water supply are provided with water supply by sinking bore wells. It is reported that the bore wells and water taps go out of use once in every two months and the time taken repair them varies from 10 to 15 days every time. Hence, all the villages go without water for 2 months in a year.

Due to irregular and indifferent maintenance of the water supply systems by the local bodies, at least one third of the schemes became defunct causing hardship to villagers. The irregular and untimely supply of water during the summer leads to tension and strife in the villages. Government has been trying to ease the drinking water supply situation in every summer on an adhoc basis by granting funds for rural water supply. Instead, governmental efforts are to be directed to provide water supply to villages on a permanent basis. This calls for the establishment of an Authority at the state level to design, execute and maintain the rural water supply systems on a permanent basis.

Suggestions

1. A Separate Agency may be created at the state level to formulate, execute and monitor the use of drinking water in rural area.
2. Permanent arrangements are to be made to provide drinking water in rural areas instead of adhoc measures implemented during summer seasons.
3. Panchayat Raj authorities are to be made responsible for the maintenance of the protected water supply systems in rural areas.
4. Awareness among the villagers needs to be created on the rational utilization of water resources in drought prone areas.

5. Involvement of voluntary agency is to be encouraged by the state government in the execution and maintenance of village water supply systems.
6. Drinking water may be supplied through the network of pipelines once in two or three days in all the villages in drought prone areas.
7. The cost of water supply may be brought down significantly by supplying clean water for not more than one hour a day on the days of supply.

References

1) Franknel, R.J., "Role of Potable Water in Community Health Planning".
2) World Bank, "Village Water Supply", Washington, D. C. 1976.
3) WHO, "Community Water Supplies", Progress Report, 1972.
4) Canuthers, I.D., "Impact of Community Water Supply", 1974.
5) Ministry of Finance, Government of A.P., Five-Year Plan Documents, Hyderabad.
6) Planning Department, Hyderabad, *Economic Survey*, 2000-01.
7) Report on Drinking Water Supply Systems in Urban Areas of Rayalaseema by Prof. K. Nageswara Rao, 1996.
8) Report on Village Water Supply in Kurnool District by Prof. K.Nageswara Rao.

7

Management of Surface and Sub-Surface Water Resources

M. Sambasiva Rao and S. Lakshmi Narayana

Introduction

Water is an important liquid gold. It is used for drinking, household, irrigation and industrial purposes. India receives high rainfall during monsoon period. The rainfall received during monsoon periods should be properly stored in surface ponds, tanks, reservoirs and under ground storage tanks for utilization of the same for drinking, irrigation, and industrial uses. Anantapur district is geographically located in a rain shadow zone and receives an average annual rainfall during the last 100 years indicated that the district experienced about 47 years of droughts are 40, moderate droughts are five and severe droughts are two. Due to frequent occurrence of droughts, there is a need for proper utilization, conservation and management of surface and sub-surface water resources in the district.

Study Area

The Anantapur district covers an area of about 19,125 Km^2 and is geographically located in the southwestern part of the Andhra Pradesh state. The district possess 36,40,478 population according 2001 census. There are 63 mandals and 927 inhabited villages in the district. Geographically the district is located in between 13°40' and 15°15' Northern latitudes and 76° 50' and 78° 30' Eastern longitudes. Topographically the district is divided in the three major regions. They are northern rolling plains consisting of black soil plains. They lie in between 150-300 meters height above MSL. The central undulating terrain consisting of poor and red sandy soils with altitudinal variation of

300-600 meters above MSL and southern and southeastern uplands with altitudinal variation of 600-900 meters above MSL.

The main objectives of the paper are:

1. To analyze the monthly, seasonal and annual rainfall of the Anantapur district,
2. To assess the recharge and surface runoff the Anantapur district and evaluate the total surface water resources,
3. To study the ground water level variations, fluctuations, recharge and potential of the district and to describe the water balance of the Anantapur district and
4. To suggest measures for optimum utilization, conservation and management of surface and sub-surface water resources of the Anantapur district.

The monthly rainfall over a period of hundred years has been collected for about 13 stations in the district. The data is used to analyze the mean monthly rainfall, mean seasonal rainfall and mean annual rainfall, rainfall intensity, rainfall variability and rainfall ratio adopting various statistical methods. The surface runoff is worked out adopting U.S. Geological method and RadhaKrishna etal. (1974) method. The average of the two methods given by Raghunath (1985). The data on monthly ground water level has been collected from 50 controlled wells in the district over a period 10 years. Based on the ground water data, ground water level variations, fluctuations, and recharge the ground water potential are worked out for the Anantapur district. Based on mean annual precipitation, potential evapotranspiration and actual evapotranspiration the water balance of the Anantapur district is described. Finally basing on available surface and sub-surface water resources optimum utilization, conservation and management are suggested.

Rainfall Analysis of the Anantapur District

From the analysis of monthly rainfall it is summarized that the mean monthly rainfall is less than 10 mm. In January, February, March, and December months. The average monthly rainfall varies from 10 mm. to 50 mm in April, May, June, July, and

November months. In August and October moths the average rainfall ranges from 50mm to 100mm. In September month the average rainfall is above 100 mm. The monthly rainfall intensity is low in January and February months. The monthly rainfall variability is very high in January, February, March, April, November and December months. The rainfall variability is low in August, September and October months. In May, June and July months the rainfall variability is moderate to high. The monthly rainfall ratios are very high with abnormalities in January, February, March, April, November and December months. The ratio values are low in September month. In other months they are moderate to high. From the study of mean monthly rainfall it is concluded that the months of July, August, September, October and November are highly favorable for cultivation of crop under rain fed conditions. The January, February, March, April, May, June and December months are not favorable crop cultivation under rainfed condition. The crops can be cultivated by providing water resources through canal, tank or well irrigation. The seasonal analysis of rainfall of Anantapur district reveals that the district receives high rainfall of 322.76 mm during southwest monsoon, followed by 149.54 mm in northeast monsoon period, 80.92 mm in summer period and 6.38 mm in water period. The seasonal intensity of rainfall shows that the intensity is low in winter. It is high in northeast and southwest monsoon periods and moderate in summer period. The seasonal rainfall ratio values are low in southwest monsoon period, moderate in northeast monsoon period, high in summer period and very high in winter period. The annual average rainfall ranges from 488 mm in Yadiki station to a maximum of 615 mm in Kadiri station. The average annual rainfall is 558.85 mm. The annual rainfall intensity ranges from 14 mm to 17 mm a rainy day. The annual rainfall variability varies from 17% to 34%. The annual rainfall ratio values range from 121% to 252%. The total surface water resources of the Anantapur district is

Average annual rainfall X Geographical area of the district

558.85 mm X 19,125 Km^2 = 10,688,006,250 m^3.

Recharge and Surface Run-Off

The recharge of the Anantapur district is worked out adopting U.S. Geological method (1985) and RadhaKrishna etal. (1974) method. According to RadhaKrishna etal. (1974) method the annual recharge is 10% of the annual rainfall. The annual recharge according to this method varies from a minimum of 48.8 mm in Yadiki station to a maximum of 61.5 mm in Kadiri station. The average annual recharge is 55.88 mm. The annual recharge according U.S.Geological method (1985) is 15% of the average annual rainfall. According to this method the annual recharge varies from 73.20 mm in Yadiki station to a maximum of 92.25 mm in Kadiri station. The average annual recharge is 83.82 mm. The average of the two methods is taken as average annual recharge for each station. The average annual recharge varies from 61 mm in the Yadiki station to a maximum of 76.87 mm in the Kadiri station. The average annual recharge is 69.85 mm. It is about 12.5% of the average annual rainfall of the Anantapur district the surface runoff is worked out according to Inglis formulae. The formulae is

Surface run-off = $\frac{(P-17.8)P}{254}$ where P is annual precipitation in cm.

According to Inglis formulate the surface runoff in the Anantapur district varies from59.55 mm in Yadiki station to a maximum of 105.80 mm in Kadiri station (Table.1). The average surface run-off the district is 83.49 mm. It is about 14.94% of the average annual rainfall.

Ground Water Resources

The average annual ground water levels in the Anantapur district vary from 5 to 17 meters. The average annual ground level of the district is 8.76 meters. During winter period the average ground water levels vary from 5 to 17 meters. The average ground water level of the district during this period is 9.0 meters. During southwest monsoon period the average ground water levels vary from 4 to 19 meters. The average of the district is 9.52 meters. In northeast monsoon period the average ground water levels are high during southwest monsoon and summer periods. The average of the district during this period is 8.60 meters. From the analysis of seasonal ground water level variations it is noticed that the ground water levels are high during southwest monsoon and summer periods. They are moderate in northeast monsoon and winter periods.

The annual ground water level fluctuations vary from 0.9 to 3.5 meters. The average annual ground water level fluctuation of the district is 2.28 meters. The seasonal analysis of ground water level fluctuations reveal that during southwest monsoon the average fluctuations is about 1.22 meters. During northeast monsoon period, it is 0.93 meters and in summer period, it is 0.79 meters. During winter period the average annual fluctuation in ground water level is low and it is 0.48 meters.

Geographically the Anantapur district is divided into three zones. The first zone is the recent alluvium. It is located along the river valleys and major stream valleys of the district. The ground water potential is high. The recharge is high. The annual ground water levels vary from 3 to 6 meters. The specific yield is above 10%. The recharge is high and ground water yield varies from 10,000 to 25,000 lph. The second zone consists of granitic gneisses terrain. It occupies major part of the district. Ground water is restricted to weathered fissured, fractured and faulted zones. Ground water potential is moderate. The annual ground water levels vary from 6 to 17 meters. The specific yield is very low and is about 3%. The recharge is very low and the ground water yield varies from 1,500 to 5,000 lph. The third zone consists of Proterozoic formations. They are formed of shales, dolomite, limestone, chert and mudstone. The recharge is moderate. The annual ground water levels vary from 5 to 10 meters. The specific yield is moderate. It is about 8% and the ground water yield is about 5,000 to 10,000 lph. The ground water is found in weathered, fissured, fractured and faulted zones. In limestone terrain ground water resources of the Anantapur district are found in sub-terranean channels. The ground water potential of the Anantapur district

= Average annual recharge x Geographical area of the district.
= 69.85 mm X 19,125 km^2 = 1,335,881,250 m^3.

It is about 12.498% of the total surface water resources of the Anantapur district.

Water Balance

The annual water balance elements of the district are worked out adopting Thornthwaite and Mathur (1955) method. The potential evapotranspiration (PE) or water loss due to evaporation and evapotranspiration varies from 1446 mm in Madakasira station to a maximum 1778 mm in Tadipatri station. The average PE of the district is 1609 mm. The annual actual evapotranspiration (AE) varies from 674 mm in Dharmavaram station to a maximum of 830 mm in Tadipatri station. The average annual AE of the district is 756 mm. The annual water deficit of the district varies from a minimum of 701 mm in Madakasira station to a maximum of 1058 mm in Dharmavaram station. The average annual water deficit of the district is 853 mm. The Anantapur district experiences high annual water deficit.

The water balance of the district is

1. Total surface water resources = 10,688,006,250 m^3.
2. Surface water resources stored in ponds, tanks and reservoirs (10%) = 1,068,800,625 m^3.
3. Water resources recharged to groundwater (12.498%) = 1,335,881,250 m^3.
4. Surface water resources lost in time form of surface run-off (14.94%) = 1,596,746,250 m^3.
5. Surface water resources lost in the form of evaporation and evapotranspiration (62.562%) = 6,686,578,025 m^3.

From the analysis of water balance it is found that out of 10,688,006,250 m^3 of surface water resources available in the Anantapur district about 10% is stored in ponds, tanks, and reservoirs, 12.498% is recharged to ground water, 14.94% is lost in the form of surface run-off and 62.562% is lost in the form of evaporation and evapotranspiration. In view of high water loss in the form of surface run-off, evaporation and evapotranspiration there is a need for optimum utilization of available surface water resources stored in the ponds, tanks, and reservoirs, ground water resources and storage of surface run-off water resources in the district in the form of watershed development programmes like construction of check dams, percolation ponds and water harvesting structures. The whole district has been divided in to 3,825 micro watersheds. Each micro watershed consists of 500 hectares of land.

Measures for optimum utilization, conservation and management of water resources of the Anantapur district

1. The surface runoff water should be stored in the ponds, tanks, reservoirs and under ground water tanks.
2. Crop calendar has to be adjusted with water availability calendar.
3. Modern irrigation methods like drip, sprinkler and trickle have to be adopted.
4. Dry land farming techniques have to be adopted carefully.
5. The ponds, tanks and reservoirs have to be regularly dredged.,
6. The bunds of the ponds and tanks have to be strengthened to minimize the breaches during flood periods.
7. Ground water should be extracted with in the tolerable limit. Over exploitations of ground water is leading to steep fall in ground water levels.
8. Watershed management practices like construction of check dams, percolation ponds and water harvesting structures should be carried out.
9. Under ayacut areas the second crop could be cultivated using groundwater.
10. The deep bore wells should be dug with a minimum of 300 meters space in between them. Due to low recharge the deep bore wells are getting dried up year after year. The farmers should consult the geologists for digging a deep bore wells. The geophysical surveys have to be carried out before digging a deep bore well because majority of the deep bores are not yielding water due to hard rock nature of the terrain.

References

1. Radha Krishna, B.P, Dushan Duba and Palmquist, W.N. (1974) Ground Water Studies, Publication No. 150, Government of Karnataka, Bangalore.
2. Raghunath, H.M. (1985) Hydrology, Principles, Analysis, Design, New Age International (P) Limited, New Delhi, pp. 98-121.
3. Thornthwaite, C.W. and Mathur, J.R. (1995) The Water Balance, Publication in Climatology, Laboratory of Climatology, Centerton (W), Vol. 8, No.1, pp.104.
4. U.S.Department of Interior (1985) Ground Water Manuual, A Water Resources Technical Publication. Scientific Publishers, Jodhpur. pp.1-462.

8

Participatory Watershed Development and Promotion of Sustainable Agriculture in a Drought Prone Region

M.S. Kallur

Introduction

India, even today, is a predominantly agricultural country. Further, 'agriculture' is a gamble in monsoons in the drought prone areas of the country and as well as the Karnataka state. However, the New Agricultural Policy of 2000 aims at attaining the growth, which is technologically, environmentally and economically sustainable, through out the country. In what follows, is the detailed the analysis of promotion of sustainable in the drought prone region of Karnataka State, particularly supported by the participatory approach promoted by the NGO by name PRAWARDA.

The objectives of the present paper are:

1. To know the nature of the region and it is the backdrop for the study;
2. To give the brief account of drought relief measures undertaken by PRAWARDA.
3. To elaborate activities of it towards promoting the sustainable agriculture in the drought prone area and
4. To examine the replicability of the model in other drought prone regions of the country.

The study is the concurrent evaluation of the activities undertaken by the NGO in two years period i.e., from March 2002-2004. The data were obtained from beneficiaries of the micro watershed through administering a specially designed questionnaire. However, annual reports of PRAWARDA are also made use of.

Before analysing the reality whether PRAWARDA has been successful in promoting the 'sustaining development' in the region or not, we have to know the nature of the concept. The Brundtland Commission set up by the United Nations way back; in 1987 defined the term 'sustainable development' as 'development that meets needs of the present generation without compromising the ability of future generations to meet their own needs'. The enhancement of value for the stakeholder would then have to be done by addressing needs and adding needs and adding environmental, societal and economic values through products and services.

Hence, the concept of sustainable development does not merely imply "a concern for the progeny" but requires intermeshing of economic, social and environmental policies 'to ensure a better quality of life for everyone, now and for generations to come'. The strategy of sustainable development includes the four basic themes of social progress that recognises the need of everyone, effective protection of the environment, prudent use of natural resources and maintenance of high and stable levels of economic growth and employment. The goal of broad-based sustainable, must replace the narrower goal of economic growth.

Poverty and underdevelopment have persisted and are even now persisting in backward regions of the country, in general, in India, and, in particular, in Karnataka. Backward regions are essentially not served with any major irrigation projects and they are essentially dry farming areas. As such, have fragile ecosystems experiencing soil erosion and moisture stress. Watershed development, therefore, has been conceived as a strategy for protecting livelihoods of the people inhabiting in them. The government of Karnataka, like that of Maharashtra and Andhra Pradesh has been implementing watershed development programme on a priority basis from early 1990's for improvement of the farming systems and conservation of the most important natural resources like soil and water. Besides State Government, a number of NGOs are engaged in this watershed development activity with a view to assist farmers to benefit from such activity as early as possible.

In a country with a population of over 100 crores of whom at least 60 percent live in villages and majority below the poverty line, initiating the process of development is no longer confined to the government agencies alone. In fact, there is a growing tendency to incorporate NGOs and seek their involvement, thanks to their professional approach in analysing a problem and a commitment to seek a solution, overcoming the bureaucratic red-tapism in the process. In the present Tenth Five Year plan, the Govt. of India and state government also have duly acknowledged their role in bringing about discernable improvement in the lives of poor people in more than one way. However, an economic evaluation of such NGO developed watersheds is essential for providing justification to the investment of scarce funds. Here, a NGO [i.e., PRAWARDA] developed mini-watershed in Bidar district of Karnataka is selected for an in-depth study. Further, it has provided support to community during the 2002-2003 when the district suffered from severe drought and an account of it is also given here.

Profile of the Hyderabad Karnataka Region [HKR]

Hyderabad Karnataka region [HKR], which consists of five districts viz: Bidar, Bellary, Gulbarga, Koppal and Raichur, is even now an economically backward region. Further, the entire region is drought prone and known occurrence of serious droughts since time immemorial. Within the region, the Bidar district is having one of the lowest HDI, a relatively high population growth rare of 20 percent during the last decade as compared to 17 percent for the State and relatively low rates of literacy, of 44 percent for men and 32 percent for women. However, during the last decade, a radical change has taken place in both the reality and the perspective for development, in conjunction with a shift in focus from a centralized programme-oriented approach to a grass-roots project-oriented approach, based on the direct participation of the people who need the improved life conditions which development creates.

Support to Community in the form of implementation of Drought Relief Measures:

The drought provided PRAWARDA an opportunity to prepare the people the district to face it more boldly through [i] assisting them in mobilising fodder for livestock to meet the urgent need, and [ii] creation of employment generation activities in the form of drought proofing measures. It arranged for the transport of fodder from the adjacent district Gulbarga and distributed to needy farmers. It was first distributed among small farmers, big, and better off farmers were asked to wait and get it afterwords. Farmers were persuaded to grow fodder and fodder seeds were distributed to them for cultivation. There was a great demand from farmers for growing 'tall fodder and 20 quintals of African Tall fodder maize seeds were provided to over 100 formers for cultivation. Employment opportunity was created to labourers and other by constructing farm ponds. Each farm pond could generate, on an average employment of 154 labour-days i.e., and total of 19173 labour days were created. Out of 123 farmers who dug farm ponds in their farms, 77 [62%] were small and marginal farmers. Similarly, the sunken ponds did create an employment of 1548 days at 59 and 41 percent for women and men, respectively.

Participatory Watershed Development Activities of PRAWARDA

PRAWARDA has been playing a major role in the participatory development involving the people of the area. It has become an integral part of community life and livelihood in the district, in general and in BasvaKalyan taluka, in particular. The present in depth study is with particular reference to micro-watershed area consisting of 2000 hectares. Seven villages namely [i] Sastapur, [ii] Mirjapur, [iii] B.N. Wadi, [iv] H. Wadi, [v] Koudiyal, [vi] Nirgudi and [vii] Illal of BasvaKalyan taluka, are included under the preview of this micro-watershed project. The study is the concurrent evaluation of the activities undertaken by the NGO in two years period i.e., from March 2002 to March 2004. The data is obtained from beneficiaries of the micro watershed through administering a specially designed questionniare.

Major Achievements

I. Natural Resource Management

The entire micro-watershed area is suffering fragile ecosystem. Inter alia, [i] soil erosion and [ii] moisture stress has made the farming process 'subsistence' one rather than 'commercial', in nature. It was actually a herculian task for the PRAWARDA to improve the fragile ecosystem but their participatory technique made it relatively easy and yielded fruits as the construction of the necessary structures of the 'project' was completed successfully within two years. Treatment in watershed area like building check dam, earthern nala bund, farm pond and waste weirs have increased moisture content of the area and, in turn, has led to the cultivation of 'fallow land', Farm ponds constructed within a farm area of a hectare has provided water for life saving to crops and far livestock consumption. In other words, the problem of ' moisture stress' was solved to a great extent.

II. Increase in Agricultural Production

Not only yields have improved but also improvement in the 'farming system' has occurred. Farmers have referred it as 'Integrated farming System' where in different crops has been raised and it has resulted in the enhancement of their returns form farming. For instance, they are enjoying increased return from the new crop combination i.e., Chilly, Ginger and Tomato. Agricultural related interventions initiated by PRAWARDA did take the form of the introduction and use of improved varieties of green gram, Pigeon Pea, Chick Pea etc. resulted in wholesome developments like [a] reducing the crop period [b] avoiding the problem of germination of seed while in pods and [c] per acre yield improvement. As to the per acre yield, improvement was ranging from 26 percent to 100 percent.

III. Maintenance of Community Assets

It is of common knowledge that the community assets are treated as ' no man's assets' and are largely over-exploited or allowed to disuse with poor maintenance unless beneficiaries of the area take interest in the development and maintenance of them. We have observed that in the mini-watershed, beneficiaries have been persuaded to maintain these assets properly. User Groups of the area are not only maintaining them but also raised their area. Treatment in the form the construction of a check dam in Bande Nawaj Wadi [B. Wadi] have increased the water level considerably in open wells of the villages at the lower reaches, which again provided sufficient water for raising the crops and animals.

IV. Introduction of Innovative Techniques

Some breakthrough in the form of introduction of innovative techniques was also made. In order to improve soil health and thereby increase the fertility of the cultivable land, use of organic manure was popularized. Establishment of 'seed banks' of local seeds of Tur, Green gram. Black gram, Sesame etc. Created awareness among beneficiaries in which about 400 farmers participated did bring awareness in them as to their conservation and multiplication.

V. Increase in Employment

Farm labour employment is substantially high under watershed-based technology compared to that under the traditional technology, It is estimated that the watershed-based technology employs about twice as many labourers as compared to traditional practices. In absolute terms employment increased by 300 to 400 person hours per hectare. Poverty and under-employment are positively related and more employment would therefore benefit the poor. This would go a long way in achieving overall growth of incomes in the backward regions of dry land areas.

VI. Livelihood Promotion

In the resource poor areas like that of the project area, the question of livelihood is interlinked with the farming system and food security. PRAWARDA aimed at sustainable livelihood activities by transcending mere subsistence and creating conditions of savings and capital formation for the families. That is why, it facilitated the process of formation of SHGs, which will not only create 'on farm activities' but also 'off-farm income-venerating activities'. While doing so women folk of the area was kept in mind and several activities such a bag making, starting a petty shop, tailoring, and other service units etc. Were encouraged. The NGO was successful in seeing to it that financial support from several [both public and private institutions] sources such as, Sri Ratan Tata Trust, NABARD, ISPWD-K and CAPART, local Taluka Panchayat and Banks, is made available to SHGs. Besides the individual livelihood options, group livelihood activities have been introduced to generate income for masses. Neem Unit of Bandenawaj Wadi village generating income for 11 women and Community Irrigation wells at Illhal village supporting the livelihood of eight women are the few examples of this kind.

VII. Human Resource Management or Capacity Building

It has taken shape in the formation of Self Help Groups [SHGs], Village Watershed Management Committees [VWMCs], and User Groups [UGs]. In the first year, PRAWARDA's role in this context was to act as a catalyst in the formation of community-based organisations such as SHGs and VWMCs. This was done after preparing the plan for the entire area, which consisted of both the Private property resources [ppRs] and common property resources [CPRs]. In this phase, firstly, the work of selection of facilitators and their training was completed.

Facilitators got themselves acquainted with the villages and their socio-economic profiles. Afterwards, people dependent on watershed resources [both directly and indirectly] were persuaded to organise into SGHs and UGs. Villagers, who became members of the SHG and UGs, in turn, later, elected their leaders.

For every 60 acres of the cultivable area one UG was formed. Farmers with patta lands and those enjoying 'government land' became members of the UG. As to the contribution of members, 'backward caste' and 'other caste' farmers in the group contributed 10 percent and SC and ST farmers 5 percent of the cost of the 'work'. The contribution was made in terms of 'cash' of 'material' and both. The group leaders established link between the 'group' and 'labourers' and organized monthly meetings. Matters like [i] construction of water harvesting structures and [ii] contribution, either in the form of 'cash' or 'labour' were discussed or decided in the meetings. To carry out the watershed planning and implementation at the village level, specific institution called 'Watershed Management Committee' [WMC] was formed in all villages and they started working in the second year. In all, seven WMCs were formed by selecting two representatives from all Shiwars [i.e., a local name for micro watershed] and they were made responsible for executing the water harvesting structures.

In the second and last year, special consideration was given to include the poorest of the poor in the project i.e., widow women, physically handicapped, landless labourers, in addition to SC and ST community people, in the project. Members of WMCs were trained in participatory watershed planning & implementation and bookkeeping. The leaders i.e., Chairman and Secretary of WMCs did play a key role in seeping that constructions like farm bunds, waste weirs, boulder checks, diversion channel and farm ponds are up to the mark as to their quality. They personally took measurements of structures, maintained records of payments, persuaded all members to contribute their share in terms of either 'cash' or 'labour' and personally performed the 'curing' activity.

Thus, PRAWARDA intervention has led to increased community involvement in watershed planning and implementation.

VIII. Planning and Monitoring and Evaluation

Planning and Monitoring and Evaluation is persued as a 'focus area' by the PRAWARDA in the micro watershed area. Firstly, views of farmers of seven villages with regard to soil and water conservation were considered with appropriate technical advice and they were included in watershed planning. Secondly, Chairperson and members of the WMCs took keen interest in the form of personal supervision of the works. This, in turn, resulted in improvement of the quality of works undertaken; be it a check dam or waste weir etc., in both PPRs & CPRs. Thirdly, it resulted in the completion of works, as per the schedule. Fourthly, it made the process of 'labour contribution' [Shramadaan] easy and compulsory. Fourthly, as to 'open grazing', which was practiced extensively before the PRAWARDA intervention, the same was controlled by beneficiaries themselves voluntarily, as they were convinced about the harmful effects of it. Lastly, by adopting Planning, Monitoring and Evaluation systems in the local language i.e. 'Kannada', transparency and accountability was achieved.

IX. Women Empowerment and Removal of Vested Interests

In addition to the above, other benefits like 'women empowerment' and 'removal of vested interests' also were realised. In the 'wage employment' generated in the project area, women labourers did get special preference. Women members in WMCs did put up valient struggle and insisted for a fail deal and this resulted in the employment of more number of women workers, especially belonging to landless families and SC and ST communities. Provision of employment opportunities will go a long way in empowering women. Empowering women and weaker sections is not just for meeting their economic needs but also has its positive impact on socio-economic development of the entire region. Not only women succeeded in getting employment opportunities, but also, they were successful in keeping stakes away from the project of theirs. This was effected by transferring the Watershed Works' Fund to the WMC itself and members themselves deciding the 'work allotment' to labourers. From time immemorial, 'external contractors' have been a bane in the history of dry land development of the 'study area' as well of the country. This sort of 'transformation' was not, in any way, that easy. In fact, 'labourers' working in the watershed faced some intimidation from Ganga Jala Nayan Samiti of Mirjapur village and especially from 'male watershed samiti' of that village. Chairperson of it created many hurdles in their path. However, finally members and women labourers took him to task, and, in addition, demanded 'transparency', in the matter that led to the conduct of three WMC meeting and he was made to keep quiet.

X. Gender Sensitisation

In addition to 'women empowerment', 'gender dimension' has been integrated at all levels of the project and in all the focus areas, in the project area. Resource-poor and marginalized women have been especially targeted for training in capacity building, with PRAWARDA acting as a facilitator in accessing credit for development purposes. Training given to women members in WMCs has enabled them to think as equal partners with men in the development of the area. The very fact that women labourers took the Chairperson to task for giving employment to members other than local ones is the positive proof that they are 'conscious' of their area and their social responsibility towards the development of it.

Concluding Observations

Just now, the project intervention period of PRAWARDA is over. It is expected that the above benefits will not only continue and they will be intensified in the years to come. Thus, this NGO promoted project has the economic viability and holds better prospects to the people of the area. Further, this model can be replicated easily in any other area of the state or the country. In the past, how to enlist people's participation was one of the most baffling problems that confronted planners and the government. Now, the entry of NGOs as facilitators has solved this problem.

References

1. Hanumantha Rao C.H: Watershed Projects, 2000.
2. D.M. Nanjundappa: High Power Committee for Redressal of Imbalance, 2002.
3. Annual Reports of PRAWARDA from 2000-2004.

9

Karraguda Micro Water Harvesting Structure

M. Sankara Reddi, M. Ramesh and M. Sundra Rao

Introduction

Palakonda sub-division of Andhra Pradesh state is geographically situated at northern and western direction of Srikakulam District Jotting into Orissa State. The hills in these areas are part of the Eastern Ghats and run into hundreds in number. The hills' general elevation is 1500 to 3000 feet. Climate of the area is characterised with a moderate and high rainfall. The average rainfall in this area is 1080 mm. The importance of the occurrence of rainfall is examined in reference to cyclones. It indicates that November month is more cyclone prone month. 52.5% of the total rainfall is received under the southwest monsoon. On an average, there are 70 to 80 rainy days in a year. The winds are generally light to moderate in velocity. Soil erosion hazard is severe due to steep slopes, badly managed farming fields, overgrazing, fallow lands, cultivable and uncultivable waste are the principle factors. The run off water causes soil erosion.

Karraguda Village of Goyidi Panchayat, Seethampeta Mandal is a small village covering an area of 420 acres. It is located at the foot of barren and rocky hills in the rain shadow area of the Eastern Ghats. With an average annual rainfall of 1050 mm, most of which falls within a span of a few days. Karraguda Village, Goyidi Panchayat, Seethampeta Mandal of Srikakulam District of Andhra Pradesh has been experiencing severe droughts for many years. The landscape is marked by heavy soil erosion. The highly eroded stony soil is largely unfit for cultivation, but for the lack of alternatives, the people of Karraguda continue to grow crops.

The Community Action Group (CAG) Committee members of Karraguda village of GOYIDI Panchayat have prepared a Community Micro Project proposal to improve their socio-economic conditions and made a request to Jana Chetana and CARE STEP to facilitate them to mobilize necessary resources and technical expertise to excavate Irrigation Tank across the Papara Konda Hill stream. The purpose of construction of the proposed Irrigation Tank is to increase the productivity and to improve the source of livelihoods of poorest among poor and vulnerable. This activity shall generate additional employment, income and prevents migration. At present, they are raising a temporary bund and diverting the water to irrigate their lands through a means of poonu. Poonu means a temporary earthen bund excavated across the hill steam to storage flow water. The structure of poonu is temporary in nature and subjected to frequent breakdowns. This is causing heavy loss of employment man days and livelihoods. On the other hand, there is heavy siltation deposited at poonu area. So, as to mitigate this problem, the Community Action Group resolved to request the concerned agencies to approve their Micro Watershed projects. The construction of New Irrigation Tank is to divert the flow of floodwater. The excavation of New Irrigation Tank at Papara Konda Stream at Karraguda Village is very good and spread in an area of approximately 60 Acres. The yield is calculated is 629 cubic meters. The storage capacity of the Tank is 629 Cubic Meters of water. The flow water will be used to irrigate to an extent of 50 Acres approximately. On the other hand, the storage water will recharge the ground water and lead to increase the water table in the village. This will facilitate to increase the water table levels of drinking water wells. This work had generated 2672 man-days of employment. The average Man-days of employment generated are 50.

People Centred Participatory Development Process

The selected site location is comprises of six villages namely Rasulupeta, Karraguda, Diguva Daraba, Jaggaduguda,

Addakulaguda and Addakulaguda Pathuru. They are situated on the bank of Chittigeda rivulet. The local Community Action Group (CAG) is identified one of the core problem as lack of assured irrigation and discussed the need to have an Integrated Micro Watershed Development Project in 2004. Initially people had doubts about the whole idea, apprehending it as an attempt by officials to evict them from the cultivation of unreserved forestland.

While responding to the issue, the CEO, Jana Chetana had conducted AOL exercise and asks them to analyse the issue in all angles and aspects. They divided into small groups and made an open enquiry and investigation into the said problem. Finally, they come up with a solution that there is an urgent need to Construction of Micro Water Harvesting Structure at Karraguda Village, Goyidi Panchayat, Seethampeta, Srikakulam to avoid run off water and divert the same to irrigate agricultural fields. Basing on their suggestion, Mr. L. Krishna Rao, Community Coordinator, carried a detailed Investigation Study by involving all the stakeholders and prepared a detailed Peoples Estimation-cum-Abstract of Detailed Activities. They had series of meetings where the purpose and plan of the project were discussed. Later, they followed whole-hearted devotion.

- The area earlier suffered the fury of seasonal rivulets commonly called the Geddalu, which caused widespread damage by inundating large chunks of arable land.
- It was predominantly a degraded scrub area where soil retained less moisture and sustained scarce vegetation.
- The area comprised disintegrated pockets, which were completely cut off from the rest of the region during the monsoon.
- Emphasis was laid on the participation of people in planning and implementation of development activities.

Learning Experiences

Various water bodies were examined to harness the water. In addition to this, gullies were plugged by constructing a number of structures along the water line on the upstream side of the catchment area. Finally, a site was selected for the construction of an earthen dam at Peparai Konda near Karraguda. They commenced the work on 11th November 2004 and completed by end of 31st December 2004. Within a short span of one month, a fifteen feet high earthen dam was built by the villagers and they used their traditional technical knowledge and skills. This dam helped to collect and retain rainwater flowing from the catchment area that has provided perennial source of irrigation to 28 families irrigating 50 acres of land. The village community had born 25 percent of the cost of construction of the dam in the form of donation of voluntary labour (*shramdan*). They are responsible for the upkeep of the dam have been organised into a user group.

According to the opinion of the Community Action Group members, this dam has proved to be a boon for villagers in one or more of the following ways: -

- Structural and mechanical measures including construction of earthern dams to harvest runoff generated during rainy season and its subsequent use during rest of year.
- Flow diversions through mechanical and vegetative measures to control rate of water flow on hill slopes and to minimize soil erosion.
- Conservation effective production. Sustained natural resource management linked to poverty alleviation.
- Participatory planning on watershed basis: from village to watershed.
- The water, which earlier inundated land, has now been channelised to the fields for irrigation.
- This has led to a change in the cropping pattern. Besides traditional crops, cash crops like tomato, ladyfinger, long gourd and fruits like lemon, guava and mangoes are being grown.
- Increment in non-farm employment.
- Increased literacy rate.

People Centred Integrated Micro Watershed Management

The twin objectives of poverty reduction and environment management are combined in this project. Locate funds by "greening" investment under rural employment programmes like Employment Assurance Scheme and from area development programmes like Integrated Wasteland Development programme.

Work executed through Village Water Users Committees consisting of User Groups, Self-Help Groups and Credit Groups. Government through Mission provides technical and financial support.

Community Action Groups (CAGs) have been constituted for planning and implementation of activities on the basis of commonly agreed action plans. Perceptible change is seen in quality of life of people through better nutrition, housing, clothing and improved literacy.

Our idea on the potential for water resources development in the tribal regions of Srikakulam is now receiving attention in various forums.

The Planning Commission, the Ministry of Tribal Affairs, Government of India has taken note of it. In order to focus on various studies in various tribal villages in Srikakulam District we have undertaken to highlight the successes cases.

Benefits

- Degradation of the catchment has been checked largely.
- Green cover on forestland and outside has been improved.
- Effective conservation and augmentation of water resources has taken place leading to better access to drinking water and increase in irrigated area.
- With the reclamation of cultivable wastelands and degraded uplands, the net sown area has increased.

- o Multiple cropping has been reintroduced with assured availability of irrigation water. This has resulted in increased crop productivity due to better soil, water and crop management.
- o Seasonal human and cattle migration has been reduced.
- o Different water harvesting techniques were used to store and conserve water for its subsequent efficient use.

Project Achievements

- Recharging of groundwater resources. Higher incomes through high crop Production.
- Improved livelihood, access to education, nutrition and health due to increased economic returns.
- Improved and sustainable source of fuel wood from shelterbelt pruning.
- Recognition of the value of the integrated management of natural resources.
- Marginal reduction in human and cattle migration.

Conclusion

Community participation is essential for getting the desired outcome of any project, as participation of people in developmental activities, gives an impetus to the working process and it makes the programme a self-sustained one. Use of commonly available resources and identifying the key areas, where the available technology can be put to use, provide a useful link in bridging the gap. A small intervention of technology in integrated Land and Water development has transformed the economy and ecology of Karraguda region while conserving the natural resources through people's participation.

The success of Land and Water development program is fully dependent on the efficiency of management and effectiveness of people's participation. In fact, land and water management is not merely anti-erosion and anti-run-off approach but also a comprehensive, integrated approach of land and water resource management. In order to obtain maximum benefit, it is imperative that the natural resource, soil and water, forest, greenery, common resources and facilities be properly protected and utilised. Then only it will help to improve and maximise productivity. It would ultimately be dependent on the strong community of people who are in the area. They have to be knit together through Self Help Group, Village Waterusers Committees and School Education Committees under Community Action Group as a people's initiative.

10

Minor Irrigation: Rationale and Objectives

K. Nageswara Rao and T. Narayana Reddy

Rational utilization and timely conservation of water resources assumes greater importance in drought prone areas where water resources are scare in their availability. In these areas ground water utilization needs to be effective, particularly in irrigation and agriculture sectors. In other words, this calls for productive utilization of water for irrigation and agricultural purposes. Minor irrigation works serve the twin objectives of effective utilization and conservation of scare water resources in drought prone areas. Minor irrigation works are intended for the improvement of irrigation so as to stabilize existing irrigation works and expand irrigation with available water supplies. These works are implemented with an objective of storing the little water available, conserving moisture by harvesting to stabilize the production of field crops. By and large, the important sources of irrigation are tanks, canals, surface wells, dug wells etc.

A Geological Survey of India report states that the surface water potentialities are limited in drought prone Anantapur district and there is no scope for sinking tube wells. In view of this sinking bore wells or tube wells for irrigation has become near impossible proposition in the district. However, minor irrigation tanks and percolation tanks provide scope for irrigation in this district. In this context, an attempt is made in this study to evaluate the impact of minor irrigation tanks on the agriculture sector of the district economy.

This paper intends to estimate the impact of minor irrigation tanks in Anantapur district in stabilizing the ayacut area under these tanks and also enquires into the changes in the cropping pattern of the district in the recent decade. For this purpose a survey of 20 of the 307 minor irrigation tanks in Anantapur district has been conducted in January 2005 and the results are analysed.

Anantapur District

The geographical positions of the district render it, the driest part of the state and hence, agricultural conditions are more often precarious. Monsoons evade this part of the state and due to this unfortunate location. The normal rainfall of the district is 552.0 mm. There are no perennial rivers in the district and the important river is Pennar. Another significant river in the district is Chitrvathi. The soils of the district are predominantly red except Kanekal, Bommanahal, Vidapnakal, Urvakonda, Guntakal, Gooty mandals. A look into the pattern of land utilization of the district reveals that then net area sown is 10,09 lakh hectares, which form only 53.00 percent of the total area of the district. The total cropped area is 10.44 lakh hectares and the area sown more than once is 0.37 lakh hectares.

The cultivated area of the district is 10.44 lakh hectares out of which 9.00 lakh hectares is under kharif and 1.44 lakh hectares is under rabi season. Anantapur district occupies the lowest position in respect of irrigation facilities with only 14.98 percent of the gross cropped area. Out of the gross cropped area 68.35 percent is under wells including tube wells, 22.22 percent is under canals, 7.10 percent is under tanks and 2.33 percent is under other sources.

Minor Irrigation Tanks

It is noted that many tanks have been in use in the district for irrigation in many villages in the past. Rainwater has been the main source of water into these tanks. However, the drought conditions affected irrigation under these tanks and many tanks became defunct for want of water. Further, due to the neglect of the administrators to maintain and sustain these tanks for use of irrigation, the bunds of many tanks became weak and failed to withhold the rainwater even in good rain fall years. On the other hand, some of the tanks breached during the years of good rainfall. As a result, agricultural and irrigational activities in Anantapur district turned out to be precarious leaving the plight of farmers pathetic.

In this context, attempts were made by the district administrators to reconstruct the breached tanks and restore them for irrigational use, apart from constructing new tanks to develop and sustain irrigation in the district. Such efforts were taken up on a notable scale under Drought Prone Areas Programmes. At present there are 307 minor irrigation tanks in Anantapur district catering to the needs of irrigation in the district.

It is found that 15 of the 20 selected tanks are old tanks, 2 are reconstructed tanks and the remaining are new tanks constructed to meet the irrigational needs of the villages in the district. Catchment area of Roddkampalli in Roddam mandal has largest Catchment area of 210.00sq. miles while Uppidipalli tank in Madakasira mandal is has the lowest catchment area of 2.90 sq. miles. This reveals that the catchment area of the tanks has been significantly fluctuating and it varied 100 times from the lowest to highest catchment area tanks. The average catchment area of the minor irrigation tanks seems to be around 50.00 sq. miles in the district.

The water holding capacity of minor irrigation tanks in Anantapur district has been different between the tanks. It is 15.82 for the smallest sized tank in Nadimpalli village of Samandapalli mandal and 195.37 mcft. for Peddakondapalli in Roddam mandal. Among the selected tanks only one quarter of the tanks have the water holding capacity more than 100.00 mcft. The cost of construction or reconstruction of the tanks also varied violently between tanks. It was Rs. 1.12 crores for the reconstructed tank in R. Anantapuram of Kambadur mandal and Rs. 25.21 lakhs for the new tank constructed in Venkatampalli village of Tadpatri mandal.

The ayacut area developed under the minor irrigation tanks in the district varied from 137 acres under Vankatamalli tank in Tadpatri mandal to 1037 acres under Gooty tank in Gooty mandal. In all, a total of 83,000 acres of ayacut area has been developed under the selected tanks at an average of 415 acres under each tank. Only 8 of the selected tanks have the ayacut area more than this average value. It indicates that many minor irrigation tanks are smaller in their size and have smaller ayacut area under them in Anantapur district.

It is a common feature that irrigation tanks provide for irrigation of crops not only in the village where the tank is located but also in other village down stream. It is found that three-fourths of the ayacut area under the selected tanks belong to the villages in which the tanks are located and only one quarter of the irrigated area under these tanks belong to the down stream villages.

It is noted that the wells in the ayacut area have been receiving water from the tanks and providing irrigation facilities. There has been a steep rise in the number of wells under the tanks between 1995 and 2005. The policy of the government to provide financial assistance for sinking new wells under various schemes has been the reason for the indiscriminate sinking of bore wells and exploitation of water in the district. This resulted in a steep fall in the irrigated area over the decade, apart from the drought conditions that shattered the irrigation in Anantapur district.

The intensity of drought has been visible from the data relating the tank filling in the preceding 10 years period. During 1995-2005 only two tanks are filled with water in 5 years while 9 of the 20 tanks received water in 4 years and other tanks had water in 3 years. The drought conditions had affected adversely the irrigation potential in the district in the last decade.

Further, it is observed that even during the years of good rainfall when the tanks received water, water is available for one half of the year in 14 of the 20 selected tanks and for less than 5 months in other tanks. This seems to have adversely affected the irrigation in kharif season under many tanks. Recurring drought conditions, indiscriminate use of water by increased number of wells contributed for the significant decline in the area under irrigation under minor irrigation tanks in the district during 1995-2005.

Cropping Pattern

Regarding the cropping pattern adopted by the farmers under the selected minor irrigation tanks in Anantapur district, it is found that several crops including minor crops like Korra, Maize etc are also raised under the tanks. However the important crops cultivated in kharif season are groundnut, jowar, sunflower, paddy etc and the lone crop raised during the Rabi season is paddy. To a larger extent paddy has grown in the district in the Rabi season under the wells.

The yield per hectare of the crops grown decreased between 1995 and 2005. The yield per hectare of groundnut, the lead crop of the district declined by nearly 0.75 quintals while that of paddy crop declined by little more than 2.00 quintals per hectare. It is also noted that the cost of irrigation in the district between 1995 and 2005 also increased steeply because of the hike in the prices of agricultural inputs. As a result, the incomes of the farmers reported have been declining over the period. Under many tanks in the district sunflower has been the crop that has been sustaining in its cultivation, as it has been an irrigable dry crop.

The important findings of the study are:

(i) Many of the minor irrigation tanks are old tanks constructed during the period of Vijayanagar rulers and later administrators. The size of the tanks varied significantly in their catchment area, water holding capacity and the irrigation potential developed under them.

(ii) As many of these tanks are old tanks they breached during the season of heavy rains. In fact, the maintenance of these tanks has been neglected for quite some time. Only when the irrigation became precarious efforts were made to reconstruct some of these tanks under Drought prone area programme.

(iii) Further, to mitigate the adverse effects of drought attempts were also made to construct new minor tanks to stabilize the irrigation potential in the district. However, the duration of construction of many new tanks was long and hence the cost of tank construction escalated significantly.

(iv) Wells including tube wells that derive water through recharge from the minor irrigation tanks have been the major source of irrigation in many villages. The financial assistance and subsidy provided by the government to the farmers to sink wells resulted in the growth of wells.

(v) Indiscriminate use and exploitation of ground water affected the irrigation potential of the district significantly. As a consequence of this the area irrigated under the minor irrigation tanks decreased during the last decade.

(vi) The cropping pattern adopted by the farmers under these tanks has been diversified. While a number of crops have been grown during the Kharif season only paddy has been raised during the rabi season under many tanks.

(vii) Absence of crop rotation and single or mono crop culture in rabi season brought down the yield per hectare of the important crops raised in the district during the last ten years period.

(viii) Liberalization policies pursed by the government during the reforms period facilitated the adoption of new technologies in agriculture sector in the form of hybrid seed, application of fertilizer and pesticides that resulted in the cost of cultivation in the district.

(ix) These factors, in addition to the recurring drought conditions worsened the economic conditions of the farmers that forced some of them to commit suicides.

11

Draught and Ecology Management of Forest Resources

D. Chenna Reddy and K. Nagendra Reddy

Forests play an important role in environment stability and contribute significantly in the process of economic development. Conservation, development and management of forests are prerequisite for maintaining a healthy ecosystem. Lack of people's participation and non-existence of any effective regulatory system for resource use has been a major cause for degradation of forests and adjoining lands. A study has been done in Anantapur District to evaluate Peoples Participation in Joint Forest Management.

Participatory approach has a major role in allocating rights and responsibilities over resources. A key concern is to identify approaches, which can enhance the efficiency and accountability of the system. The concept of JFM has been interpreted in various ways but the basic element in this concept is to establish grassroot community-based institutions and the effective involvement for protection and management of the forest.

The impact of the programme was analyzed on the basis of its performance in two major areas. Improvement in the state of forests covered by the programme and improvement in the socio-economic conditions of the communities involved in the forest management. Information for the analysis was obtained through interaction with the different stakeholders belonging to the sample Vana Samrakshna Samithi (VSS), N.C.Thanda.

Naginayanicheruvu Thanda VSS is operated under Andhra Pradesh Forest Protection Scheme formed on 16-07-1994. The total numbers of householders are 105 and the area allotted is 240 ha. The villagers are aware of micro plan contents. The investigator noticed the following works were done in the VSS.

The impact of the JFM programme is analyzed here in terms of the success in protection and regeneration of the degraded forests thereby bringing about an improvement in the environment, generation of additional income and employment and facilitating social development in the VSS members and village people.

The measures taken for the protection of forest by the VSS members had a tremendous impact on natural regeneration and the growth of trees in their areas. The important species regenerated include Bikki, Neereddi, Kalivi, Neem, Tamarind, Sandalwood, Teak, Chigara, Sandra, Pacharim, Rela, Regu, Neeruddi, Neredu and Palm trees.

As regards the reasons for natural regeneration after the formation of VSS, the member's opinions are that the control of fire accidents was the main reason for natural regeneration and illegal felling of trees by the woodcutters and tending activities undertaken by them facilitated natural regeneration. The other reasons include the prevention of cattle grazing.

Impact on Income and Employment Generation

The major impact of JFM programme, having a direct impact upon the living conditions of the members of VSS was its contribution to the generation of additional income and employment. This had taken place on account of three factors: undertaking of different works in VSS area; through the support activities and the indirect impact on agriculture.

As mentioned earlier, the support activities undertaken directly by the forest dept. and those by other agencies through providing matching grants to the thrift groups also facilitated the member's families to take up alternative economic pursuits.

Further, the SMC works undertaken by the VSS members resulted in an increase in the ground water table, which led to the availability of more water in the wells and to the digging of more number of bore wells. As a consequence, there was in increase in both the extent of cultivated area and the crop productivity.

Besides, there is some additional income, through to a limited extent, to the VSS members because of their usufruct rights over the non-wood forest produce on individual basis and selling them in the village itself or in the nearby places. It was found that the additional income generated through all the above activities was used mostly for consumption purposed and to some extent for productive purposes. Further, because of this additional income as well as due to the promotion of thrift habit, the dependence on moneylenders was reduced to a considerable extent.

Impact on Social Development

The VSS activities appear to have set in motion a kind of social change in the forest fringe villages. The most important effect could be seen in arresting seasonal migration, which is a common feature in the drought prone areas. Because of the increase in additional income and reduction in migration, there was some positive impact on education of children.

Reduction in the Dependency on Forest

As a result of various measures taken up under the programme, there was some reduction in the dependency on forests. Particular mention may be made about the distribution of smokeless chulhas. The women revealed that fuel wood consumption was reduced by 50 percent with the use of smokeless chulhas, while some others felt that these are not of much use of preparing food to larger number in big families. Further, six biogas plants were installed in Naginayanicheruvu thanda and all of them are in use.

Involvement of the Community in Decision-Making

The involvement of the community in decision-making with regard to VSS activities can be gauged from the extent of their participation in General Body and executive committee meetings as well as their participation in the training programmes conducted. The resolution books indicate that executive committee meetings are held regularly once in a month. The percentage of attendance varied between 57 percent and 87 percent, indicating that a majority of the members are attending these meeting regularly.

The forest department conducted a number of training programmes for the different categories of VSS members with a view to build up their capacities so that they could take an active part in the programme and sustain the efforts made so far.

Sustainability of VSS

An attempt was made to obtain the views of the people with regard to the functioning of the programme and their suggestions for its sustainability. The members of generally satisfied with the present rules and regulations concerning JFM. However, the members felt that restrictions with regard to the extent of rock-fill dams that could be constructed per hectare and the rates for different works could be made more flexible to suit the local needs.

In the village the forest cover is very low, the entire wasteland and government land looking plan land barren hills. There is no responsibility of villagers to protect the forest. Before village people for their primary needs of firewood rapidly degraded starting the VSS more than 200 ha forest area, illicit cutting of wood, burning of forest were occurred. In 1994, VSS is formed. The officials, Divisional Forest Officer of the Penukonda attended the meeting.

The Forest Department had taken 240 ha land for VSS to develop the degraded forest in Somandepalli forest region of Penukonda reserve forest. Before starting VSS there was no species identified. After formation of VSS firstly developed 25 ha plot in the reserved forest. 7500 plots developed in 1994-95 under the VSS committees. In 1994-95 constructed check dams, gully pits planted 75 nos. and 80% of plants survived.

In 1997, forest developed 40 ha area for plantation and other nourishing worked. One important aspect about the plantation is that the development of intensive plot on which the V.S.S members hoped to derive sufficient returns in future. In 1998-99, construction of check dams with rough stone dry packing and digged gullies with rough stones, excavating continues contour trenches. In 2001-02 10 ha plot developed under APFP scheme. Seed dibbling work done through the entire VSS like this works done by the works. All this work was done by the VSS committee.

Comparing Profile of Forest from 1994 to 2004

In the year 1994 village forest cover is very low, the entire wasteland and government land looking plain land with barren hills. There is no responsibility of villagers to protect the forest. Before starting VSS more than 200 ha forest area rapidly degraded by village people for their primary need of fire wood, illicit cutting of wood, burning of forest were occurred in 1994, the year in which VSS was formed.

Plantation Activity

About 175 ha were developed under Andhra Pradesh Forest Project (A.P.F.P) schemes i.e., natural regeneration programme. Above programme of plantation included 2000 plants consisting of Kanuga, Neelagiri, Subabul etc. The survival rate of plants was significant and which was up to 80%. One multipurpose tank was constructed in the forest, which was very useful to cattle, and people who are visiting frequently in to the forest. Out of 250 ha area, continuous contour Trenches (CCTs) were nearly about 100 ha, Rock Fill Dams (R.F.Ds) 105 ha, plantation 175 ha were developed under Andhra Pradesh Forest project (APFP) scheme i.e., natural regeneration programme. More than 4000 plants were planted in the forest area in 25 ha plot. Check dams and trenches were constructed and plain land was ploughed with tractors. In this land 500 bikki trees were planted. The V.S.S executed different works and plantation programme including steps taken to protect forest. In between 1994 to 1999 25000 plants were grown in the V.S.S forest area and nearly 110000 running meters of C.C.Ts (continuous contour trenches) were digged. More than 100 R.F.Ds (Rock fill dams) were constructed across the hill area. People expressed their feelings about condition of forest was very bad before V.S.S formation. They said that there is no co-ordination between Forest department and village people. Hence degraded forestland and forest fires were usually prevailing. With the implementation of V.S.S in 1994 established a cordial relationship with forest officials.

The people of the village took the work of developing forest, which also provided them some financial assistance through the forest works and forest resources like fruits, beedi leaves etc. The total profit was credited to the V.S.S committee through government policy.

Record of Plant Growth in the VSS Area

The plant species recorded in the VSS area in post-development scenario are:

Name of the Species		Local Name
Alangium salvifolium	:	Uduga
Dalbergia paniculata		
Givotia rottleriformis		
Cassia siamea	:	Pacchari
Dolichandrone atrovirens	:	Pothurirrodat
Erythroxylon monogynum	:	Devadaari
Syzysium eumini	:	Neredi
Gardenia gummifera	:	Bikki
Securinegal leucopyrus	:	Tellapulisiri
Edathara, Acacia leucophloca	:	Tellathumma
Albizia amara	:	Chigara
Emelima arborea	:	Kondagummudi
Carrissa spinarum	:	Kalivi
Terminalia Arjuna	:	Maddi
Hardwickia binata	:	Aari
Wrightia tunctria	:	Palavara

Ziziphus aenoplia	:	Pariki
Coculus hisutus	:	Dusara
Catunargam spinosum	:	Manga
Rivea hypocrateriformis	:	Bodhi
Pterocarpus marsupium	:	Egi
Tarenna asiatica	:	Papidi, (Bingipapiri)
Diospyros melamoxylon	:	Beediaaku
Ereria tilaeifolia	:	Jaana
Alangium salvifolium	:	Ulinja
Acacia chundra	:	Sandra
Dodonaea viscosa	:	Bandiri are commonly found

in the VSS area.

Table11.1: Natural Regeneration and Plant Growth

Plantation Programme

1. Total No. of saplings planted	:	51,600
2. Area (ha)	:	205
3. Intensive plantation programme:		
i. Important species	:	Eucalyptus
ii. No. of saplings	:	3000
iii. Area (ha)	:	7

Fire prevention in VSS areas

1. No. of fire accidents:		
i. Before formation of VSS (average per year)	:	2
ii. After formation (Total)	:	1
2. Reasons for Control	:	Formation of fire lines

Natural regeneration of plant species in the VSS area

1. Plant species	:	Satisfactory
2. Bushes and Fodder species	:	Good

Reasons for natural regeneration after formation of VSS

1. Reasons:

i. Prevention of catt!e grazing and Control of fire accidents : Yes
ii. Tending activities : Yes
iii. SMC works : Yes
iv. Preventing illegal feeling of trees: Yes

Reasons for the growth of trees in VSS areas

1. Reasons (Order of priority) : 1. Gap plantation
2. Soil moisture conservation works
3. Protection from illegal felling

Table11.1 shows the natural regeneration is good in the VSS area. 51,600 plants were planted in 205 ha area as well as 300 eucalyptus plants were planted were planted in 7ha area. Two fire accidents were done before formation of VSS. This is reduced after formation of VSS. Bushes and fodder species growth rate is satisfactory. Reason fort plant growth is prevention of illegal felling of trees, reducing of fire accidents and cattle grazing.

Table 11.2 : Impact of VSS on Socio-Economic Conditions

Employment and income generation

1. Employment generated through VSS Works (No. of person days) : 2,143
2. Amount received as wages through VSS works (Rs. in lakhs) : 2.46

Impact on Agriculture

1. Net cultivated area increased
2. Crop productivity has increased

Awareness and utilizations of forest produce

1. People are aware of usufruct rights
2. People use to collection on non-wood forest produce
3. Sale/Personnel use of NTFP is Individual
4. Place of Sale outside

Migration

No. of families migrated

i. Before formation	:	Nil
ii. At present	:	Nil

Education and health

1. Positive impact on education	:	Moderate
2. Positive impact on health	:	Yes
3. Positive impact on family planning	:	Yes

Promotion of non-conventional energy sources

1. No. of house holds provided with smokeless chulhas	:	105
2. No. of house holds using smokeless chulhas	:	105
3. No. of bio-gas plants in the village	:	6
4. No. of plants in use	:	6

Table 11.2 shows improving the economic condition of the beneficiaries.2143 man –days worked and gained 2.46 lakhs through VSS works. Cultivated land increased, crop productivity raised. They are well aware about the use of usufructs rights and sale of Non Timber Forest Produce. Migration stopped due to participation of V.S.S works. 105 smokeless chulahs were distributed, 6 bio-gas plants also distributed to promotion of non conventional energy.

Table 11.3 displayed the functioning of V.S.S. They key role of V.S.S is general body and executive committee. From 1996-01 there were more than 23 meetings conducted. Overage percent is 12.4 and 26 percent is average every meeting for general body.

The executive committee meets regularly from 1996-01. 48 meetings were held during the period.

Table 11.3: Administration of VSS

Particulars of General body meetings held		
1. No. of meetings held during 1996-01	:	23
2. Average attendance per meeting	:	26
3. Percentage of total	:	12.4
Particulars of Executive Committee meetings		
1. No. of meetings held during 1996-01	:	48
2. Average attendance per meeting	:	14
3. Percentage of total	:	82.4
Details of training programmes conducted		
1. No. of training programmes conducted:		
i. Presidents and EC members	:	3
ii. GB members	:	2
iii. SHG's	:	1
iv. Total	:	6

Average 14 percent were presented in every meeting. Total percent is 82.4. Training is the most important aspect to success every programme. Total 6 training programmes were conducted. Out of these trainings for E.C members, 2 training programmes for General Body (G.B) and 1 training for Self Help Groups (S.H.Gs). The administration is very good in the committee.

Policy Implications

On the basis of the above conclusions, the following recommendations are made for the effective implementation of the JFM programme to ensure equity and sustainability.

1. Elections may be held regularly for EC once in two years so as strengthen the democratic credentials of VSS.
2. There could be some flexibility in the norms fixed for the extent of rock-fill dams in a given area if the situation demands.

Some of the rock-fill dams have sited up and hence there is a need for undertaking desilting operations on a regular basis.

3. There is a need for planning the support activities to be taken up in VSS area/village in coordination with other government departments. Care has to be taken to build the capacities of the people to demand and achieve their tasks on their own. In other words, the philosophy of self-held needs to be promoted more vigorously.

4. There is a need to promote income-generating activities that could be built around the existing thrift groups so that alternative opportunities are created in order to sustain the efforts being made to reduce dependence on forests. The thrift groups need to be moulded self-sustaining through regular meetings conducted and saving activity will develop among the members.

5. The training programmes like capacity building, institutional building, micro finance, lively hood promotion activities undertaken so far need to be strengthened further by arranging more such programmes for the members of the VSS formed under different schemes in the district, particularly for women.

A mechanism has to be evolved for raising revenue from the forest produce being used by the members in order to create a maintenance fund at the VSS level with which the programme can be made sustainable to some extent.

Conclusion

One of the major objectives of the study was to evolve suitable strategies for making the J.F.M intervention successful and measure them against the existing parameters governing the functioning of J.F.M. This micro level of study in social, ecological and economic aspect of J.F.M activity in Naginayani Cheruvu thanda reveals the following.

Overall performance of J.F.M was found to be moderate, and impact of the programme in the study was satisfactory.

- There is a scope for improving the performance of the committee meticulously developing the capacities of the main actors.

- A well thought-out state level strategy for training and capacity development would go a long way ensuring the statewide enhancement of the J.F.M. Committees performance.
- It is felt that there is difference in the understanding of the programme at various levels of the Forest Department and NGOs play a key role in the JFM programme, involving them in training will ensure uniformity in understanding, implementation, monitoring and evaluation of the programme.
- The study also indicates that there is uniformity among the committee in preparing micro-plan, which plays a stellar role in forest department, finalized a uniform format for micro-plan preparation and this is introduced in to the state.

12

Inter-Linking Rivers Project

M.G. Basava Raja, T. Ramesh, Manu Mahesh and M. D. Umesh

The interlinking of rivers is considered as the best remedy for the two recurring problems of India viz., water scarcity in the rivers of South India and the floods that affect the north Indian States. In pursuance of Supreme Court order, Government of India has set up a Task Force to consider the modalities of implementing Inter-linking Rivers Project (ILRP) and the NDA which was in power then, declared that this task would be taken up on a war footing. The present UPA Government seems to be not much enthusiastic about this project. But Congress Party when it was in opposition during NDA Government promised that it would support this project. So, during NDA Government, more or less there was unanimity among most of political parties of India.

The idea of linking of rivers is not a new one. In the 19th Century, Colonel Sir Arthur Cotton, who is known as the father of Indian irrigation schemes, was the first to coin the idea of interlinking of rivers in the country. When the East Indian Company was planning to link up different regions which were under their control with Railway tracks, Sir Cotton suggested for linking up rivers for economical system of water transport. So Sir Cotton's prime concern was for inland navigation transport. The British Committee on Irrigation, on financial constraints grounds, dismissed the idea of linking of rivers. In 1970s, a couple of grand schemes of interlinking of rivers were proposed by Engineer / Minister K.L. Rao and Airlines Pilot Captain Dinshaw Dastur. Dr. Rao's concern was irrigation facilities and generation of electricity. Dastur's scheme was known as Garland Canal

Scheme to feed Himalayan waters to the peninsular parts of the country. Rao and Dastur schemes were rejected on the grounds of their feasibility, desirability and viability. The present ILRP has been the result of estimates worked out by National Water Development Agency (NWDA).

NWDA's Proposal

The NWDA was set up in 1982 to work out basin-wise surpluses and deficits and study the storage possibilities, links and transfers the NWDA has been working on this project for over two decades and producing reports. There are three components in NWDA's project proposal, viz., The Himalayan Rivers Component (H.C) the Peninsular Rivers Component (PC) and the Hydro Electric Components. The HC envisages for a number of links, including some within the Ganga system, some between neighbouring rivers in the Brahmaputra system, a couple between those two systems, one long link from the Sarada to the Sabarmati through the Yamuna and the Rajastan, and one from the Ganga to the Subernarekha and then on to the Mahanadi. The general idea is to transfer waters to Southern Uttar Pradesh, Haryana, Punjab and Rajastan and eventually southwards to the peninsular component. The PC involves a number of links, of which the most important would be those connecting the Mahanandi, the Godavari, the Krishna, the Pennar and the Cauvery. Other links would include the Ken-Betwa, the Parbati-Kalisindh-Chambal, the Par-Tapi-Narmada and the Damanganga-Pinjal. Another idea is the partial diversion of certain rivers flowing into the Arabian sea eastwards to link with rivers flowing into the Bay of Bengal, viz., the Bedti-Varada, the Nethravathi-Hemavathi, the Pamba-Achankovil-Vaippar.

The PC will cost Rs. 1,06,000 crores; the HC will cost Rs. 1,85,000 crores; and the HEC will cost Rs. 2,69,000. So, the total cost of NWDA project proposal will be Rs. 5,60,000 crore and a 15 year deadline. According to this plan about 300 dams and more than 1000 kms of canals will be dug. Of the 30 links proposed, 14 are in the Himalayan and 16 in the Peninsular component.

Objections Raised Against ILRP

The ILRP is criticized as a mindless dream and too ambitious. The important objections raised against ILRP are given below.

1. The ILRP would flood an estimated 8000 sq. kms of land and leave three million people homeless. This view is expressed by Sudhir Vombatkere, a retired Military Engineer. According to him, this type of river linking project was thought of in Soviet Russia under Stalin regime; When rives flowing north were to be diverted to its dry central region. But even Soviet Scientists then categorically rejected the project on the pretext that it would cause enormous environmental damage.
2. Spreading of Polluted Water - According to Ravi Agarwal Environmentalist of Delhi based NGO Srishti, the ILRP will spread pollution from rivers like Ganga to cleaner rivers. Inter-linking of toxic river with non-toxic river will have a devastating impact in all of our rivers and as result of that on all human beings and wild life. For example. Per river of Gujarat is mercury contaminated. Yamuna water are poisonous. So when rivers are linked, pollution control will be even more difficult and many more rivers will run into sewers.
3. According to some opponents of this project, there has not been much analysis as to how flow irrigation affects soil health and river health. For instance, every river's water properties are different; and the survival of a number of aquatic species, insects and birds depends on these unique properties. Proper study has not been made on these aspects.
4. It cannot be understood now that the states that are not riparian will have no claims to the Water of the rivers. Hence, a transfer of water from one region to another would be done only by consensus. But the Cauvery water dispute shows that there is simple solution to sharing river water even when the two warring states were both riparian. Since there is accord on the sharing of

river water from a surplus region to a deficit one, disputes between them could increase many fold. In this context, mention may be made of Punjabi state. This state has raised objection for the ILRP and earlier raised a hue and cry when desert state Rajastan as a non-riparian state was being given water from the Indus river system. There are other problem also. West Bengal, which is also objecting to the proposal fears that any linking of the Ganga and Brahmaputra might ease the flood situation in Assam, but worsen it in West Bengal.

5. The ILRP could also seriously severe India's relations with its neighbours, especially Bangladesh, which gets much of its water from Ganga and Brahmaputra after these rivers leave our country. When India completed Farakka Barrage in the Ganga (1974) it diverted crucial dry season flows in to the canals of the country. The relations between these countries have not been since then. So far, there has been to comment from Dhaka on the ILRP.

6. The Articles on Linking of Rivers appeared in The Hindu Survey of the Environment-2003 collectively suggest that the ILRP is not advisable project. According to Ramaswamy lyer, it will attempt to redraw India's geography with potentially grievous results. It has been argued by Neil Pelkey that the need to pump water to slightly higher place will make it an unrealistic project. According to Rohan D'Souza ILRP is our country's final step towards hydrological suicide. According to Biksham Gujja and Hazara Shaik the international experience with such projects does not suggest any room for optimism with the Indian experiment. Some another suggests for thinking a fresh about a scheme, which assures too much on paper but actually threatens to devastate the country.

7. The cost worked out by Nilakanth Rath reveal that the ILRP needs giant amount of fund, which is difficult to mobilize. Rath has worked out the likely cost of the project by taking into consideration the rate of interest at an annual rate of seven percent and the inflation rate five percent at the end of 20 years, will come to: Peninsular Rs.3,81,878 crore + Himalayan Rs.6,66,485 crore + Hydro Electric Rs.9,69,105 crore = Rs.20,17,468 crore at the end

of 20 years. Approximately, total cost comes to Rs.1,00,000 crore a year. According to Rath, it is a pity that instead of doing the first things that are crying out to be done first in regard to irrigation, people are being fed with this pie-in-the-sky type of slogan.

8. Another criticism on this project is that this project is going to benefit large number of contractors, bureaucrats, engineers, political leaders, Consultants and not the water starved people of the country.

Rejoinder to the Objections

Every economic activity will be having various initial problems and oppositions. From time to time, ways and means have been worked out to over come the problems and to get more benefits. In the initial period, even machines, Air Planes, Railways, Multi-Storeyed Buildings, Family Planning devices, Large Scale Industries etc., were opposed on various grounds. Now all these are accepted and have become an integral part of our life benefiting the people in many ways. Now, the ILRP is objected on various grounds. There is also point in the objections. But the benefits of ILRP are more than the problems / disadvantages. The objections raised on ILRP are more than the problems / disadvantages. The objections raised on ILRP can be retorted as given below:

1. The first objection is on the ground that 8000 sq. kms of land is going to be flood. This may be true. This loss can be offset by providing assured irrigation facilities to millions of hectares of land in the different parts of the country. It is definitely possible to increase many times the production of agriculture, horticultural and flouricultural items in the country. There will be very wide scope for taking up animal husbandry, fishery, social forestry and other subsidiary occupations in different parts of the country. Also, there will be more scope for the generation of electricity in the country. The ILRP is proposed with the good intention of removing poverty, unemployment, and improving economic

welfare of millions of poor persons of the country. It is imprudent to compare foreign country experience with Indian experiences.

2. Pollution is the fourth largest problem of Indian economy after poverty, population explosion and unemployment. Appropriate water treatment measures are needed in the cities where city effluent waters are reaching rivers. City wastes and waste waters management and treatment can be a big source of wealth for the country. By using these wastes, organic manure can be a produced and sold to the farmers on commercial basis. Treated city water can be used for forestation under the highly useful social forestry programme. These measures not only keep the town and cities and rivers clean, but also help to bring about ecological balance and increasing farm productivity in the agricultural sector. Hence, there is no point in raising objection on the ground of pollution.

3. The third one is really a silly objection. All waters of north Indian rivers are perfectly suitable to all soils of India. In no way north Indian river water are going to affect acquatic species, insects and birds.

4. For the fourth objection-states are bound to oblige the directives of the Central Government, An Ideal National Water use policy can be formulated by the Central Government in consultation with the States and finding of ideal solution to sharing of waters is not a problem.

5. The ILRP definitely will not create any dispute with the neighbouring countries. The ILRP can utilize floodwater to the maximum extent if any problems arise; they can be amicably set right through cordial negotiations. Neighbouring countries also understand that the ILRP is a human-friendly project benefiting millions of poor people of south Asian countries.

6. Regarding sixth objection-Pumping of water. No doubt, it is expensive and unwieldy. Experts may think of remodeling the scheme of ILRP in such a way as the necessity of pumping water will not arise. Side by side, ILRP also help to generate electricity in different places in sizable quantum,

7. Regarding the cost of the project. Since this project is worth while in the longer interest of the people of the country and the economic system as a whole, fund may be mobilized through people's contribution, floating of irrigation bonds, borrowing in the internal and external money markets, using of surplus funds of financial institutions etc., Regarding interest rate-interest rate alone will not rise; side by side national income will also increase when the ILRP starts to give benefits to the people of the country.

8. Regarding the eighth objection, we cannot expect charity from engineers, consultants, and contractors because they are professional people; they naturally expect remuneration for their services. No doubt, there will be corruption on ethical grounds. If the country is prospered people will also be prospered, if the country is ruined, people of the country will also be ruined.

Rationale of Inter-Linking of Rivers

India is endowed with abundant water resources but we are not utilizing them in an economic and efficient manner. As a result of this, even now there are millions of hectares of lands are deprived of irrigation facilities, the result is continuation of poverty in the country. Owing to alarming growth of population, the demand for water and food will also increase. For this, the number of acres of land under irrigation facilities should also increase. According to one estimate, in due course of time India will overtake People Republic of China, and by 2050 the population of the country would around 150-180 crores. Therefore, it would be necessary to increase area under irrigation to 160 million hectares for all crops by 2050. The country has to evolve other strategies like diverting and usefully utilizing the excess water from one basin to another. With four percent of water resource and 15% of global population which is expected to increase to 25% by 2050, the situation will become precarious in the percapita availability of water was 6006 cubic metres at the time of independence which is slided down to 1700 in 2004 and it is expected to fall to 1140 cubic metres by 2050. However, there will be surplus water in eastern India i.e., Brahmaputra basin and it will be 3000 cubic metres per capita. While in Pennar and Sabarmati, it is as low as 300 cubic metres per capita.

Benefits are more than the Problems

Though this project is opposed on the grounds of giant cost and ecological problems, there are also a large number of benefits.

1. Benefits in Agricultural Sector

The ILRP is thought of as the best plan to provide irrigation facilities to the Farmers. When ILRP is completed, the living conditions of crores of poor farmers will be increased. The farmers will be able to grow two or three crops a year. Crops diversification is also possible with the availability of assured irrigation facilities. They can grow food grains, pulses, horticultural and fluoricultural crops. Subsidiary occupations such as animal husbandry, fishery, rabbits rearing, honey keeping etc., are all possible with the completion of this behemoth plan. As a result, the agricultural growth and additional employment opportunities will increase in the country. Large number of acres of lands of states like Rajastan, Madhya Pradesh, Maharastra, Andhra Pradesh, Karnataka, Tamil Nadu and other states, which were hither to, not cultivate for want of water, can be used for profitable cultivation.

2. Flood Control

India is considered as the most flood affected country in the World after Bangaldesh. The average flood flows in the Ganga and Brahmaputra are in the range of 50000 cusecs. Floods ravage North Indian states, leading to soil erosion, large scale loss of life, crops, houses of the people, The flood havocs would be minimized with the completion of the ILRP.

3. Removal of Regional Imbalances

The ILRP will also help to reduce spatial uneven economic development, and bring about permanent green revolution in the country. The backward regions of AP (Telangana), Karnataka

(North Karnataka Districts), different parts of Madhya Pradesh and Tamil Nadu can be developed. The prosperity caused by supply of irrigation facilities will help for increasing welfare, happiness, peace among the people which in turn help for achieving powerful national integration.

4. Poverty Removal

Poverty is any country is among others, due to lack of opportunities. The hectic agricultural, horticultural, flouricultural activities and taking up of subsidiary occupations such as animal husbandry, fishery development, rabbits rearing, honey keeping etc., will all help to increase the living conditions of millions of farmers of rural India. The hub of activities will also help the landless to get employment opportunities around their living areas with reasonably good wages. Therefore, the ILRP can go a long way in removing poverty among the people. Besides, the forward and backward linkages of ILRP can also lead to increased employment opportunities in the country.

5. Employment Opportunities

The ILRP will help to create large number of employment opportunities for skilled / unskilled labourers, educated / uneducated unemployed persons, engineers, technicians, planners, consultants, and administrators etc. The secondary job creation effects will be in the form of growth of ancillary activities needed to supply inputs and services such as machines, transport and communication services. If, good planning and vision link this to the development of appropriate industrial and services clusters, it can be permanent source of employment.

6. Industrial Development

Primary, secondary and tertiary sectors are all inter dependent. Development of agriculture in big way brings about various advantages to industrial sector i.e., in the form of demand for fertilizers, agricultural implements, transportation services. In the stage of development works of the ILRP, the demand for cement, iron and steel products etc., will be enormous, which in turn help for the spectacular progress in the field of industrial sector of the country.

7. Electricity Generation

Generation of electricity is one of the priority areas of our country; the ILRP will help the beneficiary states to generate more electricity than needed, and the surplus electricity can be supplied to other deficient states. This will help in compensating he imbalance caused by according special emphasis to beneficiary states. The surplus electricity can also be utilized for Railway sector, to save other sources of energy. The export sector will also benefit if electricity is available at cheaper price in adequate quantum.

8. Enormous Scope for Forestation

The 2640 km link involved with the ILRP will help for the growth of high valued and useful plants in the left and right sides of the canals. In the long run this forest resource will help to earn bigger amount of income to the national exchequer. Forestation will also help to bring about ecological balance in the country. This is compatible with Kyato Environmental Agreement.

9. Fishery Development

Construction of dams and digging of Canals provide wider scope for the fishery development. There are Indian specialities like Shrimps, by increasing the production of shrimps and other marine products the country can get sizable amount of export earnings.

10. Economic Growth

The development of agriculture, industry, creation of more employment opportunities, generation of electricity will all due to the ILRP, so this project can lead to the higher growth rate of the economy. The GDP, per capita GDP will increase due to development of different sectors. On the whole, India can achieve a very high growth rate, both in the near future and distant future, due to the increased planned productive investment with a very high linkage effect.

Concluding Remarks

No doubt, the ILRP needs capital. Large number of acres of land is going to be submerged. Large number of trees will also fall leading to ecological damage. Large number of contractors, politicians, engineers, consultants will swallow scarce financial resources indirectly. Despite all these drawbacks, the ILRP is one of the best available giant development project to ameliorate the poverty and unemployment problems of India. Definitely there is need for modification of the plan. Pumping of water can be avoided. Along with this plan, there is a greater need to check the flowing of waste water of cities and industries to Ganga, Yamuna and other rivers by adapting water treatment plants in the required places. Social forestry programme is to be taken up on massive scale to facilitate the absorption of NPK elements in the wastewaters of cities. Bio- manure producing plants should be set up to utilize degradable wastes. Available plastics should be used in the road constructions and re-construction programmes. Glasses can be recycled for producing other glass products.

To sum up further, the ultimate aim of the ILRP is to ensure that India produces about 450 mts of food grains by 2050 when India will become number one country in the size of population. The final aim of the ILRP is to remove the problems of poverty and unemployment and to set the country in economic bloom.

References

1. Report of the National Commission for Integrated Water Resources Development (1999), (New Delhi, Ministry of Water Resources, Government of India).

2. Ghose, Arabinad (2003), "Inter-Linking of Rivers: Vision and Issues" Kurukshethan, Vol. 51, No.12, October.

3. Ghosh, S.N. (2002), "Linking up Rivers: A Recipe for Disaster", Mainstream 40 (52).
4. Gujja, Bhiskham and Shaik, Hajara (2003), "Linking of River: A Systainability Perspective" The Hindu - Survey of the Environment.
5. Lyer, Ramaswmay R (2003), "Linking Rivers; A Chimera of a Project" The Hindu - Survey of the Environment.
6. Pelkey, Neil (2003), "Linking Rivers: Cost of the Behemoth" The Hindu - Survey of the Environment.
7. Pillai, Karunakaran G. (2004), "Inter-Linking of Rivers in India", 87th Conference Volume, The Indian Economic Association (IEA).
8. Prabhu, Surnesh (2003), "Inter-Linking of Rivers in India", Press Information Bureau, Government of India.
9. Prasad, HAC (2002), "Ganga-Cauvery Rink: A Master Plan for Growth, (Chennai: the Hindu Business Line).
10. Rao, K.L. (1971), "India's Water Wealth" (New Delhi: Orient Longman Ltd.).
11. Rath, Nila Kanta (2004) "Linking Rivers: Some Elementary Arithmetic", EPW Vol. XXXVII, No.29.
12. Vombatkere, S.G. (2003), "Inter-Linking: Salvation or Folly II", India Together, January.

13

Economics of Micro Irrigation Systems

G. Sreedhar and N. Ravindra Babu

With the increase in population, the demand for water has been increasing on all fronts throughout the world. Clarke (1993) estimated that the world-wide water use would increase from 1360 km in 1950 to 5189 km in 2000. Agriculture has been the single largest user of water, more so in the developing countries. The existing levels of water use efficiency are quite low in the agricultural sector. Even though the demand for water in agriculture was expected to increase by 17 per cent between 1980 and 2000, the share of agriculture in water use was expected to decline from about 68 percent in 1980 to about 52-62 percent by 2000 (Hubenar, 1999). In the Indian context, the projections made by the National Commission for Integrated Water Resource Development Plan indicate that the water requirements for the irrigation sector would rise by more than 50 percent by 2050 when compared to the level in 2000. The water requirements for industry and household consumption would also grow at a faster rate. Even after fully exploiting all the usable water resources, the increasing water requirements of the irrigation sector can be met only by enhancing the level of water use efficiency from about 36 percent in 1993-94 to about 60 percent by 2050 (Government of India, 1999).

It is estimated that a 10 percent improvement in the efficiency of water use would be equivalent to adding about 14 million hectares of gross irrigated area (Saleth, 1996). Thus, there is mounting pressure on irrigation sector to make use of all technical and organizational potentials for saving water conservation technologies in agriculture, especially the micro irrigation systems such as drip and sprinkler irrigation. Studies indicate that the average irrigation efficiency can be as high as 85 to 90 percent in sprinkler or drip irrigation with proper management (Hillel, 1985: 43).

In drought prone regions of India, in addition to low levels of water use efficiency in agriculture, water scarcity due to insufficient and sporadic rainfall has been causing serious hardships to people not only in respect to irrigation but also in respect of dinking water needs. Ground water table levels have been falling rapidly indicating the depletion of ground water resources. Therefore, micro irrigation has the added relevance in the drought prone regions to overcome the problem of water scarcity and sustain the irrigated agriculture to a certain extent. In view of this, the government of India took steps in early 1980's to propagate the adoption of drip and sprinkler irrigation technologies in the drought prone regions of the country, with a subsidy of 50 percent of the capital costs.

The spread of these technologies has picked up momentum when the government took a decision to enhance the subsidy to 75 percent to other farmers and 90 percent to SC/ST/women beneficiaries from 1996-97 onwards. But, the subsidy on these systems has been reduced to a maximum of 50 percent of the unit cost since 1999-2000. Nevertheless, there has been increasing realization among the farmers about the need for these systems as a measure to save water. As a result, the spread of micro irrigation systems has been steady, even thought at a slow pace. Against this backdrop, it becomes pertinent to examine the following issues concerning these systems:

- How many and which category of farmers have actually availed the subsidy and adopted the drip and sprinkler irrigation technologies?
- Whether all those farmers adopting these technologies have utilized them to the optimum extent? If no, what are the reasons?
- What are the benefits derived by the adopter farmers and to what extent these are better when compared to conventional well/bore well irrigation systems?

- What are the problems encountered by the adopter farmers with regard to operation of these systems and what are the mechanisms available to address these?

All these issues are of crucial importance to determine the efficacy of micro irrigation systems which need to be propagated at a faster rate in the drought prone regions of the country. A glance at the available literature indicates the paucity of comprehensive, micro level studies concerning both drip and sprinkler irrigation systems across the country. In the present paper, an attempt has been made to examine the above issues in the context of drought prone regions of Andhra Pradesh, which is the fifth largest state in terms of both area and population and which also occupies a prominent place in respect of the growth of micro irrigation in the country. More specially, the present paper seeks to ascertain the extent of adoption of drip and sprinkler systems in drought prone regions of Andhra Pradesh. It seeks to examine the working of drip and sprinkler systems with a view to analyse the operational problems and the adequacy of support facilities. It also aims at examining the relative economics of drip and sprinkler irrigation when compared to conventional irrigation methods and assessing the impact of these systems as perceived by the user-farmers.

Multi- stage sampling method was followed for conducting this study. At the first stage, one district each from the drought prone Rayalaseema and Telangana regions in Andhra Pradesh was purposively chosen depending on the severity of drought and the implementation of programmes for the spread of micro irrigation systems. The study was conducted in Anantapur district from the Rayalaseema region and Mehboobnagar district sprinkler irrigation units from 1994-95 to 1995-1996 were taken in to account for drawing the sample so as to allow sufficient time for stabilisation of benefits under these systems. At the third stage, the sample farmers were selected on the basis of stratified proportionate sampling method taking into account the geographical spread and the year of sanction of the drip/sprinkler units. The sample farmers were drawn from 12 mandals in

Anantapur district and 15 in Mehboobnagar district spread over all the revenue divisions in each district. The sample for the present study comprises 141 drip farmers, 192 sprinkler farmers and 179 control farmers, totalling 512 farmers. However, the analysis pertaining to the relative benefits from these systems was confined to only those farmers who were using them as on the date of survey, i.e., 97 drip user farmers and 76 sprinkler user farmers, when compared to 79 drip control farmers and 100 sprinkler control farmers. The reference period of the study was the agricultural year 1999-2000.

The results of the study are presented in four sections, viz., 1) Grounding and Working of Micro Irrigation Systems, 2) Economics of Micro Irrigation Systems, 3) Impact of Micro Irrigation Systems, and 4) Policy Implications.

Grounding and Working of Micro Irrigation Systems

Droughts are a recurring phenomenon in the study area comprising Anantapur and Mehboobnagar districts resulting in frequent crop failure. Both these districts are extremely backward in terms of the availability of natural resources as well as the quality of human resources. The net irrigated area accounted for 14 percent and 20 percent of the nest-sown area in Anantapur and Mehboobnagar districts respectively during 1999-2000. Wells/tube wells, accounted for about 72 and 86 percent of the net irrigated area in Anantapur and Mehboobnagar districts respectively during 1999-2000 (Government of A.P., 2001). The scope for extending canal irrigation under major/medium irrigation projects is limited in these districts, and the only option is to effectively utilise the available water resources for promoting sustainable agriculture. Thus, the importance of micro irrigation systems for the study area needs no overemphasis.

The efforts for the spread of micro irrigation in the study area started during 1990's. The progress of adoption of micro irrigation in the study area is shown in Table 13.1, from which it is evident that the rate of adoption of both drip and sprinkler systems was rather slow and fluctuating, in spite of the

Table 13.1: Growth of Drip and Sprinkler Irrigation in the Study Area

S.No.	Year	No. of drip units grounded			No. of sprinkler units grounded		
		ATP	MHB	Total	ATP	MHB	Total
1.	1990-91	----------	---------	---------	56	50	106
2.	1991-92	----------	---------	---------	113	65	178
3.	1992-93	16	55	71	188	100	288
4.	1993-94	38	60	98	155	120	275
5.	1994-95	130	95	225	367	180	547
6.	1995-96	140	151	299	411	245	656
7.	1996-97	486	132	618	107	790	897
8.	1997-98	507	188	695	386	344	730
9.	1998-99	253	211	464	--------	413	413
10.	1999-2000	304	339	643	--------	--------	--------
	TOTAL	1874	1231	3105	1783	2304	4087

Note: ATP = Anantapur District, MHB = Mahaboobnagar District

Source: Office records of Agriculture and Horticulture Departments in the Study Area.

availability of schemes for the promotion of these systems and the offer of heavy subsidies by the central as well as the stage governments. While it is justified that the government offered higher subsidy to encourage the farmers to adopt the micro irrigation systems and later on reduced it, the extent of reduction from 70 and 90 percent to 33.3 and 50 percent was certainly on a high side. In addition, a cut in funding for these schemes hampered the progress in this regard, especially at a time when it is picking up.

Regarding the category of farmers who availed the micro irrigation schemes and whether the grounded units are in working condition, the analysis has been done with reference to the sample farmers in respect of two parameters, namely landholding size and caste category. The distribution of the sample farmers by landholding size group revealed that out of 141 drip farmers, 21 percent were very large farmers (>20 acres), 40 percent large farmers (10-20 acres), 29 percent medium farmers (5-10 acres) and 10 percent small farmers (2.5-5 acres). In terms of caste category, 86 percent of the drip farmers belonged to upper castes (Ucs), 13 percent backward classes (BCs), and one percent scheduled castes (SCs). On the other hand, out of 192 sprinkler farmers, 16 percent were very large farmers, 18 percent large farmers, 23 percent medium farmers, 42 percent small farmers and one percent marginal farmers (<2.5 acres). In the case of sprinkler farmers, 31 percent belonged to Ucs, 9 percent BCs, 33 percent SCs and 26 percent scheduled tribes (STs). The pattern is more or less similar in both the districts. It follows from the above that economically and socially well-off sections of the society adopted the drip irrigation systems, while a considerable number of farmers belonging to economically and socially weaker sections of the society also adopted the sprinkler irrigation systems. Thus, a nexus between the caste and landholding size prevailing in the rural areas was reflected in the matter of availing the micro irrigation schemes.

Whether all the micro irrigation units grounded in the sample farmers are in working condition? The answer is not in the affirmative, as could be seen from Table 13.2 showing the proportion of working units to those grounded in respect of the sample farmers. It may be noted from Table 13.2 that about 69 percent of the drip units grounded in respect of the sample farmers were in working condition as on the date of field visit, while the corresponding figure was lower at about 40 percent in the case of sprinkler units. The proportion of working units to those grounded was higher in Anantapur district than in Mehboobnagar in respect of both the drip and the sprinkler irrigation systems.

It becomes pertinent to trace the main reason forcing a considerable proportion of sample farmers from not retaining the micro irrigation units grounded. The main reasons reported by the non-user drip farmers could be linked to the problems encountered by them including the sub-standard materials (32 percent), low water pressure (23 percent) and lack of technical guidance (21 percent). Some others reported blockage of pipes, while one-fourth of them expressed the problem of the need for continuous supervision. Of these, lack of technical guidance, implying the absence of proper training, appears to be one of the major reasons responsible for the inability of the non-user drip farmers to manage low pressure and other problems, besides the use of sub-standard materials, in a way forcing them to dispense with the drip irrigation system. On the other hand, the main reasons reported by the non-user sprinkler farmers include the need for frequent shifting of nozzles in black soils (17 percent) and blockage of nozzles and leakages (16 percent). It was also found that the sprinkler units were given in some areas where the water table level was quite high and where there was no scarcity of water. In these areas the farmers discarded the sprinkler system mainly because it required the shifting of nozzles from one area to another within the same filed. This called for additional effort on their part, which they were not willing to put forth. Moreover, they were at ease with the conventional method of irrigation and never experienced the scarcity of water. Obviously, they were enticed by the dealers to go for these systems in order

Table 13.2: Working of the Drip and Sprinkler Units Grounded in Respect of the Sample Farmers

S. No.	Landholding Size group (acres)	Proportion of Working Units to Total Units Grounded					
		Drip Units			Sprinkler Units		
		ATP	MHB	Total	ATP	MHB	Total
1.	MF (up to 2.5)	0.0 (0)	0.0 (0)	0.0 (0)	0.0 (1)	0.0 (1)	0.0 (2)
2.	SF (2.5 to 5)	71.4 (14)	0.0 (0)	71.4 (14)	14.6 (41)	12.5 (40)	13.6 (81)
3.	MeF (5 to 10)	79.2 (24)	70.6 (17)	75.6 (41)	68.2 (22)	36.4 (22)	52.3 (44)
4.	LF (10 to 20)	72.4 (29)	55.6 (27)	64.3 (56)	76.5 (17)	52.9 (17)	64.7 (34)
5.	VLF (above 20)	82.4 (17)	46.2 (13)	66.7 (30)	70.6 (17)	57.1 (14)	64.5 (31)
	Total	76.2 (84)	57.9 (57)	68.8 (141)	46.9 (98)	31.9 (94)	39.6 (192)

Note: Figures in the parentheses indicate the number of units grounded in each category.
MF = Marginal Farmers, SF = Small Farmers, MeF = Medium Farmers, LF = Large Farmers, VLF = Very large Farmers.

to avail the subsidy. While some of them have sold off the entire unit, some others retained the pipes but sold the nozzles.

The sample farmers faced number of difficulties to get the micro irrigation units sanctioned from the government. The time lag between the date of application and date of installation worked out to about 70 days suggesting that there was considerable delay in processing the applications and there was also a delay were the cumbersome procedures and lack of readiness on the part of the dealers to supply the needed equipment, according to the sample farmers. Another reason was the delay in the sanction of budget and release of money to the dealers. The farmers were of the opinion that these delays need to be avoided so that they can pursue their crop plan as scheduled.

With regard to training in the operation of the micro irrigation systems, it was found that about two-thirds of the adopters of drip and sprinkler irrigation did not receive any training. But those who received some kind of training, largely from the dealers/company agents, found it useful. The role played by the agricultural extension officials in this respect was negligible. The important problem being faced in the case of the working drip units include the blockage of filters and drippers/emitters (21 percent), blockage of pipes (20 percent), damage of laterals and drippers by rodents/wild boars (18 percent) and low water pressure (12 percent). Some others have reported the problem like breakage of pipes during summer, supply of sub-standard materials and power supply fluctuations. In the case of the working sprinkler units, the major problems reported by the sample farmers were the need for frequent shifting of nozzles in black soils (37 percent), low water pressure and leakages (17 percent) and blockage of nozzles (16 percent). Neither the agricultural extension officials nor the private dealers who supplied the equipment could come to the rescue of the drip and sprinkler farmers when the later faced problems in operating and maintaining the micro irrigation systems. The adopters approached their neighbouring farmers, obviously with more experience, and private consultants in the wake of such problems.

Thus, the support systems necessary for the successful operation of the micro irrigation systems appear to be inadequate in the study area.

Economics of Micro Irrigation Systems

The analysis pertaining to the economics of drip and sprinkler irrigation has been done for individual crops grown on considerable scale both by the experimental group (drop or sprinkler farmers) and control group (non-drip and non-sprinkler farmers) in respect of the sample farmers, separately for Anantapur and Mehboobnagar districts. As far as drip irrigation is concerned, the analysis has been confined to orange and pomegranate in Anantapur district, while it has been done for mango, orange, sapota and guava in Mehboobnagar district. In the case of sprinkler irrigation, the analysis has been confined to groundnut in both the districts. Only those farmers who derived yield under the drip/sprinkler and non-drip/sprinkler conditions were included in the analysis and the economics were worked out per acre for the crops under reference.

Table 13.3 shows the economics of horticultural crops grown under drip and non-drip conditions in Anantapur district. It may be seen that in respect of orange, the total cost of cultivation per acre worked out to Rs. 13,084 under drip conditions as against Rs. 13,084 under non-drip conditions. The value of the output per acre was Rs. 30,944 in the case of drip farmers as compared to Rs. 26,974 for the control farmers. The net profit per acre worked out to Rs. 17,860 in the case of the drip farmers, higher by 32.2 percent when compared to the control farmers. The higher net profit per acre of orange in respect of the drip farmers when compared to control farmers was more on account of higher yield and less due to saving in the cost of cultivation. The drip user farmers could save on account of lesser cost of labour, but spent more on organic manure.

In the case of pomegranate, both the total cost and value of the output per acre were lower in the case of the drip farmers at Rs. 16,117 and Rs. 42,846 respectively as compared to the

Table 13.3: Economics of Horticultural Crops Grown under Drip and Non-drip Conditions in Anantapur District (Rs. per acre)

S. No	Particulars	Orange		Pomegranate	
		Drip	Non-drip	Drip	Non-drip
1.	No. of Sample Farmers	36	45	25	5
2.	Area under the crop (acres)	259.5	196.0	195.0	28.5
3.	Cost of organic manure	3966	2804	6825	7192
4.	Cost of chemical fertilizers	1528	1739	2031	2677
5.	Cost of pesticides/ Insecticides	2540	2272	2118	8736
6.	Cost of Preparatory works	300	495	202	473
7.	Cost of application of				

	Manure/fertilizers/Pesticides				
8.	Cost of Watering	326	334	327	385
9.	Cost of Weeding	696	891	543	1014
10.	Cost of Harvesting	616	661	377	621
11.	Cost of other operations	698	853	1117	1164
12.	Maintenance of irrigation	431	601	686	631
	Equipment				
13.	Hiring charge	1183	1480	905	1245
14.	Total Cost	800	1354	986	484
15.	Value of the output	13084	13484	16117	24622
16.	Net profit	30944	26974	42846	44912
		17860	13490	26729	20290

corresponding figures of Rs. 24,622 and Rs. 44,912 in respect of the control farmers. The net profit per acre, however, worked out to Rs. 26,729 in the case of the drip farmers, higher by 31.7 percent when compared to the control farmers. The higher net profit in the case of the drip farmers was essentially due to saving in total cost on account of less expenditure on pesticides/insecticides when compared to the control farmers.

The economics of horticultural crops grown by the drip farmers and the control farmers in Mehboobnagar district are shown in Table 13.4. It may be noted that in respect of mango, the total cost per acre was slightly lesser and the value of output per acre was slightly higher at Rs. 8,181 and Rs. 17,907 respectively in the case of the drip farmers when compared to the corresponding figures of Rs. 8,786 and Rs. 17,630 in the case of the control farmers. The net profit per acre worked out to Rs. 9,726 in the case of the drip farmers, higher by 10 percent as compared to the control farmers. The drip farmers earned higher profits in mango crop more due to saving in the labour costs and less due to increase in output as compared to the control farmers.

In respect of sapota, both the cost of cultivation and value of output per acre were higher at Rs. 7,350 and Rs. 12,590 respectively in the case of the drip farmers as compared to the corresponding figures of Rs. 6,612 and Rs. 11,538 in the case of the control farmers. The net profit per acre worked out to Rs. 5,240 in the case of the drip user farmers, higher by 6.4 percent when compared to the control farmers.

In respect of guava, the cost of cultivation and the value of output were higher in the case of the drip farmers at Rs. 5,952 and Rs. 14,250 respectively as compared to the corresponding figures of Rs. 5,212 and Rs. 12,600 in the case of the control farmers. The net profit per acre worked out to Rs. 8,298 in the case of the drip farmers, higher by 12.3 per cent when compared to the control farmers.

In respect of orange, both the cost of cultivation and value of output per acre were higher at Rs. 7,528 and Rs. 24,444 respectively in the case of the drip farmers as compared to the

Table 13.4: Economics of Horticultural Crops Grown under Drip and Non-drip Conditions in Mahaboobnagar District (Rs. per acre)

S. No.	Particulars	Orange		Mango		Sapota		Guava	
		Drip	Non-Drip	Drip	Non-Drip	Drip	Non-Drip	Drip	Non-drip
1.	No. of Sample Farmers	2	7	23	14	5	3	3	3
2.	Area under the crop (acres)	9	22	239	46	22	13	20	20
3.	Cost of organic manure	889	777	1799	1482	845	692	1325	1320
4.	Cost of chemical fertilizers	956	570	898	825	645	407	430	305
5.	Cost of pesticides/Insecticides								
6.	Cost of Preparatory works	1733	1013	2068	1417	1695	930	1100	1437
7.	Cost of application of Manure/fertilizers/ Pesticides	228	445	253	700	209	492	197	240
8.	Cost of Watering	267	211	220	317	359	269	120	110

9.	Cost of Weeding	533	386	418	591	604	450	505	225
10.	Cost of Harvesting	500	497	395	667	509	615	440	360
11.	Cost of other operations	678	463	465	654	481	669	400	255
12.	Maintenance of irrigation	222		236	380	463	423	300	140
	Equipment		304						
13.	Hiring charge	944	1254	1010	1110	1050	1246	810	615
14.	Total Cost	578	315	419	643	490	419	325	205
15.	Value of the output	7528	6235	8181	8786	73501	6612	5952	5212
16.	Net profit	24444	18181	1790	17630	2590	1153	14250	12600
		16916	11946	9726	8844	5240	4926	8298	7388

corresponding figures of Rs. 6,235 and Rs. 18,181 in the case of the control farmers. The higher cost of cultivation in the case of the drip farmers was on account of higher expenditure on organic manure, chemical fertilizers and pesticides/insecticides. The net profit per acre worked out to Rs. 16,916 in the case of the drip farmers, higher by 41.6 per cent when compared to the control farmers.

Thus, the drip farmers earned higher net returns per acre in respect of all the crops grown in Mehboobnagar district also, but the rate of return per acre was highest in the case of orange, followed by guava, mango and sputa. The only crop grown commonly in Anantapur and Mehboobnagar districts and taken up for analysis here was orange in whose case the rate of return was higher in Mehboobnagar when compared to Anantapur. The studies of Narayanamoorthy (1997), Narayanamoorthy and Deshpande (1998) and Shivakumar et al (2001) also reported higher productivity levels for the drip farmers when compared to the control farmers.

The economics of groundnut grown under sprinkler and non-sprinkler conditions in Anantapur and Mehboobnagar districts are presented in Table 13.5. In Anantapur district, the cost of cultivation was lesser and the value of output higher at Rs. 5,244 and Rs. 11,694 respectively in the case of the sprinkler farmers when compared to the corresponding figures of Rs. 5,799 and Rs. 11,339 in the case of the control farmers. The net profit per acre worked out to Rs. 6,450 in the case of the sprinkler farmers, higher by 16.4 percent when compared to the control farmers. On the other hand, both the cost of cultivation and the value of output per acre were higher in the case of the sprinkler farmers at Rs. 8.022 and Rs. 15,157 respectively when compared to Rs. 6,183 and Rs. 10,475 in the case of the control farmers in Mehboobnagar district. The net profit per acre worked out to Rs. 7,135 per acre for the sprinkler farmers, higher by 66.2 percent when compared to the control farmers. Thus, the sprinkler farmers earned higher net returns from groundnut when compared to the control farmers in both the districts, the rate of return being

Table 13.5: Economics of Groundnut Grown under Sprinkler and Non-sprinkler Conditions in Anantapur and Mahaboobnagar Districts (Rs. per acre)

S. No.	Particulars	Anantapur		Mahaboobnagar	
		Sprinkler	Non-Sprinkler	Sprinkler	Non-Sprinkler
1.	No. of Sample Farmers	46	50	29	49
2.	Area under the crop (acres)	245	204	101	128
3.	Cost of Seed	1422	1415	1729	1477
4.	Cost of organic manure	676	1046	1289	845
5.	Cost of chemical fertilizers	648	627	803	620
6.	Cost of pesticides/ Insecticides	356	408	381	306
7.	Cost of Preparatory works	191	130	291	229
8.	Cost of Sowing	73	109	205	152
9.	Cost of application of Manure/fertilizers/ Pesticides	138	126	257	222

10.	Cost of Watering	37	383	603	404
11.	Cost of Weeding	249	318	463	405
12.	Cost of Harvesting	232	192	564	450
13.	Cost of other operations	91	95	299	183
14.	Maintenance of irrigation Equipment	493	561	646	537
15.	Hiring charges	301	389	492	383
16.	Total Cost	5244	5799	8022	6183
17.	Value of the output	11694	11339	15157	10475
18.	Net profit	6450	5540	7135	4292

higher in Mehboobnagar when compared to Anantapur. Similar results were reported in the studies conducted by NABARD (1989) and Khade et al (1989).

It follows from the above discussion that both the drip and the sprinkler irrigation appeared to have been beneficial for the user farmers who maintained these systems, but the rate of return varied from drip to sprinkler and again from crop to crop as well as district to district.

Impact of Micro Irrigation Systems

It is widely known that the micro irrigation has certain tangible benefits such as conservation of water, conservation of energy, increase in the irrigated area, increase in the crop yield, improvement in crop quality, reduction in labour costs, effective application of chemical fertilizers, reduction in pest/insect attacks and convenience in management. It is important to know whether the sample farmers who maintained the drip and sprinkler systems (experimental group or user farmers) experienced these benefits, and if so, to what extent. Hence, an attempt is made here to examine the perceptions of the user farmers with regard to the impact of drip and sprinkler irrigation systems in terms of each of these benefits and the extent to which each benefit is felt.

Table 13.6 presents the opinions of the drip/sprinkler user farmers on the impact of drip and sprinkler irrigation systems. It may be noted that the single most important benefit perceived by vast majority of the user farmers was the conservation of water to a great extent, as opined by 93 percent of the drip farmers and 87 percent of the sprinkler farmers. The other two important benefits perceived by majority of the user farmers as having a positive impact to a great extent were the conservation of energy (59%) and an increase in irrigated area (57%). With regard to increase in the crop yield and improvement in the quality of crop produce, a majority of the drip farmers in both the districts taken together (69% and 72% respectively) felt that these systems had a considerable impact, whereas the opinion of the sprinkler farmers was divided on these two aspects; while 59 percent and 78 percent

Table 13.6: Opinions of the Sample Farmers on the Impact of Drip/Sprinkler Systems (Working Units Only)

S. No.	Particulars	Per cent of Sample Farmers					
		Drip Farmers			Sprinkler farmers		
		ATP (N=64)	MHB (N=33)	Total (N=97)	ATP (N=46)	MHB (N=30)	Total (N=76)
I.	Conservation of Water						
	1. To a great extent	89.1	100.0	92.8	78.3	86.7	81.6
	2. To some extent only	9.3	0.0	6.2	21.7	13.3	18.4
	3. Not at all	1.6	0.0	1.0	0.0	0.0	0.0
	Total :	100.0	100.0	100.0	100.0	100.0	100.0
II.	Conservation of Energy						
	1. To a great extent	73.4	60.6	69.1	52.2	70.7	59.2
	2. To some extent only	25.0	39.4	29.9	39.1	26.7	34.2
	3. Not at all	4.6	0.0	1.0	8.7	3.3	6.6
	Total:	100.0	100.0	100.0	100.0	100.0	100.0
III.	Increase in the Irrigated Area						
	1. To a great extent	67.2	81.8	72.2	63.0	50.0	57.9
	2. To some extent only	29.7	18.2	25.7	37.0	50.0	42.1

	3. Not at all	3.1	0.0	2.1	0.0	0.0	0.0
	Total:	100.0	100.0	100.0	100.0	100.0	100.0
IV.	Increase in the copy Yield						
	1. To a great extent	70.3	67.0	69.1	58.7	6.7	38.1
	2. To some extent only	28.1	27.0	27.8	41.3	66.7	51.3
	3. Not at all	1.6	6.0	3.1	0.0	26.6	10.6
	Total:	100.0	100.0	100.0	100.0	100.0	100.0
V.	Improvement in crop Quality						
	1. To a great extent	73.4	69.7	72.2	78.3	3.3	48.7
	2. To some extent only	2.5	30.3	26.8	21.7	63.3	38.1
	3. Not at all	1.6	0.0	1.0	0.0	33.4	13.2
	Total:	100.0	100.0	100.0	100.0	100.0	100.0
VI.	Reduction in Labour Costs						
	1. To a great extent	73.4	87.9	78.4	30.4	53.3	39.5
	2. To some extent only	26.6	12.1	21.6	34.8	43.3	38.1
	3. Not at all	0.0	0.0	0.0	34.8	3.4	22.4
	Total:	100.0	100.0	100.0	100.0	100.0	100.0

VII.	Effective Application of Chemical Fertilizers						
	1. To a great extent	9.4	33.3	17.5	0.0	0.0	0.0
	2. To some extent only	67.2	45.5	59.5	0.0	33.3	13.2
	3. Not at all	23.4	21.2	22.7	100.0	66.7	86.8
	Total:	100.0	100.0	100.0	100.0	100.0	100.0
VIII.	Reduction in pest/Insect Attacks						
	1. To a great extent	10.9	12.1	11.3	17.4	0.0	10.6
	2. To some extent only	51.6	72.7	58.8	50.0	56.7	52.6
	3. Not at all	37.5	15.2	29.9	32.6	43.3	36.8
	Total:	100.0	100.0	100.0	100.0	100.0	100.0
IX.	Convenience in Management						
	1. To a great extent	81.2	54.5	72.2	8.7	6.7	7.9
	2. To some extent only	14.1	45.5	24.7	32.6	36.7	34.2
	3. Not at all	4.7	0.0	3.1	58.7	56.6	57.9
	Total:	100.0	100.0	100.0	100.0	100.0	100.0

of the sprinkler farmers respectively from Anantapur district felt that crop yield and crop quality improved to a great extent, the corresponding figures for the Mehboobnagar district were only 7 percent and 3 percent respectively. As regards the reduction in labour costs, while 78 percent of the drip farmers perceived that drip irrigation resulted in the reduction of labour costs to a great extent, the corresponding figure was only 40 percent in the case of the sprinkler farmers.

A majority of the user farmers did not perceive the impact of micro irrigation in respect of other benefits. While a majority of the drip farmers (60%) felt that the drip irrigation systems resulted in the effective application of chemical fertilizers to some extent only, as many as 87 percent of the sprinkler farmers felt that the sprinkler systems did not lead to effective application of chemical fertilizers. In this context, it may be stated that the practice of fertigation (application of fertilizers through water) is not prevalent in the study area; even in research stations it is being followed only to a limited extent. Over half of the drip and sprinkler farmers felt that the impact of micro irrigation systems on the reduction of pest/insect attacks was also to limited extent. Regarding the convenience in management, while 72 percent of the drip farmers felt that the drip system was convenient to manage, about 58 percent of the sprinkler farmers opined that sprinkler system was not at all convenient to manage.

Thus, while a majority of the drip farmers perceived the positive impact of drip irrigation system in terms of all but two benefits (effective application of fertilizers and reduction in pest/insect attacks) to a great extent, the corresponding figures were relatively lesser in the case of the sprinkler farmers. This could be mainly because of the inconvenience the sprinkler farmers experienced in operating the sprinkler irrigation system especially due to the supply of inadequate number of nozzles and the need to shift them from one place to another.

Policy Implications

What could be the policy implication of the study based on the above findings?

It follows from the above discussion that there are four issues that merit attention here:
1) Reasons for the slow progress in the propagation of micro irrigation systems, 2) non-retention of the micro irrigation units grounded, 3) problems being encountered by the user farmers and 4) optimisation of benefits from the micro irrigation systems.

Slow progress in the propagation of micro irrigation systems in the study area could be traced to four main reasons. Firstly, there were considerable variations in the subsidy and funding policy of the government with regard to the micro irrigation systems. There is a need for adopting a rational formula for arriving at the optimum subsidy for the these systems because of the involvement of huge capital costs, especially in drought prone regions where the cost of extraction of ground water is on the continuous rise and the farmers are the worst affected lot. The state government's policy of an upward revision in the subsidy for drip farmers is seen as a welcome measure both by the farmers and the agricultural extension officials, especially in the context of two successive droughts in Anantapur district.

This policy needs to be extended to other drought prone districts also and the central government should reverse its subsidy policy in respect of micro irrigation. There is a need for increased allocation of funds for the propagation of drip and sprinkler irrigation systems in the drought prone regions to meet the demand from the farmers and the need for judicious use of scarce water resources in the wake of inadequate rainfall and lowering of groundwater table level. The funding available and the pattern of release of funds under different schemes of central and state government should be made clear by the respective governments in the beginning of the financial year itself so that the agriculture and horticulture departments at the district level could plan for making allocations to different mandals based upon demand survey.

Secondly, the procedure for sanction of micro irrigation units appears to be cumbersome. The procedure for sanction of drip/sprinkler units should be simplified in such a manner that the decision-making is brought down to the level of Horticultural Officer and Mandal Agricultural Officer instead of AD (Horticulture) and JD (Agriculture) at the district level. There should not be any cut-off date for receiving applications from the farmers for the sanction of drip/sprinkler irrigation and the installation of the units should be arranged as per the convenience of the farmers.

Thirdly, there is need to incorporate certain changes in the administrative set-up for the implementation of schemes for promoting micro irrigation such as installation of Management Information Systems in the Agriculture and Horticulture departments, and posting of one Assistant Director at the district level in these departments to focus undivided attention to the promotion of micro irrigation.

Lastly, there is a need to have a tie-up with the nationalised banks and cooperative banks to arrange a loan for at least a part of the non-subsidy portion, which has to be paid by the farmers at time of application itself, to the needy farmers.

The other three issues, viz., non-retention of the units by some farmers, problems being encountered by the adopters and optimization of benefits from micro irrigation, could be traced to adequacy of support systems; these may include the supply of standard equipment, agricultural extension systems and after-sales service facilities. The drip and sprinkler farmers faced certain problems in operation and maintenance of the system mainly concerning technical aspects and on-ground difficulties, but the agricultural extension officials and dealers/company agents did not come to their rescue in the wake of such problems.

The inability of some farmers to effectively deal with the systems, the support facilities required for the proper functioning of drip and sprinkler systems such as the extension and training facilities and after-sales service and repair facilities, both in the public and the private sectors, appear to be inadequate in the study area. It appears that the government did not provide for adequate training inputs and continuous extension-cum-technical support alongside the campaign for the propagation of the micro irrigation systems.

There is a need to evolve a mechanism to ensure that the companies supplying the drip/sprinkler irrigation equipment should fulfil the warranty for one year and service for five years as per the agreement. There is a need to set up a monitoring cell in the agriculture and horticulture departments for this purpose. The companies should operate after-sales service centers in the study area, preferably at the mandal level in each district. There is a need to strengthen the extension/training system and ensure the supply of standard equipment at reasonable rates for the faster propagation of drip and sprinkler systems in the drought prone regions. The agriculture/horticulture departments have to organise awareness-cum-demonstration campaigns in collaboration with the manufacturing companies on a regular basis so as to educate the farmers on the specific features of the drip/sprinkler equipment and ways of dealing with the operation and maintenance problems. The agriculture/horticulture departments should arrange exposure trips for the potential adopters of drip/sprinkler systems to the fields of progressive farmers where such systems are functioning successfully including the practice of fertigation and other improved practices so as bring home the various advantages of these systems in clear and operational terms.

Thus, provision of adequate funds, a rational policy for subsidy, arrangement for bank finance, and adequate support systems are required for the propagation of micro irrigation systems in the drought prone areas. Besides, the provision of continuous extension support to the adopter farmers would facilitate the optimisation of benefits from micro irrigation systems, which would, in turn, contribute to the expeditious adoption of these systems by more and more potential farmers. The mechanism for monitoring the implementation of schemes for promoting micro irrigation, duly incorporated in the existing administrative framework at the district level, would facilitate the faster spread of these systems in an effective manner.

NOTES

a) It is estimated that agriculture accounted for about 68 percent of the world's fresh water resources exploited, while the corresponding figures for the industrial sector and the household/domestic sector stood at about 24 percent and 8 percent respectively. Further, more than 70 percent of the world's irrigated area is located in the developing countries (Wolf, 1999: 13-14).

b) More than 90 percent of the world's irrigated area is watered by traditional methods of gravity irrigation, which have an average irrigation efficiency of no more than 40 percent due to poor planning, construction and operation (Hubenar, 1999: 149).

c) The area under drip irrigation has increased from 1500 ha in 1985 to 70,859 ha by 1998-99. Within the country, the area under micro irrigation accounts for less than 0.1 percent of the net irrigated area (Kannan and Gurumurthy, 1999: 15). These figures are contradictory to the estimate made by M.L. Manrai according to whom the area under drip irrigation stood at 358000 ha during 1998-99 (as quoted in Dhawan, 2000: 3779).

d) There were more studies on drip irrigation when compared to sprinkler irrigation. Further, these studies were confined to a few pockets of the country. Besides, these studies focused mostly on economic aspects, and did not deal in detail with the operational problems and adequacy of support systems. Very few studies were concerned with both drip and sprinkler irrigation (For details, see Sreedhar, 2003).

e) Andhra Pradesh, with an area of 11585 ha under drip irrigation (16%), stands second in the country, next only to, but far behind Maharashtra with an area of 32924 ha (46%) under drip irrigation during 1998-99 (Kannan and Guruswamy, ibid.).

f) The average annual rainfall is 544 mm and 942.6 mm, and the area under forests accounted for 10.2 percent and 14.4 percent of the geographical area respectively in Anantapur and Mehboobnagar districts, which are far lower when compared to the state averages.

g) The overall literacy rate and female literacy rate worked out to 57 percent and 44 percent respectively in Anantapur district, while the corresponding figures for Mehboobnagar district stood at 46 percent and 33 percent according to 2001 Census, which are very low when compared to the state averages of 61 percent and 51 percent.

h) The fluctuations in the number of drip and sprinkler units from one year to another could be traced to variations in the proportion of subsidy and funding pattern from time to time. It was learnt that because of the cut in the subsidy and also because of the lack of funds since1998-99, the progress of grounding the drip and sprinkler units was adversely affected from 1999-2000 onwards.

i) In the selected districts, sprinkler irrigation has been promoted under the erstwhile National Oilseeds Development Programme and now under three schemes, viz., Oilseeds Production Programme, National Pulses Development Programme and Agricultural Development Fund. On the other hand, drip irrigation is being promoted under the centrally sponsored schemes and the special package programme of the central and state governments respectively.

j) With regard to drip irrigation units, the farmers desirous of setting up them are required to approach the concerned Horticultural Officer (HO), who after field inspection to verify the existence of tube well and electricity connection, gives them the prescribed applications. The farmers are selected on 'first come-first serve' basis subject to the fulfilment of eligibility conditions and availability of funds. The farmers have to submit the applications along with a demand draft (DD) for the non-subsidy amount in favour of the company to the HO who forwards them to the ADH, for placing the indent order with the respective companies. In respect of sprinkler irrigation units, the MAO identifies the beneficiaries at the mandal level. He would inspect the filed and after satisfying himself with the suitability of the systems of the system in the given location, recommends the applications of the beneficiaries and forwards them through the ADA at the sub-divisional level to the JDA at the district level. The list of companies and approved rates are supplied to the farmer along with the application. The farmer has to pay the non-subsidy component in the form of a DD in favour of the company and enclose it to the application. The JDA places the indent order with the concerned companies. The companies have to supply the equipment and install it in the farmer's field within one month from the date of placing the indent order.

References

1. Dhawan, B.D. (2000), "Drip Irrigation: Evaluating Returns", Economic and Political Weekly, Vol. 35, No.42 pp. 3775-3780.

2. Government of India (1995), Water Related Statistics, Central Water Commission, Ministry of Water Resources, New Delhi.

3. Hillel, Daniel (1988), "The Efficient Use of Water in Irrigation: Principles and Practices for Improving Irrigation in Arid and Semi-arid Regions", The World Bank, Washington, D.C.

4. Hubener, Rolf (1999), "The Evolution of Irrigated Farming", Natural Resources and Development, Vol. 49/50, pp. 143-159.

5. Kannan, S. and Gurumurthy, S. (1999), "Drip Irrigation and Water Management", Yojana, Vol. 43, No. 2, pp. 15-16.

6. Khade, V.N. et al (1989), "Evaluation of Sprinkler Method of Irrigation for Green Gram and Groundnut", Journal of Maharashtra Agricultural Universities, Vol. 14, No. 1, pp. 117-118.

7. NABARD (1989), "Sprinkler Irrigation in Semi-arid Areas of Rajasthan", Economic Analysis and Publications Department, NABARD, Bombay.

8. Narayanamoorthy, A. (1996), "Impact of Drip Irrigation on Consumption of Water and Electricity", Asian Economic Review, Vol. 38, No. 3, pp. 350-364.

9. Narayanamoorthy, A. (1997), "Economic Viability of Drip Irrigation: An Empirical analysis from Maharashtra", Indian Journal of Agricultural Economics, Vol. 52, No. 4, pp. 728-739.

10. Narayanamoorthy, A. and Deshpande, R.S. (1998), "Economics of Drip Irrigation: A Comparative Study of Maharashtra and Tamil Nadu", Agricultural Situation in India, Vol. 44, No. 1, pp. 25-29.

11. Saleth R. Maria (1996), "Water Institutions in India: Economics, Law and Policy", Commonwealth Publishers, New Delhi.

12. Shivakumar, H.K. et al (2001), "Economics Analysis of Drip Irrigation Systems in Sunflower", Karnataka Journal of Agricultural Science, Vol. 14, No. 4, pp. 924-927.

13. Sreedhar, G. (2003), "Economics of Micro Irrigation Systems in Drought Prone Regions of Andhra Pradesh", Report of the Major Research Project, University Grants Commission, New Delhi.

14. Wolff, Peter (1999), "On the Sustainability of Water Use", Natural Resources and Development, Vol. 49/50, pp. 9-28.

14

Watershed Development Programme: Potential and Importance

K. Dasaratha Ramaiah, D. Sreenivasa Rao and M. Krishna Naidu

Water is undoubtedly a biological need of all the living things. It is one of the most important natural resources and is vital for the socio – eco - system and sustainable socio-economic development. Though water availability depends on different climate conditions it is a renewable resources. The majority of the population in rural India depends on agriculture and the agricultural sector depends on water for irrigation facilities. A sustainable socio-economic development of rural areas depends on the availability of natural resources like soil, water and tree. These are possible through the Watershed Development Programme in rain fed areas.

In recent years, the Watershed Development Programme is being undertaken extensively by both national and external donors, as a means of addressing land degradation, drought and poverty. The Treatments in Watersheds comprised developing forests, pasturelands, raising soil conservation measures and building water-harvesting structures (gully plugs, check dams) along watercourses. It also includes developing appropriate land use and economic strategies that meet both the conservation and production needs. Such an initiative requires approximately 4-6 years for the treatment of micro Watershed i.e., approximately 10 Sq. kms.

The Watershed Development Programme is the conservation and regeneration of an entire catchment area of a drainage line through different physical and vegetative measures. The objective is to prevent soil erosion and increase soil moisture content, increase the ground water level and conserve the biomass cover of the soil. It results in improved land productivity, ensure availability of water for protective irrigation and the increased fodder, fuel, fibre availability. Watershed Development Programme activities may also result in doubling of the annual yields as well as in adopting improved technologies, diversified land use pattern and other economic activities like dairy development programmes.

Need and Importance

Dry land areas in the country account for about 70 percent of the cropped area and contribute more than half of the country's food grains production. These areas share 60.80 percent of the output of coarse cereals, major oilseeds and fibre crops. Even after realizing the entire irrigation potential in the country, about half of the area will still remain unirrigated. The sheer weight of this is crop economy alone can suppress of enhance the growth performance at the country. Stagnation of production and productivity has been observed in all the major food crops of dry land agriculture.

The Watershed Development Programme is the basic need for integrated development and management of the land and water resources, which provide life support for rural communities. Thus the prospects for agriculture in the dry land areas are severely constrained by the specific features of their natural resource endowments and the changed context. In a situation of low pressure on resources, viability was possible through traditional land cultivation practices. Watershed Development Programme ensures supply of water to every field, removes hunger and poverty from poor areas, provide green cover over denuded areas, bring in more rains and improve the environment. Watershed Development Programme is also described as a programme that holds the key to solve problems of employment, economy, ecology, export and equity.

In the changed circumstances with the high pressure on agricultural resources, the required high resources use intensity for high productivity with conservation and possible through traditional measures. This requires application of modern science and technology blended with the rationale of indigenous practices. The necessity for purposive measure to check soil erosion, improve the moisture retention capacity and the natural fertility of the soil. The Central Government initiated a National Watershed Development Programme for Rainfed Areas (NWDPRA), which was implemented by each State Government with some modifications.

Watershed Development Programme in India

Traditionally, India depends on agriculture and the Indian farmers themselves maintained the watersheds like ponds, tanks and other irrigation systems for centuries. As noted activities such as desiltation of water channels and ponds, protection of vegetative and soil conservation activities were affected collectively under the guidance of village councils. Increase in population pressure and erosion of socio-religious and political institutions degraded the land, water and vegetation.

The importance of micro Watershed Development was recognized and is being practiced in the country since 1973 due to the recommendations of the Task Force on Integrated Development of Drought Prone Areas. From 1979-80, the Watershed Development Programme was transferred to the State Governments as per the recommendations of the National Development Council. The farmers and villagers themselves undertook the programme through direct participation. Watershed Development Programme in India, at the stage of about 50 years of development, appears both fantastic and frightening. After 73rd Constitutional Amendment, Watershed Development has been included in the schedule of subjects to be handled by the Panchayats. This provides opportunities for combing development of grassroots democracy and natural resources in a systematic manner. Watershed Management would ensure supply of water to every field and restore ecological balance.

The Watershed Management was started in India in 1962-63 with the launching of the government scheme, "Soil conservation works in the catchments of River Valley Projects." The chief aim of it was the prevention of siltation of reservoirs built with huge government funds. The National Watershed Development Programme for Rainfed Agriculture (NWDPRA) started in 1995-96. Watershed community is now being encouraged to participate in the government/donor/NGOs projects and contribute labour or cash. Watershed Development programme technology should meet the watersheds of the community if the government has to be accepted and replicated by the people. The priority of water should be in the following order – human drinking water, domestic use, animal drinking, agriculture, horticulture etc.

The development strategies in India have been stressing upon the optimum utilization of natural resources such as land, water, vegetation etc. Conservation, regeneration and protection of these natural resources are essential for the overall development of the people. The failure to do so in the past resulted in over exploitation of natural resources and caused problems such as land degradation, denudation of vegetation, depletion of water resources which in turns resulted in promoting drought, famine and desertification. Watershed Development Programme has gained much importance especially in drought prone areas. The ultimate objective of this programme is to develop the natural resource base, sustain its productivity, improve the standard of living of millions of poor farmers and landless labourers and endeavour for restoration of ecological balance.

Objectives of Watershed Development

Watershed Development Programme in India envisages promotion of multiple objectives. They include the following:

1. To promote the economic development of the village community which directly of indirectly depends on the watershed through:

- Optimization of the watershed's natural resources like water, vegetation, etc., that will mitigate the adverse effects of drought and prevent further ecological degradation.
- Employment generation and development of the human and other economic resources of the village in order to promote savings and other income -generation activities.

2. To encourage restoration of ecological balance in the village through:

- Sustained community action for the operation and maintenance of assets created and further development of the potential of the natural resources in the watershed by promoting simple, easy and affordable technological solutions and
- institutional arrangements that make use of, and build upon, local technical knowledge and available materials.

3. Special emphasis to improve the economic and social conditions of the resource poor and the disadvantaged sections of the Watershed Community such as the asset less and the women through:

- More equitable distribution of the benefits of land and water resources development and the consequent biomass production.
- Greater access to income generating opportunities and focus on their human resource development.

The Watershed Development Teams play an important role in promoting the Watershed Development programme. The Watershed Development Team shall work exclusively and full-time for the Watershed Development Projects in the selected villages. The funds given to watershed committee are to be used exclusively for the works component.

The allocation of 25 percent finance to Project Implementation Agency (PIA) is meant for administration, training, community organization and for initial work component. The watershed committee can receive funds directly of through the Gram Panchayats to a separate account opened exclusively for this purpose.

Watersheds Development Programme in Anantapur District

Anantapur is a hot arid district and falls in rain shadow zone with a very long estimated annual rainfall of 520 mm. Which is second lowest in the country after Jaisalmer in Rajasthan. In the district, the area is fully undulating with ridges and valleys with an average elevation of 1000 feet above mean seal level. Out of the total rainfall received only 10 to 15 percent is utilizable for agriculture, the rest of the rainwater is going waste, through streams in to sea and evaporation. Due to large number of water conservation and water harvesting structures taken up in the district in 1993-94 and 1994-95, 1000 m. cum. of additional ground water recharge was made possible.

The entire district is declared as hot arid zone due to severity of soil erosion, high temperatures, low and erratic and uneven distribution of rainfall which resulted in soil and moisture stress, excessive evaporational losses and crop losses. Trends of desertification are also seen in some parts of the district. Ground water levels are alarmingly decreasing and degraded forests had happened in the last four decades. All these factors are creating tremendous concern and awareness regarding the danger that is looming large among the masses of the district.

Anantapur district mainly depends on south west and north east monsoons. But failure of two monsoons for last three years hits the district drastically leading to drought. Anantapur district has declared as hot arid district and programme of DDP introduced in the year 1995 onwards. In this Programme a concerted micro Watershed Development approach was envisaged under Dr. Hanumantha Rao's new guidelines of government of India. According to this, area of watershed would be approximately 500 hectares. In micro watersheds the developmental works are being taken up by watershed committees with the help of Self -Help Groups (SHG) and Users Groups (U.G) under the supervision of Watershed Development Team, Project Implementation Agencies and Multi disciplinary teams. Table 14.1 shows the details of Watershed Development Programme in the district, since 1995-96.

Table 14.1: Year-wise and Scheme-wise No. of Watersheds in Anantapur District

S. No.	Year	Name of the Scheme	No. of Watersheds Sanctioned	Completed	Still over	On going
1.	1995-96	DDP	96	96	--------	------
		EAS	141	141	--------	--------
2.	1996-97	DDP	10	10	--------	-------
3.	1997-98	APHM&ECRP	20	20	---------	------
4.	1998-99	DDP	100	---------	100	-------
5.	1999-2000	DDP	96	---------	96	------
6.	2000-01	DDP	60	----------	-------	60
7.	2001-02	DDP	80	---------	-------	80
8.	2002-03	APRLP	100	--------	-------	100
		DDP	110	--------	-------	110
9.	2003-04	Hariyali	110	--------	-------	110
10.	2004-05	Hariyali	110	---------	--------	-------
TOTAL			1033	392	196	460

In Anantapur District, the Watershed Development Programme was launched in 1995-96, in order to improve the quality of life of the farmers. In the initial year 1995-96, 237 watersheds were sanctioned under Desert Development Programme and Employment Assurance Scheme. In the next year i.e., 1996-97, only 10 watersheds were sanctioned under D.D.P. Its number increased to 100 during 1998-99. From 1995-96 to 2002-03 the total number of watersheds sanctioned under D.D.P in the district were 572 and under EAS, the number of watersheds were 141. Hariyali scheme was implemented in 2003-04 and 2004-05. The total number of Watersheds sanctioned in the district was 1033, out of these 1033 watersheds, 392 were completed, 196 are spillover and 460 watersheds are ongoing.

The Scheme-wise expenditure on watersheds during 2004-05 is shown in Table 14.2. Under Desert Development Programme, 446 Watersheds were sanctioned for the financial Year 2004-05 with a financial outlay of Rs. 1945.81 lakhs and out of this Rs. 1119.78 lakhs were utilized up to November 2004. Under DDP-Hariyali 220 Watersheds were sanctioned with a financial outlay of Rs. 866.25 lakhs. Under A.P Rural livelihood Programme 100 watersheds were sanctioned and out of 766 watersheds sanctioned 535 are on going. However, out of 766 watersheds sanctioned under different schemes for the financial year 2004-05, 3192 watersheds are ongoing by spending on amount of Rs. 1806.79 lakhs against Rs. 3566.19 lakhs sanctioned for Watershed Development Programme in the District.

Through the implementation of Watershed Development Programme in the district water conservation works like soil conservation, check dams, check walls, contour bunding, percolation tanks etc:, have been going on. Through these works, ground water levels in the Watershed areas will be increased during the good rainfall years. Under Watershed Development Programme, various types of works have been taken up in the district during 2004-05. (See Table 14.3)

In 2004-05, avenue plantation has been taken up in the district in 12 hectares with an amount of Rs. 8.30 lakhs and nearly 16,060

Table 14.2: Scheme-wise Expenditure during 2004-2005

(Rs in lakhs)

S. No.	Name of the Scheme	No. of Watersheds	Funds available	Expenditure Up to Nov 2004	No. of work On going
1.	DDP	446	1945.81	1119.78	2657
2.	DDP & Hariyali	220	866.25	3.04	-------
3.	APRLEP	100	754.13	683.97	535
	TOTAL	766	3566.19	1806.79	3192

Table 14.3: Works Proposed During 2004-2005, Under Ongoing Watersheds

S. No.	Type of work	Physical in nos\Hectors		Man days of Employment Generation
		Physical in Nos\hectors	Expenditure (Rs. in lakhs)	
1.	Avenue	12	8.030	16,060
2.	BHA	16	13.550	27,100
3.	Breaching closings	02	1.800	3,600
4.	CCT\PPT	41	36.498	72,996
5.	Check dams	397	577.408	5,77,408
6.	Check walls	16	11.670	11,670
7.	Contour binding	6	12.150	24,300
8.	DLH	4	3.923	3,923
9.	Fodder plot	7	0.670	1,348
10.	FO\DP\SP	671	246.620	3,28,826
11.	Gabion structure	2	0.820	1,046
12.	Kinas	91	117.70	23,540

13.	Mini percolation Tanks	20.2	282.188	2,82,188
14.	Nischinta	5	2.048	2,048
15.	Other works	188	151.363	2,01,817
16.	Paved wash	14	11.540	11,540
17.	Percolation Tanks	55	19.870	33,117
18.	Percolation Tanks	53	101.219	1,55,722
19.	Rock Fill Dame	47	41.890	55,853
20.	Soil Conservation works	23	70.169	93,559
21.	Strengthening Tanks	51	37.64	37,640
22.	Supply Channels	13	15.97	21,940
23.	Surplus weir	05	9.250	12,333
24.	Water Through	3	0.150	200
	Grand Total:	1,924	1,774.136	20,00,368

man days of employment was generated. The major works taken up under Watershed Programme are water conservation works, Rock Fill dams, Percolation tanks, Form ponds, Fodder plots, Afforestation etc. All these programmes covered in 1924 hectares and 20,00,368 man days of employment was generated directly and indirectly to the agricultural labour in rural areas in the drought prone district of Anantapur.

Conclusion

Through Watershed Development Programme, the problems of employment, economy, ecology, export of and equity will be solved. With the implementation of the Watershed Development Programme in a drought prone district like Anantapur, the employment opportunities are increasing in rural areas during the lean agricultural season. The Watershed Development Programmes is providing additional man days employment by way of dairy development, sheep rearing, afforestation etc., Due to water conservation works in the Watershed areas, the ground water levels are increasing during the good rainfall years. Due to the increase of ground water levels in the watershed areas, the area under cultivation, the productivity of agriculture will also be increased. In Anantapur district, the area under forests, covers only 10 per cent of the total geographical area. To maintain the ecological balance in this drought prone district, it is necessary to increase the area under forests. This is possible at some extent through the afforestation programmes in watershed areas. To generate employment opportunities for wage seekers it is necessary to implement Watershed Development Programmes in a drought prone district like Anantapur.

References

1. Ahluwalia, M.S., (1978), "Rural Poverty and Agricultural Performance in India", National Institute of Rural Development, Hyderabad.

2. Blaikie, Piers. (1985), "The Political Economy of Soil Erosion in Developing Countries", Longman, London.

3. Devies, S. (1991), "Adaptable Livelihoods", Macmillan, London.

4. Dilip Fouzdar, "Watershed Development Concepts and Strategic Land Water Management Options", Yojana, Vol. 43, No. 10, October, 1999.

5. Hanumappa, H.G., (1994); "Agro-climatic Regional Planning and Watershed Development", Yojana, Vol. 39, January.

6. Seth S.L., (1996), "Watershed Management in India", Kurukshetra, Vol. No. 9, June 2000.

15

Impact of Watershed Development

U. Sankara and P. Ramappa

In India majority of the people living in rural areas still depend on rainfed agriculture for their livelihood. But rainfed areas are characterized by low productivity, high risk, vulnerability to degradation of natural resources and low level of technological change. Droughts occurs frequently resulting in acute shortage of water for irrigation and drinking. Even huge investment in irrigation projects could not mitigate the problem of drought. Soil erosion is another problem caused by surface run-off and mismanagement of lands. Hence there is need for preventing degradation of soil, water and related resources in order to enhance agricultural productivity and incomes of the people of rainfed areas. In pursuance of that watershed development programme was viewed as the key programme which could meet the challenges of rainfed and drought-prone areas.

Watershed is a geographical area where in rainwater falling in, drains in to a common point. Hydrologically, watershed could be defined as an area, the run-off from which drains through a particular point or the drainage system. It is an aerial expanse of land surface from which the run-off flows through a defined drain, channel, stream or river. On reaching the land, a part of rainwater that evaporates or percolates into the soil, drains into ditches, streams of lakes. The land area from which water drains to a given point is a watershed. According to Carl B. Brown and Warren T. Murphy "Watershed" implies a drainage area containing a few thousand or a few hundred thousand acres, from which water drains towards a single channel. It is a social and economic unit for community development and conservation of water, soil, forests and related resources.

An attempt has been made here,

(1) to present a brief history of watershed development; (2) to understand the role of NGO in watershed development and (3) to examine the overall impact of Watershed development on soil water, vegetation and socio-economic conditions of the people.

For the purpose of evaluating the impact of watershed development Kothakunta watershed where watershed development works were started in 195 by a Non Government Organisation namely Jana Jagruthi has been selected. The data relating to watershed development works, expenditure and other necessary information has been collected from the records and progress reports of NGO. Discussions are held with the organizers to understand their approach to watershed development and activities taken up. Field visit was made in February 2005 to verify physically all the watershed development works of Kothakunta watershed, with the help of the employees of NGO. The members of watershed committee, Self Help Groups and user groups were also consulted. The people benefited through government schemes/institutions are also contacted. Based on these discussions and the information given by them the overall benefits of watershed development accrued to the people of Kothakunta watershed are estimated.

History of Watershed Development

The idea of conservation of natural resources like land, water and vegetation on watershed basis is not new. Watershed as an approach to development was adopted in the U.S. in Tennessee valley for reducing soil erosion in the valley areas during early 1920s. The history of watershed management in India was started in 1880 with the Famine Commission and then with the Royal Commission in 1928. After Independence the Government supported programme was started in mid 1950s with the establishment of the soil Conservation Research, Demonstration and Training Centers at eight centers. Afterwards, the Central

Soil and Water Conservation Research and Training Institute (CSWCRTI) was established by linking all the eight centers in 1956. This center started watershed activities in 42 locations mainly to understand the technical process of soil degradation and to find out ways to conserve soil.

The first large-scale government supported watershed programme was started in 1962-63 to check siltation in the multi purpose reservoirs as "soil conservation works in the catchment of river valley projects". This was followed by another mega project in 'Drought Prone Area Programme (DPAP) in 1972-73. In the same manner the 'Desert Development Programme' (DDP) was added for the development of desert areas and for drought management in the fragile, marginal and rainfed areas. Recognising the importance of watershed programmes the Ministry of Rural Development also adopted the approach in 22 locations in rainfed areas in 1984. Many projects assisted by bilateral donors and international agencies like the World Bank were also started. A number of non-government organizations also started working for integrated watershed development programme. In 1986-87 the National Watershed Development project for rainfed areas (NWDPRA) was launched for optimizing the production of importance crops. It was subsequently decided to adopt a common approach for implementation of various programmes, which led to the formulation of the Watershed Development Guidelines in 1994.

Kothakunta Watershed

Kothakunta watershed is situated at Tavalam village of Tanakallu mandal in Anantapur district of Andhra Pradesh. The area of this watershed is 670 acres, which covers the lands of Mogalichetla Thanda, Ramla naik Thanda and a part of the lands of Tavalam village. The two thandas (villages of Lambadas) are the hamlets of Tavalam revenue village. Kothakunta Watershed covers 112 households of which 90 are Scheduled Tribes, 11 Backward Castes and the rest are of forward communities. All households own some land. Main occupation of the people is agriculture and the subsidiary occupations are sheep rearing, dairying and some people engaged as labourers. Of 112 farmers 98 are marginal and small farmers and the remaining 14 are big farmers. Out of 14 large farmers 10 are Scheduled Tribes and the rest forward castes. The soils of this watershed are not so fertile and there are slope lands along with some patches (15 acres) of saline lands. Upper catchment is a semi-hilly tract. Prior to the development of Kothakunta Watershed people living here faced many problems like scarcity of water for irrigation and drinking, unemployment, migration, crop failures due to severe droughts, insufficient medical and housing facilities, soil erosion which made lands less productive and illiteracy.

So in order to develop this area a Non-Government Organisation (NGO) namely Jana Jaagrithi, with its office at Tanakallu came forward and started implementing watershed development activities in 1995 under Rayalaseema Watershed Development Programme with a combination of farmers' knowledge and experience and the advices of outside experts. In the first phase of watershed development programme importance was given to improve the natural resources of land, water and vegetation with watershed development works. In the second phase attempts were made to; popularize the improved agricultural practices among all the farmers. The entire land of 670 acres was treated starting from the ridge line. Earthen and stone contour bunds were constructed in agriculture lands. Also, rock fill dams and gully checks were constructed in the drainage courses. The cost of constructing different structures in private lands was equally shared (50:50) by the NGO and the farmers while in common lands (joint land) the farmers shared 25 percent of total cost. People directly participated in the works and contributed their share in the form of labour.

Watershed Development Works

Table 15.1 shows the particulars of watershed development works completed and expenditure incurred between 1995 and 2002. Earthen and stone bunds, waste weirs (309), gully checks

Table 15.1: Particulars of Works Completed in Kothakunta Watershed between 1995 and 2002
(cost in Rs.)

Nature of work	Area Covered (Acres)	No. of units	Cost of construction		
			Share of NGO	Share of people	Total
A. In Private lands					
Earthen bunds	353	---	83,469	83,469	1,66,838
Stone bunds	94	---	38,000	38,000	76,000
Waste weirs	---	309	32,737	32,737	65,474
Strengthening of bunds	587	---	52,749	52,749	1,05,498
Gully checks	---	1,890	38,673	38,673	77,346
Repairs to Gully checks	---	23	30,047	30,047	60,094
Drinking water pond for cattle	---	1	1,300	700	2,000
B. In common land					
Common Land Development	210	---	1,17,065	29,266	1,46,331
Gully checks	---	259	27,480	9,160	36,640

Water harvesting structures	---	7	2,27,067	56,767	2,83,834
TOTAL			6,48,587	3,71,568	10,20,155

Source: Records and Progress Reports of NGO.

(1890) and one drinking water pond for cattle were constructed in private lands. Earthen and stone bunds cover 353 acres and 94 acres of land respectively. The common land (Joint property) area covers 210 acres. Here also gully checks (259) across streams and seven water harvesting structures were constructed. In addition to the construction of new bunds the old bunds were also strengthened. To complete all these works an amount of Rs. 10,20,155 was spent.

Table 15.2 shows the details of other works taken up in Kothakunta watershed. Attempts were made to develop horticulture in 32 acres and fodder in 10 acres by providing fodder seed. The NGO also supported the Self Help Groups by providing sheep and 13 milch animals. Seed for farmers and the food grains bank is to meet the demand for food grains in drought years. A nursery was maintained and a total of 100000 seedlings were distributed for plantation in watershed area. The total expenditure incurred for all these activities was estimated at Rs. 670878. Of this the peoples' share was 33.5 percent.

Different committees and groups like Watershed Committee, Finance Committee, User groups, DWCRA groups, Self Help Groups etc were formed representing both men and women of the people living in watershed area. These are independent and hold the responsibility of developing watershed and community. Meetings are held once in 15 days or a month to view the situation and discuss the problem and activities to be taken up.

Assistance through Government Schemes

Table 15.3 presents the information relating to different benefits extended to the people of Kothakunta Watershed through government schemes. For providing drinking water facilities an overhead tank was constructed and taps were also arranged with an expenditure of Rs. 4,50,000. As a result there is no drinking water problem especially for two thandas. Another important assistance of the government is construction of 42 pacca houses for the people of Mogalichetla thanda. These houses cost Rs. 7,35,000. Sree Anantha Grameena Bank extended crop loans to

Table 15.2: Particulars of Other Works/Activities taken up in Kothakunta Watershed During 1995-2004

(Amount in Rupees)

Item	Area Covered (Acres)	No. of units	Expenditure incurred		
			Share of NGO	Share of People	Total
Horticulture	32	---	41,980	41,980	83,960
Falow land development	17	---	42,000	42,000	84,000
Fodder seed	---	2	6,300	5,000	11,300
Support to SHGs	---	5	1,00,000	1,00,000	2,00,000
Milch animals	---	13	1,30,000	---	1,30,000

Seed bank	---	1	5,000	---	5,000
Nursery	---	1,00,000	90,820	25,055	1,15,876
Seed dibbling and plantation	210	---	5,000	1,667	6,667
Watch and ward	210	---	25,075	9,000	34,075
TOTAL			4,46,175	2,24,702	6,70,878

Source: Records and Progress Reports of NGO.

Table 15.3: Benefits Extended through Government Schemes and Institutions

Purpose	No. of items/persons	Amount extended (in rupees)
Overhead water tank	1	4,50,000
Pacca houses	42	7,35,000
Milch animals	22	2,75,000
Oxen	4	21,000
Carts	2	18,000
Sanitation	20	55,000
Pensions to pregnant women	43	12,900
Kirana shop	1	10,000

Fair price shop	1	30,000
Crop loans from SAGB	73	9,20,000
Others (GCP+STC)	11	80,000
Total :		26,06,900

Source: Records and Reports of NGO.

the tune of Rs. 9,20,000 for 73 farmers. At present the farmers are not approaching private money lender for loans. A total of 22 milch animals were given to women. The cost of these animals was estimated to be Rs.2,75,000. An amount of Rs. 12,900 was given for 43 pregnant women as pension. Four bullocks, 2 bullock carts, 20 sanitation facilities, one Kirana shop and one fair price shop were also given to the people of Kothkunta Watershed. For all these purposes government and banking institution provided a total amount of Rs. 26,06,900.

Impact of Watershed Development

Discussion held with the people of Kothakunta watershed reveal that the value of land significantly increased from say Rs. 5000 per acre in 1995 to Rs. 30,000 per acre in 2004. One breached tank was repaired and 6 another water harvesting structures (Kuntas) were constructed. These constructions helped to increase ground water table and reduce soil erosion. In 1995 there were 15 open wells constructed for getting irrigation facilities. As all these wells have run dry farmers give up those wells. Later on sixteen community borewells were drilled under A.P. wells programme and all these wells were energized by A.P.S.I.D.C. Each community borewell benefits five to six farmers. With the drilling of borewells an area of 210 acres was brought under irrigation. The cost of each borewell was estimated to be Rs. 1.00 lakh including the cost of energization. Of the total cost, the farmers' contribution was 15 to 20 per cent.

The important norms framed to spread the benefits of community borewells equally among all the farmers are as follows. Each community borewell has to cover 5 to 6 farmers. New borewells should not be sunk by any farmer within 10 acres of land. No farmer should sell his land without the permission of other farmers. Rice and sugarcane should not be grown. Only half of the command area should be used for growing crops in Rabi season. The depth of each bore well is restricted to 200 feet. There should be 200 mts. distance between one well to another. All the farmers have to share the charges of electricity and repair expenses. Care was taken to distribute the borewells uniformly across the watershed. All the farmers agreed these norms and have been following them.

Due to improvement in the availability of fodder and drinking water the livestock consisting of cows including jersey, oxen, buffaloes, goats and sheep increased from 980 in 1995 to 4230 in 2004. Due to lack of employment opportunities especially in lean season people of this watershed used to migrate from their village to neighbouring villages and urban areas. After developing watershed and sinking borewells they have stopped migration. This is a major achievement of watershed development. There are 7 DWACRA groups with 70 members. These groups received an amount of Rs. 38,000 as revolving fund loans from the banks to the tune of Rs. 2.00 lakh. They saved an amount of Rs. 90,000 out of their income.

Awareness among the people has increased. Even the women started participating in public meetings. Watershed committees are represented by women members and their contribution to watershed is significant. Besides DWACRA groups 10 Self Help Groups were formed with 100 women members. Sheep costing Rs. 1,12,000 were given for 50 members. A total of 13 jersey cows were also distributed to increase employment opportunities and income levels of women.

More employment opportunities were created during the construction of watershed development works. As shown in Table 15.4, a total of 40729 mandays were generated between 1995-96 and 2003-04. Every year on an average 4525 mandays were generated. It is also observed that men and women are paid equal wages. Even after the completion of watershed works the employment opportunities continued through intensive agriculture and live stock management.

Following the suggestions of watershed implementing agency the farmers of Kothakunta watershed have decided to grow only irrigable dry crops like groundnut, bajra, ragi and vegetables under community borewells. These wells helped them a lot to increase their income levels. But this watershed development could not reduce the problem of drought in rainfed areas.

Table 15.4: Employment Generated through the Construction of Watershed Works

Year	No. of mandays created
1995-96	1754
1996-97	4761
1997-98	7860
1998-99	4512
1999-00	4966
2000-01	8365
2001-02	4283
2002-03	2112
2003-04	2116
Total:	40,729

Source: Progress Reports of NGO

Total food grains productions increased from 2300 quintals in 1995 to 3900 quintals in 2004. Productivity levels also increased. Say for example the yield of groundnut per acre increase from 250 kg in 1995 to 500 kg in 2004.

There was a denuded forest covering 210 acres of land in upper catchment area of watershed. This forest was developed by growing trees like neem, Sandra etc. and careful protection. Forest products like gross, wood, moduga leaves and that are available. Hence watershed development programme helped to improve vegetation in watershed area.

Conclusion

The role of Janajagriti – a Non-Government Organisation in the development of Kothakunta watershed was impressive. At the same time the people of the watershed in question wholeheartedly participated in all watershed development activities and worked hard for the development of watershed and themselves. Watershed development reduced rainwater run-off and conserved soil and water resources, improved groundwater and drinking water, increased the availability of fodder and changed the composition of livestock, generated employment opportunities, increased cropped area, productivity levels, vegetation and awareness among the people. But this development could not reduce the impact of drought on rainfed areas.

References

1. Deshpande, R.S. and G. Thimmaiah, "Watershed Development Approach and Experience of National Watershed Development Programme in the Country", Journal of Rural Development, Vol. 18, No. 3. 1999, pp. 453-469.

2. Farrington, J.C., Torton and A.J. James, "Participatory Watershed Development", Oxford University Press, Delhi, 1999.

3. Joshi, P.K., et al., "Watershed Development in India: Synthesis of Past Experience and Needs for Future Research", Indian Journal of Agricultural Economics, Vol. 59, No. 3, July-September 2004.

4. Purandare, A.P., and A.K. Jaiswal, "Watershed Development in India", NIRD, Hyderabad, 1995.

5. Rao, Hanumantha C.H., "Watershed Development in India: Recent Experience and Emerging Issues", E.P.W., Vol. 35, No. 45, November 4, 2000, pp. 3943-3947.

6. Seshagiri Rao, K.V., "Watersheds Comprehensive Development", B.S. Publications, Sultan Bazar, Hyderabad.

16

Water Resources Management: A Note

C. Basavaiah

A National Water Policy was formulated by the National Water Resources Council in 1987. It states that water is one of the crucial elements in developmental planning and as such, it should be planned, developed and conserved in an integrated and environmentally sound basis keeping in view the needs of the States concerned. A National Water Board was formed in September 1990 to review the progress made in implementing the national water policy. The issues under consideration of the Board included setting up of river basin authorities in the States, formulation of a national policy for rehabilitation and resettlement of oustees in the river valley projects and strengthening the data base in the water resources sector.

Recently, a national perspective for water resources development was prepared by the Government to optimally utilise the available water resources by storage and inter-basin transfer of water from surplus to deficient areas, as mentioned earlier. It has two components viz., the Himalayan Rivers Development Component and the Peninsular Rivers Development Component. The former, apart from linking the main Brahmaputra with the Ganga envisages construction of storage reservoirs on the Ganga and the Brahmaputra and their tributaries in India and Nepal along with inter-linking canal systems to transfer surplus flows of eastern tributaries of the Ganga to the West. In the case of peninsular rivers, the proposal is to transfer surplus water of Mahanadi and Godavari to the States within these basins.

The Centre for Science and Environment (CSE) has been involved in raising awareness about the need of community based water management for a number of years. Unless people from individual households, farmers and industrialists are involved, the water management programme cannot be successful. The potential of rain to meet water demands is tremendous. Theoretically, the average rainfall of 100 mm of rain falling on one hectare of land in arid regions like Jaisalmer can yield up to one million liters of water. As a technological solution CSE is therefore promoting the concept of community and household-based water harvesting as this decentralized technology can be adopted by all concerned and also promote a participatory paradigm of water management.

India has the World's largest irrigated area. The gross irrigated area in the country has touched more than 92 million hectare. There is an urgent need to utilize the available water resources in more efficient and cost effective manner by increasing the yield per unit of water used. The major opportunity in increasing irrigation efficiency at the farm level lies in adopting suitable methods of water application. Drip irrigation is a recent development in irrigation technology, provides an efficient method of water application helps in achievement of twin objectives of higher productivity and better water management.

The National Water Development Agency was registered under the Societies Act in 1982 to take up surveys, investigation and studies for the above purp9ose. A primary assessment show that about 224 cubit km of additional water can be put to use with this programme after meeting the water requirements of the surplus basins. However, it is necessary for the State Governments with surplus water basins to agree to such transfer of water in the national interest. With the implementation of the proposals for inter-basin transfer it would be possible to cover additional 350 lakh hectares under irrigation facilities over and above 1130 lakh hectares which can be covered through conventional means.

The rationale behind private sector participation in the water sector is that it may lead to introduction of innovative ideas, generation of financial resources and the adoption of corporate management in improving service efficiency and accountability to users. The private sector can be involved in planning, development and management of the water resources projects. Water Users` Associations and local bodies should be involved in the operation, maintenance and management of water infrastructure at appropriate levels progressively for transferring eventually the management of such facilities to them.

The new water policy is the need of the hour so that it attaches importance to the socio-economic component of water management. Water resource development, it has to be realised, should not only provide for drinking water, irrigation and hydro-power generation but also for conservation of the eco system. In sum, looking at the impact on environment, desertification, deforestation, increasing salinity, lowering ground water level, etc., one can see that the water scenario in the country is to be grim. The need of the hour is a scientific management policy of water resources with a rational pricing policy as its fulcrum.

17

Water Resource Management in Andhra Pradesh

G.Satyanarayana, M.V.Raghavulu and
M. Reddi Ramu

Introduction

Water is a basic need of life. Yet, about 80 percent of people inhabiting the rural regions of the developing world in general and India in particular have no access to safe drinking water. The non – availability of safe drinking water has a direct bearing on level of health of the people and their capacity for doing work. Importance of drinking water to human beings can realize from the fact that two – thirds of the human body consists of water. A reduction f percent in this water comment of the body can causes serious disorders and a reduction of 20 percent can cause disease.

Water Resources

Water is important to the survival of human, plant and animal life. Earth is the only planet in the planetary system endowed with water resources. Nearly 80 percent of earth's system is covered with water in the form of Oceans, Lakes, and Rivers etc. The Oceans contain most of the water; nearly 97 percent of the total water and cover most of the water surface on earth. The rest is freshwater and at any time, about 22 percent of fresh water is stored in ice capes and glaciers. The water is precious and needs in almost all human activities, irrigation, industry, mining, power generation, and domestic and so on.

Water Cycle

Much of the water is stored in Oceans and this water undergoes evaporation by solar energy. High winds distribute water vapour around the globe. Water gets condensed on to the land in the form of rain, snow and fog and supports land based eco – systems. All living organisms need water for their survival and water is responsible for metabolic processes within cells so as to maintain nutrient flow in eco – systems.

Sector-wise Utilization of Total Water Resource in India (1997)

Purpose	Percentage
Domestic	4.9%
Industries	3.3%
Irrigation	82.9%
Power generation	3.3%
Others	5.6%
Total	**100.00%**

It is attempted to assess the source – wise water resources for irrigation in all the three regions of Andhra Pradesh – Andhra, Rayalaseema and Telengana.

Recent policy measures point towards a shift in the emphasis on the judicious management of water at the policy level in the state. The proportion of area under Canal and Tank Irrigation has declined while the importance of well irrigation has gone up substantially. This may be attributed to the decline in public investment in agriculture in recent years. These changes have environmental consequences. The increase in area under well irrigation coupled with the decline in tank irrigation invariably results in over exploitation of groundwater resulting in environmental problems a\such as desertification. Across the regions, Telengana and Rayalaseema have experienced drastic shifts in the composition of irrigation.

By 1980s well irrigation has become the dominant source of irrigation replacing tank irrigation in Telengana and Rayalaseema regions. Though Canal irrigation still dominates in the Coastal Andhra regions, well irrigation replaced tank irrigation for the second place. Here we focus our discussion on the status and changes in well and tank irrigation in the state, as these two are inter-linked, especially in drought prone districts have recorded a decline in their relative shares of all the three sources of irrigation, while the non-drought prone districts have recorded an increase. This reflects the growing division between these two regions as far as access to protective irrigation is concerned. The lopsided policy initiatives of neglecting minor irrigation are resulting in aggravation of this divide. In the long run this may result in irreversible ecological divide.

Ground Water

Ground water development in Andhra Pradesh is about 42 percent leaving apparently a large potential for future development. At present there are 22.23 lakh wells in the State, 13.36 Lakhs in Telangana, 4.71 Lakhs in Rayalaseema and 4.16 Lakhs in coastal Andhra regions. Further, 11.46 Lakh wells as estimated to be feasible with a distribution of 3.89, 1.38 and 6.9 lakh wells in the respective regions (with ground water development of 85 percent). It is clear that the potential for well irrigation is limited in Rayalaseema, as groundwater development in this region has crossed 50 percent. Similarly, Telangana has also limited potential. Between 1975 and 1999 number of wells increased from 8.20 Lakhs to 22.22 Lakhs, and the area irrigated under wells increased from 10 Lakh hectares to 2.44 Lakhs hectares. This problem seems to be more serious at the local level. For, 62 percent of the villages in 9 dark Mandals in Rayalaseema region fall under dark category due to over exploitation of groundwater.

In both Rayalaseema and Telengana regions majority of the wells are of 10 – 20 meter depth. This is reflected in the growth in tube wells in these regions. Well population is increasing at the rate f 56000 wells per year if which 60 percent is in the Telengana region alone. Given they present low irrigation levels in these regions (Rayalaseema and Telengana) coupled with the absence of any potential canal irrigation possibilities, these regions have to depend more on tank irrigation and improving the groundwater potential through rain water harvesting and percolation tanks. The increased stress on groundwater is clearly reflected in the faster growth of bore wells (compared to dug wells, which are drying up in most of the areas) and the declining are irrigated per well.

The further classification of regions on the basis of average rainfall shows that the improvement of groundwater is depending on rainfall. Both Coastal and Telangana region are divided into two regions namely Northern and Southern region on the basis of rainfall. The North Coastal region is getting more rainfall than South Coastal region. This is clearly reflected in terms of positive sign of indicators of groundwater development. The level of groundwater development is 31 percent in North Coastal region leaving more potential for future development, through the groundwater development f Southern Coastal region is slightly more (34 percent) than the Northern Coastal region, but below the state average of 42 percent. Similarly, Telangana regions has been divided into south Telangana and North Telangana regions has been divided into south Telangana and North Telangana regions. Southern Telangana region gets less rainfall than the Northern region. This aspect is also reflected in ground water development indicators. The level of groundwater development in both the regions has crossed the state Level development. Both the regions have recorded around 50 percent of groundwater development.

As far as the percentage of groundwater development in drought prone and non – drought districts is concerned, the drought prone districts are ahead of non – drought prone districts. Drought prone districts recorded around 46 per cent of groundwater development, where as in the case of non-drought prone districts it is 41 per cent even lower than the state average. This is also reflected in number of wells and their depths. That is the proportion of wells having more depth is found to be higher in drought prone districts than in non – drought prone districts. As is expected, the percentage of locations recording groundwater tables falling is higher (97 per cent) in drought prone districts where as it is 86 percent in non – drought prone districts.

Tank Irrigation

There are about 70 thousand tanks in the state. Of which Telangana region has 44 percent followed by Andhra (38 per cent) and Rayalaseema (18 per cent) regions. Interestingly, the region with highest dependence on groundwater (Rayalaseema) has the lowest number of tanks. Effectively only 18 percent of the tank ayacut (command area) is being irrigated. The decline, quantitative as well as qualitative, in tank irrigation may explain the low feasibility of groundwater development in Rayalaseema and Telangana regions. Whereas, the situation is different in Andhra regions due to the existence of perennial river basins like Krishna, Godavari, etc. Given the high complimentarily between well and tank irrigation, it is necessary to strengthen the tank systems in Rayalaseema and Telangana regions.

The status of tanks in drought prone and non-drought prone districts in Andhra Pradesh is as follows. Around 60 per cent of the tanks in drought prone districts ad 73 percent tanks in non-drought prone require repairs, costing Rs.12,152.51 Lakhs and Rs. 29,382 Lakhs respectively. Even in drought prone districts tank irrigation is not on priority. Tanks serve only 3.6 per cent of the net sown area while is non-drought prone districts tanks serve above 7 per cent of the new sown area. Further, given the status of tanks the effective are covered by tanks is less than 1 percent of the net sown area in the drought prone districts prone districts.

Watershed Development in Andhra Pradesh

Andhra Pradesh has also adopted the watershed development programmes by strictly adhering to the new watershed guidelines.

As per the guidelines, implementation of the watershed has to be completed in four years covering 500 hectares of area to be treated with an amount of Rs.20 Lakhs per watershed (Rs.4,000 per hectare). Anantapur district receives Rs.22.5 Lakhs per watershed (Rs. 4,500 per hectare) due to its severe agro – climatic conditions. The average area under watershed is about 500 hectares in line with the guidelines. However, there is a gap in terms of amount sanctioned and utilized by the Watershed Committee.

Seventeen districts are covered under this programme till 1998 – 99. In terms of distribution across districts, coverage is more in dry districts. Though there are variations across districts; the utilization ratio is about 58 percent, which varies from 23 percent in Adilabad district to 99 percent in West Godavari district. Till 1998 – 99 the proposed number of watersheds in the state was 3109, covering about 19 percent of the unirrigated area.

The coverage ranges from 2 per cent in Nizamabad district to 56 per cent in Chittoor district. Though the coverage is impressive, it would have been better if some of the low irrigated districts like Anantapur were given higher priority.

A comparative analysis between drought prone and non-drought prone districts with regard to watershed development programme shows a natural bias towards drought prone districts. Out of 3109 watersheds, 2121 watersheds are allocated to drought prone districts, which is around 68 per cent. Area per watershed is more in non-drought prone districts, that is 510 hectares, where as it is 455 hectares in drought prone districts. Interestingly, percentage of rainfed area covered by watershed is almost double in drought prone districts when compared to non-drought prone districts. Around 24.81 per cent of rainfed area is covered by watershed in drought prone districts where as it is 13.48 per cent in non-drought prone districts.

Conclusion

Hither to, the policy initiatives were biased against the drought prone regions. Such policy bias resulted in the widening of ecological divide between these two regions. The neglect of drought prone regions in the provision of protective irrigation is further weakening their fragility. Even the recent policies in water management fail to take the needs of these regions. Groundwater, the single most important source of irrigation, is totally left out of the purview of the water user association legislation. There were no efforts to integrate well and tank irrigation. While Water User Associations are found to be effective in the canal commands, they are not serving the purpose in the case of tank irrigation though 80 per cent of associations are for tanks. Unless the needs of these regions are identified and addressed effectively, drought regions will face irreversible ecological problems like desertification.

References

1. Government of India, "Reassessment of Water Resources Potential of India", Central Water Commission, 1993.
2. Shah, Mihir, "Water Policy Blues", The Hindu, June, 2002.
3. Ramaswamy R. Iyer, "Water - Perspectives, Issues and Concerns", Sage Publications, 2003, India.
4. Gleick, Piter, "The Human Right to Water", Water Policy I (1998), Elsevier Science Ltd., 1999.
5. Biswas Jellali and Stout, "Water for Sustainable Development in the 21st Century", Oxford University Press, Delhi.
6. Y.V.Krishna Rao and S.Subramanyam, "Development of Andhra Pradesh: 1956 – 2001: A Study of Regional Disparities", N.R.R. Research Centre, Visalandhra Book House, Hyderabad.

18

Impact of Irrigation on Agriculture Production in India

M. Ramanjaneyulu

India had experienced several famines, scarcities and droughts since 1765. During the period of East India Company rule there were twelve famines and four major scarcities occurred. During 1860 and 1908, nearly 20 famines were occurred in a period of 49 years. Bengal Famine 1943 has increased the death toll due the famine, disease was of the order of 1.3 million persons, and unofficial number of death on account of famine was 3.5 million. During 1876 to 1987, over a period of 100 years nearly 36 years were treated as drought years, of which 5 years were most calumnious which were 1877, 1899, 1918, 1972 and 1987 - in each of the year more than 50 percent area of the country was affected. Rainfall can be considered the most important factor determining agriculture production. Water is basic need and indispensable for realizing the full potential of the agriculture production. Water is a basic need and indispensable for realizing the full potential of the agriculture sector and country's development.

Optimum development and efficient utilization of our water resources therefore, assumes great significance. Agriculture production and productivity depends largely on the availability of water sources. Irrigation facilities are being made prime effort since the First Five-year plan of the economy. However, the irrigation facilities are still inadequate although the planned effort could able to achieve from 17 percent of gross irrigated area as a percentage of gross cropped area in 1950-51, which has increased to the extent of 40.2 per cent in 2000-01 It was the contribution of the First Prime Minster of India Late Pt. Jawaharlal Nehru, who created a significant base for irrigation development of nation.

India has made considerable development in the field of water resources since independence. It is largely on account of this development that today we are self sufficient in respect of production of food grains and we have been able to provide drinking water supply ton almost all the villages around the country. India has become one of the richest countries of the world in surface water resources. Average annual rainfall is nearly 4000 cubic km, and the average flow of the river system is estimated to be 1880 cubic km. Because of concentration of rivers only in three monsoon months, the utilizable quantum of water is about 690 cubic km. However, conditions are very wide from region to region, where as some regions are drought affected, others are frequently flooded, with rapid increase in population, the demand for irrigation, human and industries consumption of water has increased considerably, thereby causing depletion of water resources. The consumption that fresh water is a gift of God, which would continue to be available in perpetuity and in abundance, is under challenge.

The main pre-occupation of water resource development in the country is the extension and improvement of irrigation and hydel power generation. Water requirements for industrial and domestic uses are, met partly from reservoirs constructed and managed by the irrigation department. Agriculture production technologies have put a lot of stress on ground water resources. Rivers are the lifeline of majority of population in cities, towns and villages and most of these are considered as scared. Every river stretch has a distinct water use like bathing, drinking, municipal supply, navigation, irrigation and fishing sports etc. Water supplied to the soil from one of three sources: rain fall, surface irrigation supplies, and ground water. This supply has to be considered. The basic sources of river water are rain and snow, but uneven rainfall patterns and rapid snowmelt it is expected for the resulting river discharges to fit requisites of agriculture. It is possible to store during water at times of surplus for release during period of storage.

The productivity on irrigated land is more than the productivity of unirrigated land. The Planning commission has estimated the productivity of irrigated land to be almost double (93% more) compared to that of unirrigated land. B.D. Dhawan has ascertained that the land productivity on irrigated lands averaged about 22 quintals per crop hectare in 12983-84, whereas it was less than 9 quintals per crop hectare on unirrigated land. He again estimated the productivity of irrigated land in 1992-93 which tended to be 2.3 times that of unirrigated land. Surface resources for irrigation water storage are generally expensive. Thus, keeping in view the above importance, the following objectives have been outlined.

The present paper is based on two objectives.

1. To estimate the agriculture production through the different sources of irrigation in India.
2. To estimate the agriculture production through net irrigated area, gross irrigated area, net sown area and cropped area.

The hypotheses are framed on the basis of the study objectives, which are as follows.

1. With the increase in different sources of irrigated area, there will be an increase in agriculture production.
2. With the increase in gross irrigated area, there will be an increase in agriculture production.

The analysis of this paper is based on secondary annual time series data from 1970-71 to 2000-01 used for dependent variable agriculture production and the variables considered to be a set of determinants consists of canal irrigated area, tanks, wells and other sources of irrigation to agriculture. Another set comprised of gross irrigated area, and percentage of net sown area and percentage of cropped area, which are also determining the level of agriculture production. The specification of the variables was estimated to arrive at the final model. Description of the variables in the final equation along with source of data is presented in Tables 18.1 and 18.2. In the light of existing empirical analysis

Table 18.1: Sources of Irrigation (in million hectares)

Year	Canals	Tanks	Wells	Other sources	Total Net Irrigated Area
1970-71	12.84	4.11	11.90	2.26	31.10
1971-72	13.11	3.73	12.28	2.41	31.54
1972-73	12.10	3.62	12.96	2.25	31.83
1973-74	13.06	4.00	13.28	2.29	32.54
1974-75	13.51	3.54	14.22	2.42	33.70
1975-76	13.79	3.97	14.44	2.38	34.59
1976-77	13.86	3.90	15.08	2.30	35.14
1977-78	14.57	3.90	15.58	2.48	36.54
1978-79	15.14	3.93	16.42	2.54	38.05
1979-80	14.77	3.48	17.86	2.40	38.52
1980-81	15.29	3.18	17.69	2.55	38.72
1981-82	15.94	3.37	18.73	2.44	40.50
1982-83	16.18	2.93	19.34	2.22	40.69
1983-84	16.76	3.53	19.39	2.26	41.94
1984-85	16.27	3.02	20.39	2.45	42.14

1985-86	16.18	2.76	20.41	2.50	41.86
1986-87	16.49	2.67	20.82	2.57	42.56
1987-88	15.74	2.52	21.79	2.82	42.89
1988-89	17.10	3.00	23.21	2.93	46.24
1989-90	17.12	2.94	23.88	2.75	46.70
1990-91	17.45	2.94	24.69	2.93	48.02
1991-92	17.30	3.34	26.03	3.20	49.86
1992-93	16.98	3.17	26.92	3.21	50.29
1993-94	17.11	3.15	27.76	3.42	51.45
1994-95	17.28	3.27	28.91	3.53	53.00
1995-96	17.12	3.11	29.70	3.46	53.40
1996-97	17.35	3.34	30.82	3.62	55.14
1997-98	17.09	3.10	30.88	3.49	54.98
1998-99	17.70	2.93	33.15	3.27	57.07
1999-00	18.00	2.70	33.63	2.90	57.23
2000-01	15.98	2.52	33.27	2.89	54.68

Source: Centre for Monitoring of Indian Economy, (CMIE), March 2005.

Table 18.2: Irrigated Area and Agriculture Production in India

Years	Gross Irrigated (m. hectare)	Net Irrigated as % of Net Sown	Gross Irrigated as % of Gross Cropped area	Agricultural. Production (in million tonnes)
1970-71	38.19	22.17	23.04	108.42
1971-72	38.43	22.58	23.26	105.17
1972-73	39.05	23.21	24.09	97.03
1973-74	40.28	22.85	23.71	104.67
1974-75	41.74	24.46	25.42	99.83
1975-76	43.36	24.42	26.31	121.03
1976-77	43.55	25.20	26.03	111.17
1977-78	46.08	25.75	26.75	126.41
1978-79	48.30	26.62	27.64	131.90
1979-80	49.21	27.73	29.02	109.70
1980-81	49.77	27.66	28.83	129.59
1981-82	51.41	28.54	29.09	133.30
1982-83	51.83	29.02	30.00	129.52
1983-84	53.82	29.37	29.98	152.37

1984-85	54.52	29.91	30.92	145.54
1985-86	54.28	29.71	30.42	150.44
1986-87	55.75	30.50	31.61	143.42
1987-88	56.03	32.02	32.94	140.35
1988-89	61.12	32.59	33.53	169.92
1989-90	61.85	32.81	33.93	171.04
1990-91	63.20	33.61	34.03	176.39
1991-92	65.68	35.24	36.04	168.38
1992-93	66.76	35.29	36.00	179.48
1993-94	68.00	36.21	36.48	184.26
1994-95	70.63	37.07	37.56	191.50
1995-96	71.35	37.55	38.25	180.42
1996-97	73.27	38.61	38.66	199.44
1997-98	73.00	38.70	38.31	192.26
1998-99	75.95	40.03	39.43	203.04
1999-00	76.33	40.53	40.23	209.80
2000-01	75.14	38.75	40.18	200.00

Source: Centre for Monitoring of Indian Economy, (CMIE), March 2005.

the following Multiple Linear Regression Model has been used to find our factors influencing agriculture production. The model specified below:

APROt = αo + β1(CANAL) + β□(TANK) + β□(WELL) + β□(OTHSOUR) + e... (1)

APROt = αo + β1 (GROIRRI) + β□ (NET SOWN) + β□ (CROPAREA) + e... (2)

α and β terms equal parameters; e equal error term in the above equation.

The interpretation of the equation is as follows. Agriculture production is considered as dependent variable and canals irrigated area, area under tanks, wells and other sources of irrigated areas is considered as independent variables. If canals, tanks, wells and other sources are fixed at zero, the average value of production perhaps minus 60.680 million tones during 1970-71 and 2000-01. The partial regression co-efficient 5.732 means that as canals irrigated area increased 1 million hectors, the average production increases by 5.732 million tones of production. In the same manner, the average production is estimated at the rate of 8.905 million tones of production by increase of 1 million hectare of tank irrigation. Moreover, 1 million hectare of well irrigation is resulting to increase of 4.205 million tones of production. Other source of irrigation is influencing negative production, but it is significant. The R^2 value of 0.964 shows that all determinants explain at 96 percent of variation and still adjusted R square explains 95.8 percent variation in agriculture production. All variables are significant with D.W test value at 2.012.

APRO=-60.680 + 5.732(Canal) + 8.905(Tank) + 4.205(Wells) – 0.035(Othsour)
(-2.064)* (3.511)* (1.904)** (7.289) (-0.006)

$R^2 = 0.964$ Adjusted $R^2 = 0.968$ F = 171.862 D.W = 2.012

*1% level of Significance,**5% level of Significance,***10% level of significance

Agriculture production also depends on increasing net area irrigation; gross irrigated area, percent of net sown area and percent of gross irrigation to cropped area. The average production of agriculture is estimated approximately 59.209 million tones in keeping other explanatory variables constant. The partial regression coefficients net sown area and percent of cropped area have shown negative sign for production of agriculture but they are significant and the coefficient of gross irrigated areas has influenced by an increase of 1 million hectare led to an increase of 7.670 million tones of production. The R square value 0.977 presents the variation explained by independent variables with D.W test statistics at 1.915.

APRO=59.209+ 7.670(GROIRRI) – 4.887(NET SOWN) – 6.078(CROP AREA)

(3.544)* (6.199)*** (-1.630)* (-2.340)***

$R^2 = 0.977$ Adjusted $R^2 = 0.874$ F = 375.572 D.W = 1.915

*1% level of Significance,**5% level of Significance,***10% level of significance

Net Irrigated and Gross Irrigated Area

The total net irrigated area of the nation during 1970-71 to 2000-01 has increased from 31.10 million hectares to 57.23 million hectares. The canal and well irrigation has been contributing maximum level in the total net irrigation. In India, only four states viz., Delhi, Haryana were able to increase from 78.6 percent 100 percent during 1990-91 to 2000-01. Haryana could able to increase the net irrigated area from 72.71 per cent to 83.89 percent. In the state of Punjab it has also increased from 92.71 per cent to 94.48 per cent during 1990-91 and 1999-2000 and it has declined to 84.47 in 2000-01, further it has increased to 96.05 percent in 2002-03. Net irrigated area of Utter Pradesh also increased from 60.94 per cent to 72.76 per cent. The states such as Andhra Pradesh, Gujarat, J&K, Karnataka, Manipur, Orissa, Rajasthan and West Bengal could not able to cross at least 50 per cent of net irrigation. The details can be seen in Table 18.3.

Moreover, gross irrigated area also has increased from 38.19 million hectares to 75.14 million hectares during 1970-71 to

Table 18.3: State-wise and Year-wise Percentage of Net Irrigated Area

States	1990-1991	1991-1992	1993-1994	1994-1995	1995-1996	1996-1997	1998-1999	1999-2000	2000-2001
Andhra Pradesh	39.06	39.41	37.54	38.20	38.76	40.57	41.35	41.32	40.74
Arunachal Pradesh	20.79	20.83	24.00	19.46	19.46	19.46	21.69	21.08	25.60
Assam	------	21.14	21.14	20.58	20.58	20.85	21.18	21.18	6.22
Bihar (inc. Jharkhand)	43.45	43.48	47.52	47.90	50.27	49.39	49.54	48.74	48.74
Chattisgarh	-----	-----	-------	-------	22.25	24.69	22.19	-----	20.60
Delhi	78.60	77.52	82.61	82.98	93.62	93.62	95.12	97.56	100.0
Goa	-----	18.19	16.67	16.67	16.55	16.55	15.49	15.49	16.30
Gujarat	25.74	25.52	25.05	31.06	30.10	31.69	31.88	30.82	31.55
Haryana	72.71	76.00	75.80	76.40	76.99	76.21	78.34	81.31	83.89
Himachal Pradesh	17.07	17.37	17.48	17.78	18.49	18.82	18.76	18.51	22.70
Jammu &Kashmir	40.80	42.62	42.39	41.61	52.59	42.72	42.16	41.34	41.58
Karnataka	20.36	21.55	21.57	22.32	22.09	21.91	23.76	24.83	25.39
Kerala	14.84	14.82	14.48	15.99	15.10	15.73	16.60	16.97	17.25
Madhya Pradesh	22.06	23.90	27.08	29.61	30.01	32.33	36.45	37.56	28.26

Maharashtra	14.89	15.23	14.87	14.22	14.33	14.36	16.61	16.80	16.78
Manipur	-----	46.43	46.43	46.43	46.43	46.43	46.43	46.43	46.43
Meghalaya	22.88	22.30	22.39	22.39	21.84	20.83	21.72	20.00	-------
Mizoram	-----	12.31	12.31	10.77	6.42	6.42	8.26	9.89	9.50
Nagaland	31.02	30.40	32.28	30.10	29.38	27.56	24.14	24.14	24.00
Orissa	30.68	30.52	33.16	33.16	33.66	35.02	34.56	34.40	33.16
Panjab	92.71	93.48	93.19	93.68	92.95	92.95	94.48	94.48	84.42
Rajasthan	23.84	28.04	28.32	28.54	31.57	33.28	34.21	36.18	30.98
Sikkim	------	16.84	16.84	16.84	16.84	16.84	16.84	16.84	17.89
Tamil Nadu	42.53	45.50	47.43	50.12	49.14	52.72	53.58	55.39	54.45
Tripura	18.51	19.03	12.64	12.64	12.64	12.64	12.46	12.54	13.29
Uttar Pradesh	60.94	64.17	67.04	67.40	67.10	68.66	72.16	72.16	72.76
West Bengal	-----	34.89	35.01	34.97	34.99	34.98	35.13	34.93	43.45
ALL INDIA	33.61	35.24	36.21	37.07	37.55	38.61	40.03	40.53	38.75

Source: Centre for Monitoring of Indian Economy, (CMIE), March 2005 and November 2000.

2000-01. The maximum gross irrigation have been achieved in four states viz., Delhi (69.87% to 79.25%), Haryana (71.58% to 85.41%), Punjab (94.05% to 101.41%) and Uttar Pradesh (57.97% to 71.6%). The gross irrigated area of Tamil Nadu has increased from 43.64 percent 55.97 per cent. All other states registered below the 50 percent of Gross irrigation. The state-wise and year-details of gross irrigation area, is presented in Table 18.4. Irrigation facilities for agriculture have not been equally distributed across the agriculture land of the nation. Presently the efforts are being implementation stage of interlinking of rivers for equitable distribution of water for dry land cultivation.

Framework of Water Resource Policy

The country, which has now 4,300 dams, would need many more in the next 50 years. At the time, traditional methods like small scale water harvesting are to be encouraged. Water is important in the continuing well being and development of mankind. Efficient water resource management is needed for a sustainable development is needed for a sustainable development. The new sources of water becoming scarce, more expensive to develop, require, technology, design implementation and water management is needed in agricultural activities and major source of waster is used for agriculture purpose which accounts for more than 75 percent of all water used. Since waster use in agriculture is inefficient and not sufficient, there is a need of appropriate framework of water resource policy. Investment on irrigation during plan period has increased from Rs. 455 crore in the First Plan to Rs.36,649 crore in the Eighth Plan. The outlay for irrigation and flood control in the Ninth Plan was Rs.63, 682 crore and it has been further increased to Rs.1,03,315 crore in the Tenth Plan (2002-2007). Substantial investment has been made on the development of irrigation in India.

The thrust areas, as embodied in the National Water Policy 2002, now cover sustainable development, prioritization and completion of ongoing projects before taking up new projects, rationalized water rates, encouragement to participatory irrigation,

Table 18.4: State-wise and Year-wise Percentage of Gross Irrigated Area

States	1990-1991	1991-1992	1993-1994	1994-1995	1995-1996	1996-1997	1998-1999	1999-2000	2000-2001
Andhra Pradesh	40.70	40.76	46.97	40.56	40.67	43.12	44.71	44.12	43.68
Arunachal Pradesh	13.06	12.79	13.95	15.23	14.75	15.00	14.40	13.64	16.35
Assam	15.00	14.82	14.99	14.73	14.53	14.37	14.51	13.98	5.56
Bihar (inc. Jharkhand)	39.38	40.97	43.21	44.61	45.72	45.99	47.82	48.18	47.79
Chattisgarh	------	------	-------	-------	19.52	20.33	22.55	21.83	1958
Delhi	69.87	74.37	80.00	73.53	95.52	140.4	80.00	80.33	79.25
Goa	-----	22.78	21.60	22.09	21.82	21.82	19.88	19.88	21.05
Gujarat	27.24	27.43	28.93	32.50	34.71	33.12	34.46	35.72	33.92
Haryana	71.58	77.91	77.64	77.01	78.22	78.78	79.78	84.99	85.41
Himachal Pradesh	16.95	17.80	17.54	17.59	18.31	18.59	18.87	18.80	19.09
Jammu &Kashmir	40.90	41.17	41.11	40.72	41.01	41.50	41.35	45.63	40.23
Karnataka	21.10	22.86	23.90	24.33	23.79	23.36	25.35	26.14	26.66
Kerala	12.69	12.82	13.58	16.60	15.30	15.40	14.43	15.69	15.16
Madhya Pradesh	18.55	20.60	22.27	24.59	24.67	25.80	27.18	28.54	23.90

Maharashtra	15.18	16.22	15.27	14.75	14.77	14.50	17.01	16.86	17.39
Manipur	41.67	38.96	37.69	39.68	41.21	36.95	34.72	37.68	35.85
Meghalaya	19.54	18.77	18.83	18.91	18.22	18.44	20.68	20.68	------
Mizoram	10.39	8.35	7.48	8.04	8.26	8.26	8.62	12.09	13.83
Nagaland	28.61	27.94	29.03	29.41	31.58	21.67	25.52	25.75	24.80
Orissa	30.59	29.93	25.75	25.81	27.18	17.55	27.99	29.47	26.99
Panjab	94.05	94.59	94.95	95.14	95.16	94.07	96.74	90.86	101.4
Rajasthan	24.00	29.09	29.06	28.53	32.34	32.58	31.81	35.95	31.90
Sikkim	10.53	11.94	12.60	11.51	11.27	11.27	12.60	13.22	14.29
Tamil Nadu	43.64	46.68	49.51	51.07	50.79	51.84	54.86	54.99	55.00
Tripura	11.25	11.11	13.04	13.13	14.08	13.10	12.30	12.50	13.79
Utter Pradesh	57.97	61.02	64.06	65.36	65.80	66.85	72.93	------	71.65
West Bengal	22.06	29.12	28.70	28.57	27.76	27.50	26.81	26.10	36.90
ALL INDIA	34.03	36.04	36.48	37.56	38.25	38.66	39.43	40.23	40.18

Source: Centre for Monitoring of Indian Economy, (CMIE), March 2005 and November 2000.

cost control in projects, regulation in use of ground water, inter basin transfer, dam safety, review of projects clearance procedure etc. Proper planning and by introducing the needed reforms in the Water Resources Sector, we can definitely develop and manage the precious water resources of the country and be ready to meet the challenge of the future.

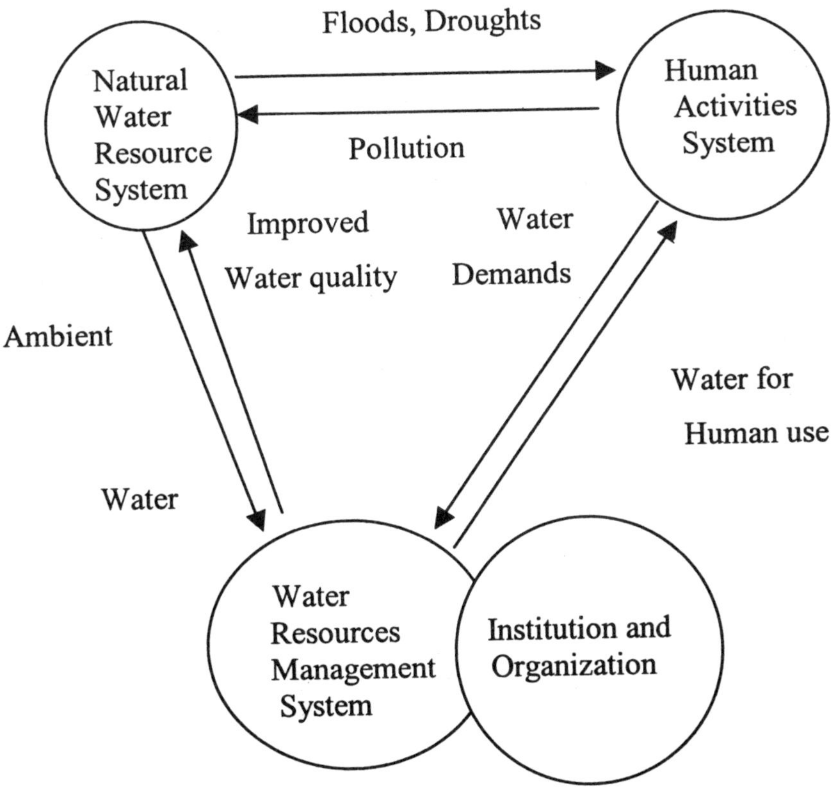

Conclusion

Irrigation is one the major infrastructure inputs of the production of agriculture and its development. In spite of several famines, scarcities, droughts, floods, cyclones, and earthquakes, irrigated land of India accounts 24 percent world irrigated area, still there is a was amount of un irrigated land remains without adequate facility. The planned effort in this regard is enormous and appropriate for development of irrigational facilities by considering increased level of net irrigated and gross irrigated areas and increase of production of agriculture. The hypothesis proved that there is a significant increase in production on account of increase in irrigational source and gross irrigated area. Only four states are enjoying the full utilization of irrigational facilities and achieving 80 to 100 percent of gross irrigated area. Majority of the states are facing acute shortage of irrigational facilities, which could not able to achieve 45 per cent of irrigated area. Therefore, India is need of water resource management and water policy to provide justice to the unirrigated area of the mother India.

References

1. Centre for Monitoring Indian Economy (2005), Basic Statistics on Agriculture, March, Mumbai.

2. Dhawan, B.D (1968), "Studies in Irrigation Impact: Issues and Productivity, Stability and Equity", Institute of Economic Growth, Delhi.

3. Dhawan, B.D (1988) "Indian Irrigation: An Assessment", Economic and Political Weekly, May 7, p.965, Mumbai.

4. Government of India, Central Statistical Organisation - 2002, "Compendium of Environmental Statistics", New Delhi.

5. Gopal Reddy, G. (2004), "Economics of Irrigation – A Case Study of Costs and Returns under Different Sources of Irrigation in Andhra Pradesh" in Conference Volume (Ed.) G. Gopal Reddy, Institutional Policy options for Sustainable Agricultural Development, April, 2004.

6. Maynard M. Hufschmids (1993) "Water Policies and Sustainable Development" in Asit K. Biwas, Hommed Jellali, Glen E stout (Eds.)

Water Sustainable Development in the Twenty First Century; Oxford University Press, New Delhi.

19

Micro Water Harvesting Structure Through People's Participation

M. Ramesh, M. Sankara Reddi, and M. Sundara Rao

"We can definitely handle the work without government help. We still don't know many things, but we will learn everything soon" – Latchumayya.

Kodisa Village Social Map

Kodisa Village, Seethampeta Mandal of Srikakulam District is a small village covering an area of 840 acres in the Srikakulam District of the state of Andhra Pradesh State. It is located at the foot of barren and rocky hills in the rain shadow area of the Eastern Ghats. With an average annual rainfall of 1050 mm, most of which falls within a span of a few days. Kodisa Village, Seethampeta Mandal of Srikakulam District has been experiencing severe droughts for many years. The landscape is marked by heavy soil erosion. The highly eroded stony soil is largely unfit for cultivation, but for the lack of alternatives, the people of Kodisa Village continue to grow crops. At out set, the Kodisa Villagers requested us to convey their deep sense of gratitude to Shri Rahul Bojja, PO, ITDA, Seethampeta of Srikakulam District and to the officials of Care Step for their cooperation and support.

Site History

Palakonda sub-division is geographically situated at northern and western direction. The hills in these areas are part of the Eastern Ghats and run into hundreds in number. The hills' general elevation is 1500 to 3000 feet. Climate of the area is characterised with a moderate and high rainfall. The average rainfall in this area is 1080 mm. The importance of the occurrence of rainfall is examined in reference to cyclones. It indicates that November month is more cyclone prone month. 52.5% of the total rainfall is received under the southwest monsoon. On an average, there are 70 to 80 rainy days in a year. The winds are generally light to moderate in velocity. Soil erosion hazard is severe due to steep slopes, badly managed farming fields, overgrazing, fallow lands, cultivable and uncultivable waste are the principle factors. The run off water causes soil erosion.

Micro Water Harvesting Structure Pre-Construction Location

Kodisa Village, Seethampeta Mandal of Srikakulam District has 60 inhabitants, 95% the families belong to Scheduled Tribe. A socio-economic study conducted in early 2002 revealed a very grim picture. Because of recurrent drought and the resulting poor economic condition, the 70 inhabitants often experienced hunger and were prone to many diseases. The women were the worst affected. Drinking water was not available within the village and they had to walk long distances to get water and fuelwood. More often than not, this task was given to young girls, who had to leave school to help in household chores and were, as a result, deprived of education.

In 1984 Jana Chetana, a voluntary agency that has been working in the district for two decades, decided to work in the village because of its poor condition. When Jana Chetana approached the village, the people expressed a desire to start a fruit preservation unit. Jana Chetana helped them in this endeavour and assisted to obtain a bank loans to go for alternative. Thus, a relationship of trust was established.

Participatory Micro Water Harvesting Structure

Participatory Micro Water Harvesting Structure helps to conserve and manage land and water on an area basis so that the basic needs of people (food, fodder, fuel, water and livelihood) are met in a sustainable and socially just manner. The operational strategy is to work on Micro Water Harvesting Structure building. It is not confined to just soil and water conservation activities, but includes land and water development.

It basically focuses on:

- Engineering measures related with the soil and moisture conservation.
- Institutional Development.
- Emphasis on grassroots mobilisation in the form of community participation.
- Plantations under Micro Water Harvesting Structure.
- Prompt, clear and accurate reporting.
- High degree of accountability, transparency and integrity.
- Replicating its development model in newer areas.

Participation in Water Harvesting Structure Construction

The formation of village institutions is vital to empowerment, socio-economic stability, leadership and overall development in the lives of the people. The key objective of forming the village organization is to encompass more people in the decision-making processes on policies impacting their lives. Ultimately this empowers the community to manage their assets and programmes. This may also include other activities such as:

- Environment Building
- Creation of Water Users Committee
- Preparation of Community Action Plan
- Soil and Water Conservation Works
- Fodder Production - Plantation Activities
- Regeneration of Degraded Forests

Preparation of Community Action Plan

The Community Action Group (CAG) Committee members of KODISA Village, KODISA Panchayat in Seethampeta Mandal of Srikakulam District have prepared a Community Micro Project proposal through Gram Sabha Meeting. The objective of the proposed activity is to improve the socio-economic conditions of Kodisa Villagers. They passed a resolution to seek Jana Chetana's cooperation to mobilize resources to construct a Recharging Percolation Tank across the Hill stream called Loddala or Naddula Maddigedda either from ITDA or CARE STEP. The purpose is to increase the productivity and to improve the source of livelihoods of poorest among poor and vulnerable. This activity shall generate additional production, employment and income. At present, they are raising a temporary bund and diverting the water to irrigate their lands through a means of "**poonu**". "**Poonu**" means a temporary earthen bund excavated across the hill steam to storage flow water. The structure of poonu is temporary in nature and subjected to frequent breakdowns. This is causing heavy loss of employment mandays and livelihoods. On the other hand, there is heavy siltation deposited at poonu area. To mitigate this problem, the Community Action Group resolved to request the concerned agencies to approve their Micro Watershed projects. The construction Recharging Percolation Tank at Kodisa village across the hill steam is to divert the floodwater for irrigation purpose. The Construction of Water Recharging Percolation Tank at **Kodisa** village will recharge the ground water table. The catchment area is very good and spread in an area of approximately 60 Acres. **The yield calculated is 629 cubic meters.** The storage **capacity of the Percolation Tank is 629 Cubic Meters of water.** The flow water will be diverted to irrigate their lands. The overflow water shall irrigate an extent of 50 Acres approximately. The work had generated 375 man-days of employment.

Areas of Success

In 2004, Jana Chetana has decided to build a Micro Water Harvesting Structure in Kodisa Village, Seethampeta Mandal of Srikakulam District as per the wishes of the community. The villagers were taken on an exposure visit to Gajapathi District of Orissa, Khammam, Warangal and Vizianagaram Districts of

Andhra Pradesh where experiments of participatory watershed development had been successful. The villagers were very impressed and enthused. They saw the benefits of Micro Water Harvesting Structures and decided to try out the same in their village. The conditions laid down for successful implementation of Micro Water Harvesting Structure were quite rigid and demanded a change in the prevailing lifestyle of village community. However, the motivated people readily accepted the conditions.

Construction of Micro Water Harvesting Structure involves the complete participation of the affected people, where they are responsible for the planning, implementation and monitoring of the project. The people of Kodisa Village, Seethampeta of Srikakulam District formed a Village Water Users Committee (VWC) to oversee the activities involved developing their Micro Water Harvesting Structure. This body was nominated or elected by the villagers in a democratic way. Representative of all geographical regions within the village is taken care to ensure equity. This was again a novel experience as the women who had never really been part of the village affairs now had fair representation on this decision-making body. As the VWC had been unanimously nominated by the villagers, the better-off farmers lobby could not dominate it.

- A ban was imposed on free grazing and free felling. The villagers decided to levy a fine on defaulters. The villagers also sold off their scrub cattle and replaced them by good quality cattle. Goats were sold off, because of which children who otherwise had to tend them could go to school. The villagers then decided to take up measures to conserve soil and water.
- Jana Chetana gave them support for technical surveys and other managerial assistance. A nursery was set up by a small farmer. Treatment measures like contour trenching, contour bunding, gully plugging, construction of check dams and percolation tanks were taken up. The villagers contributed

free labour on the basis of four man-days per month or four days wages in lieu of labour.

- The villagers were trained to carry out tasks like surveying and leveling. The activities were monitored by a supervisor who was also from the village. The result was that the people began to feel responsible for the project and so worked hard to make it a success.

Social Achievements

Before the implementation of building Micro Water Harvesting Structure the women were considered as not part of the social life. The building Micro Water Harvesting Structure movement brought about a change in this attitude of the people of Kodisa Village, Seethampeta Mandal of Srikakulam District. Social taboos have been lifted and these women are now allowed freely in the village. The women have a fair representation in the VWC and participate actively in the decision-making process. As more children could go to school, literacy in the village improved and today the literacy rate is about 80%. LPG stoves were set up in some households in the village and their fuel wood consumption declined. As drinking water had become available within the village, the women did not have to go far for water and so they could contribute more positively to the development of the village. They set up a revolving credit and made loans available to the needy at the low interest rate.

Economic Achievements

The soil and water conservation measures increased the water levels in the village wells and water was available for about 11 months in the year. Before the construction of micro water harvesting structure at Kodisa Village, Seethampeta Mandal of Srikakulam District water is available for only for just 8 months in a year. Now the farmers could irrigate their fields optimally and the agricultural productivity is increased by 30%. Horticulture was introduced in the village on wastelands and bringing more land under productive use. 20 acres is under dry land horticulture, while the remaining 22 acres under mango; orange and turmeric cultivation is irrigated. As more opportunities for employment have become available within the village, the migration to urban areas and other agricultural wage labourers has stopped. In fact, some families who had earlier left the village have now returned.

Natural Resources

Positive impacts on natural resources are also observed. The once rocky hillsides around Kodisa Village, Seethampeta of Srikakulam District are now covered with grasses and shrubs, because of the ban on free grazing and free felling. In spite of the drought situation, nearly 80% survival rate is seen in the 200,000 saplings planted by the people. Soil erosion had declined considerably and grasses are growing along the waterways. Streams, which would flow only up to November, now flow up to January even in a dry year. Drinking water is available even in the dry years. This year, for example, the monsoons did not arrive in Kodisa Village, Seethampeta Mandal of Srikakulam District until September, but the people had drinking water, and could also irrigate their horticulture plots. Today, Kodisa Village, Seethampeta of Srikakulam District acts as a role model for other village communities that wish to help themselves and better their conditions. The people of Kodisa Village, Seethampeta Mandal of Srikakulam District have even decided to adopt another village community in their vicinity and introduce it to watershed development, thus giving an impetus to a watershed movement.

Community Participation

The proposed site is selected keeping the strategic and multiple uses of natural resources to promote biodiversity in the area. The Kodisa Village is inhabitant by 56 households. They had little misconception as regards to the ownership, control and maintenance of the proposed micro water harvesting structure. Therefore, as to dispel the misconception, we have organised a series of meetings and exposure visits with a view to raise their critical self-confidence and to understand the usefulness of micro water harvesting structures. The exposure visits have provided peer group learning facility to know about the concept of Critical Path Method (CPM) and community ownership. Further, they learnt the concept of "Seeing is Believing" and convinced themselves about the usefulness of the proposed micro project.

Budget Details

S. No.	Description	Qty.	Rate (Rs.)	Amt. (Rs.)
1.	Earth work excavation for percolation tank	629	270	16,983
2.	RR Masonry	2.358	1188	2,801
3.	Cement Plastering	15.72	775	1,218
4.	Excavation for cut off wall at existing check dam	10.32	300	310
5.	RR Masonry for cut off wall	5.40	1188	6,415
6.	Earthwork excavation for recharging pond	225	32	7,200
7.	Revetment to the up stream side slope	5.40	365	1,971
8.	Revetment to toe wall	4.92	365	1,796
	Total			**38,694**
9.	Soil Fertility			16,200
10.	Forest Plantation			1,800
11.	Kitchen Garden			900
12.	Training			1,350
13.	Social Audit Wall			2,500
14.	Administration Cost			1,500
15.	Technical Experts Cost			3,000
	Total			**65,944**

After realising the need and importance of Community Participation, they boldly execute the work with true spirit and self-confidence. In spite of their busy and hectic harvesting operations, they could able to provide their human capital for execution the work with a view to posses a community asset. They completed the task well in advance. This activity has provided access to micro irrigation facility and fresh water inland fishing. They had introduced the CPM technique to speed up the work without compromising with quality and safety.

The Traditional Water Harvesting Structure method is followed, which is passed the test of time and suited to the local environment and culture. They have evolved efficiently in different social, economic and political environment.

1. These systems are eco-friendly as they laid more emphasis on ecological conservation in contrast to environmental over use by our modern systems.
2. These structures can be built with locally available material. It contributes to social cohesion and self-reliance.
3. Traditional community managed system is adopted, where the responsibility of taking decision is left with community. This encourages the community independence and optimisation of local resources.

20

Sustainable Tourism and Watershed Management

M.Rajaduraj and Dhulasi Birundha Varadarajan

Tourism has become a major and an integral part of economic, social ad physical development. It comprise complete system of nature, the universe, the space and the galaxy, which includes the man and his activities, wild life, mountains and valleys, rivers and waters forests and trees, social and cultural system, flora and fauna, the sea

Economic Impact

Most countries rightfully view tourism as part of their development strategy and as and economic alternative to traditional economic sectors such as agriculture and industry. Rapid development in the means of transport and communication has made the world into practically one single neighborhood. Indeed, there are several benefits to tourism. First and foremost, tourism plays a sizeable role in national prosperity. The foreign exchange earned by the industry increases the foreign exchange reserves and positively affects the balance of payments position of the countries. Indeed, tourism it is an important sector in the Indian economy, "where it has become the third largest source of foreign exchange, after ready made garments and gems and jewelry. The foreign exchange earnings from tourism during 1997-1998 were estimated to be about Rs. 1.1 trillion (US$ 3,173 million). The rate of growth in foreign exchange earnings from tourism is also high". The Ministry of Tourism of India estimates that the foreign exchange earned by tourism was Rs. 142,380,000,000 during 2000-2001.

Ecological Impact

Ecological impacts of eco tourism are as important as economic but they are not always positive instead they have more negative impacts. The unmanaged unmanaged growth of floating population. Tourists have to endure heavy disturbance for instance, in protected areas the lions and cheetah decrease their hunting activities when surrounded by six or more vehicles. The expansion of tourism mostly levels behind a trail of litter and destroys the fragile forest habitat and wildlife. Seasonal influx increases the population and densities resulted in physical congestion in areas like-beaches, ski slopes and historic centers.

Tourist Arrivals in Kodaikanal

Year	Domestic Tourist Arrivals	% Growth	Foreign tourist Arrivals	% Growth	Total tourist Arrivals	% Grow -th
1993	1427679	-	37110	-	1464789	-
1994	1587274	11.18	40201	8.33	1627475	11.11
1995	1621352	2.15	44675	11.13	1666027	2.37
1996	1625187	0.24	45087	0.92	1670274	0.25
1997	1629462	0.26	45399	0.69	1674861	0.27
1998	1490895	-8.50	40724	-10.30	1531619	-8.55
1999	1532985	2.82	43357	6.47	1576342	2.92
2000	1522802	-0.66	45694	5.39	156896	-0.50
2001	1547184	1.60	45697	0.01	1592881	1.55
2002	1662616	7.46	50906	11.40	1713522	7.57
2003	1842995	10,85	56774	11.53	18997669	10.87

Source: Tamil Nadu Tourism Development Corporation, Chennai.

Sustainable Tourism

Modern tourism industry heavily depends on outstanding natural features and unique cultural aspects. Sustainable development of tourism aims at the continuous maintenance of these along with equitable distribution of social- economic benefits of tourism to the resident population at the destination. The globe 90 conference of environmental and industry defined sustainable tourism as the management of tourism resources in such a way that it fulfils economic, social and aesthetic needs while maintaining cultural and life support system (Tourism Action Strategy Committee, 1990).

The Eco-tourist indulges himself in number of activities that are related to nature the most popular are trekking, hiking, bird watching, natural Photography wildlife safaris, camping mountain claming, river refilling canoeing and botanical study (Whelan Tensic, 1991). Eco tourism is in enlightening nature travel experience that contributes to conservation of the Eco system while respecting the environment. It also implies that need for taking utmost care not to alter the integrity of the Eco system while tapping the economic benefits from the resources of nature and the environment. (Vijaykumar, 1995)

Possible Solution for the Sustainable Tourism

For sustainable utilization of tourism potential the growth of this activity must be there without causing irreversible damage to the natural environment, activities relating to tourism development should take the following into consideration.

Carrying capacity of this tourist must be assessed for tourism promotion. Development of tourism should be in harmony with environment. Tourist must be given with sufficient awareness about the fragility of the ecology of that locality to be visited by them. Tourist must be involved in conservation efforts.

Public Policy Must be Reformulated

It was formed in 1863, by then retired Madurai district collector Sir Henry. The lake is under severe threat from anthropogenic activities and its watershed is fast becoming a cesspool. The lake has a watershed area of around 57 acres, and a perimeter of 5km. It is fed by natural springs that originates from the marsh and the shoal forests around its watershed. Apart from being a beauty spot the lake also serves the needs of Kodaikanal and Plani towns for drinking water. During the season times that tourist inflow, hotels and resorts at Kodai around use the lake water for all. Kodaikanal, located amidst the folds of the verdant Pali hills is one of the most popular serene hill stations in India, which mesmerizes any visitor. With her wooded slopes, mighty rocks, enhancing waterfalls and a beautiful lake, Kodaikanal is a charming hill station of South India. Kodaïkanal is situated at an altitude of about 2,133-m high and covers an area of 21.45-aq-km. The hill town is renowned for its educational institutions of international repute. The pride of Kodaikanal is the 'kutinji-gloert', which blossoms once in 12 years. The hill-plantain fruits and plums are known for their freshness and taste.

The Summer Festival in Kodaikanal

There are several beautiful hill stations in Tamil Nadu. With the Summer Festivals, the hills are even hospitable to welcome the visitors. The summer festival I held in the 'Queen of Hill stations', the evergreen Ooty; the exquisite Kodaikanal or the salubrious heights of Yercaud. Cultural programs, adventure sports, boat races, flower and fruit shows add to the splendour of the Festival

Kodaikanal Lake

One of the main attractions for the tourists of Kodaikanal is the Kodai lake which is at a distance of 3kms from the bus stand. In 1863, Vera Levinge, a former District Collector of Madurai settled in Kodaikanal after his retirement. He was the man of resource and creative ideas for this lake. By spending his own money he converted the marshy land with several streams of lake by constructing a strong bund and brought boats from Tuticorin. It is reported that the foreign resident's even used to swim in the lake.

The lake is situated at 10degress 14'n latitude and 77 degrees 28' longitude at an elevation of 2285m above sea level and it looks magnificent with star shaped glittering water, in the midst of evergreen lush slopes. The hills receive the rainfall during North-East Monsoon months of October, November and December. The lake is spread over 60 acres and surrounded by fine tarred road of

5 kms. Length, the maximum depth in 1962 was 11.5m but it is now about 9m due to siltation. The average depth is 3.0m. The boat club provides for hire. There are luxury boats also. The famous Carlton hotel is facing the lake and the hotel is having their own boats for their customers.

Today, lakhs of tourists walk around, sail on, ride on horses & cycles and admire the lake. Fishing can also be done obtaining permission from Inspector of Fisheries. Pony rides by children and adults walking around the lake are part of Kodai Holiday.

Kodaikanal Lake is a magnificent man-made lake, which spreads out in a star shape over sixty acres is a main attraction as it is set among the greenery. The boat club here offers several pleasure and racing trips.

Sources of Water

The spring that feeds the lake comes from the Gymkhana marsh. This has been badly contaminated by the building of a huge resort complex adjacent to the marsh. The construction activity around the lake is disturbing the soil and this has led to the blocking of many small springs. Wherever soil has bee disturbed situation and nutrient discharge into the lake one taking place. The lake was 11.5 mts. deep in 1970s but now it is only 5 mts. There are 19 feeder roads leading to the lake.

The Uses of Lake Waters

With whatever objective in mind the then collector Mr. Levinge built the lake is not clearly known. But today it is the main source of water for drinking and domestic use at Kodaikanal in summer. The inflow of tourists is maximum is summer and at this time that the drinking water reservoir, that is intended to supply water to the township dries up. The hotels and resorts have no choice but to rely o the waters of the lake. This apart, the entire town pilgrim of Palani depends on the water following out of the lake for its water supply. Hence the quality of water for human consumption is of utmost importance that the recreational value attached to the lake waters.

Water quality

The water that was once clear up to three meters deep today presents an appalling sight. It is like pea soup and the visibility is only around 90 cms. The reason for this state of water is the growth of algae in large number leading to Algal Blooms. There are about 800 toilets in commercial and residential living quarters that are situated in the lake watershed.

Some Recommendations to Save Kodai lake

- From a Kodaikanal lake management board, and involve all the stakeholders in the watershed- House Owner, commercial establishments
- The commercial establishments must immediately pipe their sewage after treatment out of the watershed (schools, hotels, clubs)
- Provide well-maintained public amenities for the public to use and pipe the sewage out of the watershed.
- The toilets around the lake should be connected to a common waste collection system that will pipe the sewage out of the watershed

References

1. Prabhas Chandra, 2003, "Global Eco Tourism – Codes, Protocols and Charters", Kaniskha Publishers Distributors, New Delhi.
2. V. Dhulast Birundha, 2003, "Environmental Challenges Towards Tourism", Kaniskha Publishers Distributors, New Delhi.
3. O.P. Kandari, Ashish Chandra, 2004, "Tourism Biodiversity and Sustainable Development", Isha Books, Delhi.
4. J.K Sharma, 2000, "Tourism and Development: Design for Ecological Sustainability", Kaniskha Publishers Distributors, New Delhi.
5. Department of Tourism, Government of Tamil Nadu, Chennai.
6. Palani Hills Conservation Council, Kodaikanal, Report 2004.
7. Vijayakumar 1995, "Sustainable Eco tourism in Kerala" unpublished thesis submitted to Kerala University.

21

Role of Women Entrepreneurs in Water Management

P. Regina Devi and N. Saraswathy

'Entrepreneur' in the current Indian context is an adapter and imitator much more than a true innovator. He is one much in common with Marshall's organizer of the factors of production rater than Schumpeter's creative disturber. Women entrepreneur is meant the women or group of women responsible for the existence of a new industrial enterprise. The concept is more akin to Marshall's organizer of the factors of production.

A prime, natural indivisible resource is water. Water though bitterly to human survival has a conditioned availability due to the mediation of several factors in the eco system. Water scarcity is a direct outcome of the deforestation and leads to disturbance of the hydrological cycle and further shortages of existing water base. However, the reality confronting the word is the need for planning and development of this finite resource-water. There is an ever-increasing demand of water for domestic industrial, navigation, irrigation or hydropower purposes. Besides, water is needed for other aspects of development such as health, nutrition, and education. This situation calls for a convergences of thought and action for judicious use of water. We have a scenario of "water everywhere but not a drop to drink".

A national perspective has to pervade the planning and development of water resources at the micro and macro level it is all very well to state that immediate local needs should dictate the use of water. But it is pertinent remember that water is a national resources inter linked with the fulfillment of a basic human need which common to all living beings.

Functions of a Women Entrepreneur

Frederick Harbsion in his article "Entrepreneurial organization as a factor in economic development" specifies the following functions for a woman entrepreneur.

1. Explore the prospects of starting new enterprises,
2. The undertaking of risks and the handling of economic uncertainty,
3. Introduction of innovation,
4. Co-ordination, administration and control, and
5. Routine supervision.

Role of Women Entrepreneurship

The countries, which are in the industrialization process, have a congenial climate for women entrepreneurship. These countries are stressing the importance of small scale and cottage industries. These types of industries are very suitable for women.

Women entrepreneurs can generally undertake three types of work:

1. Operate purely as a sub-contractor on raw materials provided by the customer,
2. Manufacture an item to the long – or – short – term order of another enterprises, usually a large scale enterprises, and
3. Manufacture the item for direct sale in the market

Development of Women Entrepreneur – Recent Trends

Development of women Entrepreneurship should form an internal part of all development efforts. With this vies of special chapter in the Seventh Plan has covered the integration of women in economic development. In this regard the plan documents have suggested the following:

1. To treat women as specific target groups in all development programmes.
2. To properly diversity vocational training facilities for women to suit their varied needs and skills.
3. To encourage appropriate technologies, equipment and practice for reducing their efficiency and productivity.

4. To provide marketing assistance the state level.
5. To increase women's participation in decision – making.

Issues in Water Quality Domestic Consumption

1. Important aspects in water quality which special reference to safe drinking water. The term would include non-polluted water with hygienic handling till it reaches the mouth for consumption purpose.
2. Contamination sources are many-the supply pipes-intermittent diversion through taping for a local area supply, pilferage at various points simple things washing vessels or cloths teeth pressing at the different street water sources seepage of drain water in the domestic water supply; at home, the handling of polluted water using that dipping method.
3. In places were hand pumps and piped water supply system are in conveniently installed the preference for piped water is evident. Hand pump design mechanisms are cumbersome and strenuous for women who are the main water carriers for domestic consumption.
4. One issue to be addressed is "why water supply schemes are not designed taking in to consideration the needs, habits, culture of the women who are the service provider to the family".
5. Further the pollution, degradations and neglected of traditional of water sources (tanks and ponds) have deprived the women poorer house hold of their sustenance sources leading to an increased reliance on distant water sources.

Alternative Paragon

Women Water Committee

Every village or township having elected women representative at the village or ward level form a core committee for identifying the water demand vs. supply in entire area and in the respective village or ward.

Women Street Committee

- Would be formed at the very grass-roots level to pay attention to the following issues, Need, Habits, Culture and others of the ethos of people particularly women vis-à-vis water.
- Ownership rights, accountably, control over water resources in that particular area. This could include involvement in terms of installation of water supply system, maintenance and repair activities and control of over usage of pilferage.

Water Rationing

- Checking storage facilities in household in the community and curbing wastage of stored water in household.
- Take cognizance of the ecological factors affecting traditional water sources.
- Resource mobilization and allocation of funs to strengthen existing supply system and build alternatives.
- The related developmental activities such as health, nutrition, income generation and education would be dealt alone with water management at the local level.
- Water supply in village at township would be inter linked with income generation activity provide employment opportunities to the village youth and women as also resulting in creation of infrastructure in the community.

Conclusion

The shouldering of such an activity for water management rests with the government agencies that would initiate the activity at various levels and make efforts to co-ordinate activities to sustain community usage.

Even the state government strategy should also be planned as per the activities and priorities. Judicious use of water through SHGs, watersheds/NSS/DWACRA/CMEY etc. is required, if the government strategy has to be a success, which in turn will be of greater help to women and their empowerment.

References

1. Agarwal, G.K., "Empowerment of Women through Rural Industrialisation - An Indian Experience", National Bank News Review, January-March, 1997.

2. Bisht, N.S., Misra, R.C., Srivastava, A.K., "Entrepreneurship Reflections and Investigations", Chugh Publications, Allahabad.

3. Desai, Vasant "Profile of a Woman Entrepreneur", Entrepreneurial Development, Himalaya Publishing House, Mumbai.

4. Gupta, C.B.., Srinivasan, N.P., "Entrepreneurship Development in India", Sultan Chand and Sons, New Delhi, 1992.

5. Acheson, J.M., (1989), "Management of Common Property Resources" in S Plattner (ed.), Economic Anthropology (Stanford University Press, Stanford, California).

6. Beck, T., (1994), "Common Property Resources - Access by Poor and Class Conflict in West Bengal", Economic and Political Weekly, p. 294.

7. World Bank, (1984), India: Himalayan Watershed Management Project (U.P.) Staff Appraisal Report (Washington, DC; World Bank).

22

Water Budgeting and Planning in India

S. Mani Kandan and N. Saraswathy

India has predominately agricultural economy and water lands are amongst its most valuable natural resources. The prosperity of the people demands into small measure on how judiciously these are used. For evolving policies for the best use of water resources, it is important to make an assessment of their magnitude, distribution and scope of utilisation. It is also necessary to have an idea of the present and future demands of water for various uses, such as irrigation, industries, thermal power generation, public health river conservancy etc.

Water Consumption Pattern in India

If per capita water availability is any indication, 'water stress' is only just beginning to show. This index is based on the minimum per capita level of water required to maintain an aggregate demand and proper resource management. Water availability on the Indian subcontinent is strongly influenced by a number of climatic and geographic factors. Together these combine to provide India with enough freshwater to meet the various demands arising from the agricultural, industrial and domestic sectors. However, the actual distribution of water resources over space and time limits access to certain geographic regions and a few months of the year. Government policies and economic incentives have also influenced the water distribution and consumption across India.

Water harvesting structures used in India are based on ancient models and are therefore highly adapted to the prevailing climatic and hydrologic conditions of the area. The potential of these systems to supply adequate freshwater to all areas and sectors is high. However, since colonial times – and especially after independence in 1947, these systems have been increasingly abandoned and neglected in favor of large dam and canal irrigation projects. So far, these 'modern' structures have been successful in providing water to portions of rural and urban India; yet high economic, social and environmental costs have reduced their overall benefit. The highly variable nature of the climate makes groundwater the most popular alternative for irrigation and domestic water use across India and accounts for over 400 km→ of the annual utilizable resource in the country. This dependence on ground water resources is particularly critical where dry season surface water levels are low or where wet season flows are too disruptive to be easily tapped. In addition to being accessible, groundwater quality is generally excellent in most areas and presents a relatively safe source of drinking water for Indians in rural and urban centers. Agriculture remains central to the Indian economy and it therefore receives a greater share of the annual water allocation. According to the World Resources Institute (2000), 92%, of India's utilizable water is devoted to this sector, mostly in the form of irrigation.

Major and Medium Irrigation-Budget Allotment/Planning Limit during Year 2001-2002

Item	Budget Allotment
1. Construction Work (State Budget) (Rs. 150.00 crore AIBP including State contribution)	239.5328
2. Tools and Plants & Walmi (8.3181+1.00)	9.3181
3. Establishment	96.1448
Sub Total:	344.9957
4. AIBP	350.00
5. NABARD	145.00
6. Externally Added	150.00
TOTAL	989.9957

Participatory Approach to Water Resources Management

Management of the Water resources for diverse uses should incorporate a participatory approach; by involving not only the various governmental agencies but also the users and other stakeholders, in an effective and decisive manner, in various aspects of planning, design, development and management of the water resources schemes. Necessary legal and institutions changes should be made at various levels for the purpose, duly ensuring appropriate role for women. Water Users' Associations and the local bodies such as municipalities and gram panchayats should particularly be involved in the operation, maintenance and management of water infrastructures/facilities at appropriate levels progressively, with a view to eventually transfer the management of such facilities to the user groups/local bodies.

Private Sector Participation

Private sector participation should be encouraged in planning, development and management of water resources projects for diverse uses, wherever feasible. Private sector participation may help in introducing innovative ideas, generating financial resources and introducing corporate management and improving service efficiency and accountability to users. Depending upon the specific situations, various combinations of private sector participation, in building, owning, operating, leasing and transferring of water resources facilities, may be considered.

Drinking Water and Sanitation

All drinking water schemes brought under the Rajiv Gandhi National Drinking Water Mission; emphasis to be on providing drinking water facilities in the remaining uncovered rural habitations; and on tackling water quality in about 2.16 lakh habitations; Total Sanitation Campaign to be extended ton all districts;

Water Resources Planning

Water resources available to the country should be brought within the category of utilizable resources to the maximum possible extent. Non-conventional methods for utilization of water such as through inter-basin transfers, artificial recharge of ground water and desalination of brackish or sea water as well as traditional water conservation practices like rainwater harvesting, including roof-top rainwater harvesting, need to be practiced to further increase the utilizable water resources. Promotion of frontier research and development, in a focused manner, for these techniques is necessary.

Water resources development and management will have to be planned for a hydrological unit such as drainage basin as a whole or for a sub-basin, multi-sectorally, taking in to account surface and ground water for sustainable use incorporating quantity and quality aspects as well as environmental considerations. All individual development projects and proposals should be formulated and considered within the framework of such an overall plan keeping in view the existing agreements/awards for a basin or a sub basin so that the best possible combination of options can be selected and sustained.

Watershed management through extensive soil conservation, catchment-area treatment, preservation of forests and increasing the forest cover and the construction of check-dams should be promoted. Efforts shall be to conserve the water in the catchment. Water should be made available to water short areas by transfer from other areas including transfers from one river basin to another, based on a national perspective, after taking into account the requirements of the areas/basins.

Ground Water Development

There should be a periodical reassessment of the ground water potential on a scientific basis, taking into consideration the quality of the water available and economic viability of its extraction.

Exploitation of ground water resources should be so regulated as not exceed the recharging possibilities, as also to ensure social equity. The detrimental environmental consequences of overexploitation of ground water need to be effectively prevented by the Central and State Governments. Ground water recharge projects should be developed and implement for improving both the quality and availability of ground water resource.

Integrated and coordinated development of surface water and ground water resources and their conjunctive use, should be envisaged right from the project planning stage and should form an integral part of the project implementation. Over exploitation of ground water should be avoided especially near the coast prevent ingress of seawater into sweet water aquifers.

Adequate safe drinking water facilities should be provided to the entire population both in urban and in rural areas. Irrigation and multipurpose projects should invariably include a drinking water component, wherever there is no alternative source of drinking water. Drinking water needs of human beings and animals should be the first charge on any available water.

Water Quality

- Both surface water and ground water should be regularly monitored for quality. A phased programme should be undertaken for improvements in water quality.
- Effluents should be treated to acceptable levels and standards before discharging them into natural streams.
- Minimum flow should be ensured in the perennial streams for maintaining ecology and social considerations.
- Principle of 'polluter pays' should be followed in management of polluted water.

Necessary legislation is to be made for preservation of existing water bodies by preventing encroachment and deterioration of water quality.

Rain Water Harvesting

The harvesting of rainwater involves the collection of water from surfaces on which rainfalls, and subsequently storing this water for later use. Normally water is collected from the roofs of buildings and stored in rainwater tanks or allowed to recharge ground water and thus providing a perennial source of water. In Indian scenario with its monsoons, the water harvesting experience is millennial and born of local wisdom; scientific and still in use; participatory and the basis of people's movements; the focus of innovation in the present and the best way to a non-scarce future.

Urban Rainwater Harvesting

Rainwater harvesting is increasingly being modeled and implemented successfully in urban centers where the likelihood of privatization is the maximum. Traditionally, Chennai city in South India has been dependent on the ground water to a large extent for its water needs. But large-scale construction activity has led to rapid deletion of the groundwater. Now experts maintain their view that the silver lining in the clouds that do not bring enough rain lies in a simple, economical and demonstrably successful answer-Rainwater Harvesting (RWH). Chennai gets an average annual rainfall of 1,290 mm per year. A group of concerned activists-of which Shekhar Raghavan, an RWH activist is a founder-member-has now come together under the aegis of the Akash Ganga Trust to popularize rainwater-harvesting.

Water Sharing/Distribution amongst the States

The water sharing/distribution amongst the states should be guided by a national perspective with due regard to water resources availability and needs within the river basin. Necessary guidelines, including for water short states even outside the basin, need to be evolved for facilitating future agreements amongst the basin states.

The Inter-State Disputes Act of 1956 may be suitably reviewed and amended for timely adjudication of water disputes referred to the Tribunal.

Conclusion

In view of the vital importance of water for human and animal life, for maintaining ecological balance and for economic and development activities of all kinds, and considering is increasing scarcity, the planning and management of this resource and its optimal, economical and equitable use has become a matter of the utmost urgency. Concerns of the community need to be taken into account for water resources development and management. The success of the National Water Policy will depend entirely on evolving and maintaining a national consensus and commitment to its underlying principles and objectives. To achieve the desired objectives, State Water Policy backward with an operational action plan shall be formulated in a time bound manner say in two years. National Water Policy may be revised periodically as and when need arises.

References

1. Finance and Development – A Quarterly Publication of the International Monetary Fund and The World Bank, June 1994.
2. http:// www. Angelfire.com/bc/nihhrre/NWP.html.
3. National Water Policy *(As adopted by National Water Resources Council in its 5th meeting held on April 1, 2002).*
4. World Bank, (1984), India: Himalayan Watershed Management Project (U.P.) Staff Appraisal Report (Washington, DC; World Bank).

23

Strategy for Sustainable Water Use in Future

N. Saraswathy

Water is critical for human survival, economic development, and the environment indeed; few other resources affect so many areas of the economy or of human and environment health.

Unsafe water can be fatal. Water borne disease are implicated in the deaths of 3 million people annually-mostly children-and cause over billion episodes of illness a year. Yet insufficient progress has been made in supplying adequate water and sanitation, especially to the poor. Over 1 billion of the world's 5.4 billion people lack access to safe drinking water, and 1.7 billion lack access to adequate sanitation. These problems are not limited to developing countries.

Water plays a vital role in the economy, through its use in agriculture and industry, as well as supplying energy through hydropower. A third of the world's harvested crops are produced by irrigated agriculture.

Much of the natural environment – from coastal ecosystems to water lands-depends on water. Degrading the quality or supply of that water can have disastrous effects of the environment and on biodiversity.

Clearly, the availability of good quality water is central to economic progress and to maintaining a natural environment that can help to sustain such progress: Yet in most countries, water resources are not being managed in an efficient and sustainable manner-a situation that cannot continue.

To begin with, the world's population is growing rapidly, especially in urban areas. This implies a greater demand for good and hence for irrigation. At the same time, the demand for water by households and industries, further stimulated by economic growth, is rising. These factors imply escalating competition for irrigated agriculture, which already takes a hefty share of available water.

Second, the supply of good-quality water is being contaminated through pollution originating from domestic wastes, industry, agricultural chemicals, and disguised land use, thereby effectively decreasing the amount of water available.

Third, the engineering and environmental costs of developing new water sources are much higher than those of sources already tapped. For many cities, the cost of water provided by "the next project" can be two to three times the cost of current supplies, even before environmental costs are factored.

As the increasing scarcity of water threatens to worsen the quality of life, impair the potential for economic development, and endanger vital ecosystems, a number of countries and development agencies, including the World Bank, have begun to rethink their approaches. This is particularly important for the Bank lending during the past four decades. While significant achievements have been made, investments have often encountered implementation, operational and social problems, most of which stem from the weakness in the current water resources management. In recent years, a consensus has begun to emerge on what needs to be done to correct the problems.

Why has government typically assumed responsibility for the overall management of water? Water's special characteristics make it difficult to use unregulated markets to deliver water efficiency or to allocate it equitably. The large capital requirements and economics of scale in water infrastructure tend to create monopolies, warranting regulation to prevent over pricing. Public investments in water infrastructure are often necessary given the large size and long time horizon of projects: underdeveloped capital markets in many lower-income countries and the potential for political interference reduce incentives for private investments. Water's natural supply is subjects to extreme variability over time and space. Certain aspects of water-related activities, such as flood control, are public goods, which cannot easily be changed for on the basis of use. Finally, water moves through an intricate cycle within the ecosystem that makes water activities highly inter-dependent and results in numerous spillover effects, many of which affect the environment. These effects cannot be reflected in market prices.

Pricing water well below its economic value is prevalent throughout the world, sometimes for cultural and religious reasons. Under pricing often results in misallocation and inefficient use. In many countries, expanding the supply is politically more expedient than raising fees: therefore, pricing and demand management have received much less attention. Farmer in both industrial and developing countries often pay little for their publicity supplied irrigation water and so have few incentives crops or to conserve water. This can lead to gross misallocation, whereby agricultural, which absorbs the lion's, share, often includes low-value uses compared with higher-value domestic and industrial uses.

Neglect of Public Health, Water Quality, and the Environment

Countries have generally paid too little attention to water quality and pollution control. Besides contributing to serve public health problems, poor water resources management causes widespread degradation of land and water. Many countries do not have standards to control water pollution adequately or the capacity to enforce existing legislation. Furthermore, new types of pollution-often stemming from public investment projects-have arisen involving small quantities of non-degradable chemicals that are invisible, toxic, persistent, and costly to treat.

The weakness highlighted above have particularly adverse effect on the poor (see "poverty and water supply: How to move forward", by John Briscoe, Finance & Development. December 1992). Because public services are overextended and under funded, the inadequate supply is pre-empted by wealthier and more influential groups. Paradoxically, large numbers of poor people in urban areas depend on water vendors, paying a much higher price than a middle-class person pays.

New Approaches

How to overcome the weakness in water resources management has been the subject of much international discussion. At the June 1992 United Nations Conference on Environment and Development in Rio de Janeiro, member countries endorsed policies that stress integrated water resources management "based on the perception of water as an integral part of the ecosystem, and natural resources and social and economic good". They also stressed "the implementation of allocation decisions through demand management, pricing mechanisms, and regulatory measures".

These policies reflect the current worldwide consensus on moving away from past approaches that tended to center on developing new sources of water-a "supply" focus. The new emphasis is on economic behavior, policies to overcome market and government failures, and technologies for increasing the efficiency of water use-a "demand" focus (see "water management in the maghreb") in this approach underlines the Bank's new policy for managing water resources. Among the measures countries are increasingly adopting:

Water resources should be managed in the context of a national water strategy that reflects the nation's social, economic, and environmental objectives and is based on an assessment of its water resources. Such a framework ensures that cross-sectoral and environmental implication of water investments and use are taken into account and can overcome the problems caused by fragmented through appropriate coordination mechanism.

Placing Greater Emphasis on Incentives for Efficiency and Financial Accountability

Establishment of proper incentives induces better performance by providers of water services and efficient use by consumers, leading ultimately to a better allocation of water among different uses. A key component of an appropriate incentive system is the pricing of water.

Establishing Strong Laws and Regulations

Laws and regulations covering monopoly organizations, environmental protection, and other aspects of water management that are not adequately handled by unregulated market forces can be a foundation for effective water resources management.

This will help to stop the spread of disease in crowded low-income areas. Besides building water delivery infrastructure, fee schedules can be structured so that consumers receive a limited amount of water at a low cost and pay a higher fee for additional water. Water charges up to a minimum to meet basic health requirements are kept particularly modest. This system requires that individual consumers be metered. In areas where metering is not possible, connections to sewage and sanitation may need to be subsidized for the poor. However, it is important that water entities not be driven to financial unsustainability to being charged with social objectives.

Putting Ideas into Practice

Each of the measures illustrated above is worthwhile in it, but their full potential will be realized only if they are all integrated in a country's water resources management practices. Many countries have already put some of these elements into place, while others are just beginning.

The challenge of meeting the water requirements of the planet is enormous-for developing countries alone; an estimated $600-700 billion over the next decade is needed for investments in irrigation, hydropower, water supply, and sanitation. World Bank lending will provide a small part of this amount, roughly $18 billion over the next five years. Most will have to come from domestic resources. An important way in which countries can help is by following policies that encourages cost recovery, provide economic incentives to manage water efficiently, and induce private sector investment. In the future, the comprehensive framework for water resources management and the attendant policies outlined above will be crucial for countries to sustain this vital resource for economic growth.

Reference

1. Finance and Development - A Quarterly Publication of the International Monetary Fund and World Bank, June 1994.

24

Land Utilization and Watershed Development Programme

A. Muralidhar Rao

An important concern in watershed development is the equitable distribution of the benefits of land and water resources development and the consequent biomass production. Public investment of a large magnitude is being made in both private lands and in common public property. Therefore the right of each individual in the village to an equitable share of the common lands, forest and water resources of the village regardless of his individual private land holding would be recognized and addressed through effective means

The support for micro-watershed development will be routed through the SGHs of the poor to ensure that the works taken up are demand driven and based on their left needs, thereby ensuring better targeting of the interventions in favour of the poor. Promotion of rapid rural Growth in drought-prone and rain fed areas of state is another important mean of enhancing the livelihood opportunities to the poor. Towards this end government will promote horticulture, forestry and livestock in these areas.

A 10-year (1998-2007) action plan aimed at treating 10 million hectares of wastelands/degraded lands and degraded reserve forests using participatory processes, has been initiated in the state. So far about 3 million hectares is being treated. The Government has recently embarked on a program, named A.P. Rural Livelihoods Project, in five districts (Anantapur, Kurnool, Mehboobnagar, Prakasham and Nalgonda), with the financial support of Department for International Development (DFID), government of United Kingdom, at a cost of over Rs. 307 crores.

This program addresses the issue of sustainable rural livelihoods in a framework of employment, and better conditions of living for the poor and conservation of natural resources. It provides supports for strengthening participatory processes and providing sustained capacity building for the community- based organizations involved in watershed management.

Andhra Pradesh has taken bold steps to demonstrate that a convergence of conversation and development objectives can be achieved through Joint Forest Management (JFM). Pursuing one of the most proactive JFM programs in India, the State has committed to the user groups, 100% of usufruct forest produce secured from the area entrusted to the JFM committees. Widespread implementation of JFM is leading to an increased flow (both value and volume) of forest products to communities and an increase in environmental benefits resulting form improved forest condition (Principally with respect to soil and water regimes). Formation of JFM Committees in Andhra Pradesh has successfully targeted remote an under served communities, in particular tribal populations. Government is committed to ensure the success and spread of this process.

Table 24.1: Trend Growth Rates in Area, Production and Yield of Food grains and all Crops: 1990s and 2000s

Period	Foodgrains		All Crops			
	Area	Production	Yield	Area	Production	Yield
1980-81 to 1989-90	0.22	2.81	2.71	0.09	3.13	2.52
1990-91to 2003-2004	0.07	1.98	1.30	0.41	2.30	1.19

Source: RBI 2003

Table 24.2: Growth Rate of Agriculture Production in India

S. No.	Particulars	Pre-reform period 1990-91 over 1980-81	Post-reform period 2003-04 over 1990-91
I.	Food Grains	3.1	1.66
	a)Rice	3.3	1.76
	b)Wheat	4.3	3.04
	c)Coarse Cereals	1.2	0.06
	d)Pulses	3.0	-0.58
II.	Oil Seeds	7.1	0.66
III.	Sugar Cane	4.6	2.62
IV.	Cotton	3.4	2.62
V.	Jute & Mesta	1.2	0.7
	Index of Agricultural Production	3.8	1.73

Source: RBI 2003

Table 24.3: Selected Economic Indicators

	1990-91	1991-92	1992-93	1993-94	1994-95	1995-96	2000-01
Food grains (Million tonnes)	176.4	168.5 (4.5)	179 (6.5)	184.3 (2.7)	191.5 (-3.9)	185.1 (-35)	195.9

Availability of credit for farmers is important for working capital and investments in agriculture.

Despite having a wide network of rural branches and implementation of many schemes and programmes for expansion of credit for agriculture and rural development, a large number of very poor people still continue to remain outside the fold of the formal banking system. The Growth Rate of agricultural credit for small farmers declined in the 1990s as compared with 1980s

(RBI-2002). There was a decline of credit for large farmers in the same period.

The credit deposit ration increased from 55.1% in 1980 to 97% in 1990, but declined significantly to 49.3% by 2000. The incremental credit deposit ration also declined from 106.1% in the 1980s to 36% in the 1990s.

With rising income, there will be diversification of crops, investment needs for the production of high income – elastic agricultural products, Such as dairying and livestock, horticulture, agro forests would rise much faster now. Due to these factors, rural credit has to expand at a rate faster than in the recent post

Table 24.4: Water and Seed Fertilizer Technology Programmes: 1970-71to 1980-81, 1990-91 to 2003-04

High Yield varieties	1970-71 to 1980-81	1980-81 to 1990-91	1990-91 to 2003-04
	10.5	4.2	4.44
	12.5	4.1	2.3
	9.5	2.7	1.1
	--	2.7	1.9
	3.6	1.7	2.1
	1.4	2.3	1.1
	2.6	1.7	2.0
	--	2.7	1.8
	2.7	1.3	1.2
	4.2	3.3	2.3
	9.6	8.5	3.7

Source: Economic Survey, 2002-03

Cumulative effects of all these changes through economic reforms are causing declining crop yields, shift in the cropping pattern in favour of high risky crops under the conditions of low risk baring capacity of the farmers, decline in surface irrigation and increase in ground water irrigation, inadequacies in public investment and institutional credit.

Table 24.5: Credit – Deposit Ratio by Population Groups

Population Group	C.D. Ratio			Incremental CD Ratio	
	December	March, 1990	March, 2004	December, 1980 to 1990	December, 1990 to March, 2004
Rural	55.1	97.1	49.3	106.1	36.0
Semi-Urban	47.9	48.3	40.0	48.5	37.6
Urban	56.5	52.9	42.1	51.9	39.0
Metro	81.1	58.0	73.2	51.6	76.8
TOTAL	64.0	60.7	56.0	59.8	54.8

Source: Economic Survey, 2002-03

Suicides: As a result of this, the farmers' incomes have declined thereby leading to a miserable life. It is manifested in a large number of suicides committed by them in different part of the country particularly A.P. and Karnataka. Majority of the farmers committing suicides are small and marginal farmers. This could be due to non-availability of institutional credit. The farmers take loans from money lenders at high interest rates and fall in to a debt trap. There may be many other reasons further research is needed.

Inequalities: Rural and Urban inequalities have increased. The salaries of Public Sector employees have grown at 5 % per annum while agricultural wages grew at the rate of 2.5% per annum. In the post –liberalization period Growth rates of SDP in States such as Karnataka, West Bengal, Maharashtra, Gujarat and Tamil Nadu increased faster than other States. They are better placed today because of initial conditions and because of favourable economic infrastructure that is conductive to growth. The higher rate of capital formation also helped these states to forge a head in the post-reform phase.

Inflation: Inflation is hitting the poor the most as the increase in the prices is mostly noticed in respect of rice, oil, and vegetables. One side increasing condition of inflation on the other side low prices for farm products is the paradox.

Diversification: Small farmers' consumption pattern have been shifting from cereals to non-cereal food, e.g. shift from corn and maize to rice and wheat). This has led to diversification of agriculture, which results in risk and uncertainty.

A watershed starts at mountain peaks and hilltops Snowmelt and rainfall wash over and through the high ground into rivulets which drain into fast-flowing mountain streams. As the streams descend, tributaries and ground waters add to their volume and they become rivers. As they leave the mountains, rivers slow and start to meander and braid, seeking the path of lest resistance across widening valleys, whose alluvial floor was laid down by millennia of sediment-laden floods. Eventually the river will flow into a lake or ocean. Where the river is muddy and the land flat, the sediments laid down by the river may form a delta, slitting the river into a bird-foot of distributaries which discharge into the sea. The river's estuary, the place where its sweet waters mix with the ocean's salt, is one of the most biologically productive parts of the river and of the ocean. Most of the world's fish catch comes from species which are dependent for at least part of their life cycle on a nutrient-rich estuarine habitat. The diversity of a river lies not only in the various types of countries it flows through but also in the changing seasons and the differences between wet and dry years. Seasonal and annual variations in the amount of water, sediment and nutrients drained by a watershed can be massive, especially in dry areas where most of a year's rain may fall in just a few individual storms.

Rivers, and the rich variety of plants and animals which they sustain, provide hunter-gatherer societies with water for drinking and washing, and with food, drugs and medicines, dyes, fibres and wood. Farmers reap the same benefits as well as, where needed, irrigation for their crops. For pastoral societies, who graze their herds over wide across of often parched plains and mountains, perennial vegetation along the banks of rivers provides life-sustaining food and fodder during dry seasons and droughts. Towns and cities use (and misuse) the rivers to carry away their wastes. Rivers also serve as roadways for commerce, exploration and conquest.

The role of rivers as the sustainers of life and fertility is reflected in the myths and beliefs of a multitude of cultures. In many parts of the world, rivers are referred to as 'mothers': Narmadai, "Mother Narmada': the Volga is Mat' Rodnaya, ' Mother of the Land'. The Thai word for river, mae nan, translates literally as water mother'. Rivers have often been linked with divinities, especially the female ones. In ancient Egypt, the floods of the Nile were considered the teras of the goddess Isis. Ireland's River Boyne, which is over looked by the island's most impressive prehistoric burial sites, was worshipped as a goddess by Celtic tribes.

Significance

Better water quality facilitates more availability of water based recreational services. Boating and fishing can be enlarged and swimming would be possible in a lucrative way. People would be better off by taking advantage of these services would be better off. With vast opportunities for recreation, the beneficiaries have to pay a sum of money for these. Their willingness to pay is a measure of the benefit of the cleaner river (Haveman and Knesse, 1973).

Due to pollution control, there is reduction of discharge to rivers, and lakes, growing of fish stock and reduction of the cost of harvesting. People who live in cities and towns obtain their drinking water from the river. With a cleaner river the cost of purifying and treating of water will be reduced. This will enhance social benefits (Freeman, 1973).

Distribution of Water

Fresh water can be analysed from three types of water sources such as rivers, lakes and ground water. There are 214 international rivers and lake basins in the world (CNRET, 1978). CNRET defined a river basin as an "Area within feed a given river". It considered only those international river basins which were "Separate" (That is not tributary basins) and were connected with final recipient of the water to ocean)." The study indicated that nearly 47% of the world's landmass (excluding Antarctica) falls with in international basin s. It ranged from a high of nearly 60% of the landmass in Africa and South America to a low about 40% in North and Central America.

Issues in Water Conflicts

Water is not stagnant, it is movable and doesn't confine to a political boundaries of countries. When a river forms a boundary between two countries, the countries have equal authority over it. It also generates several types of across boarded water conflicts. Due to conflicts between co-basin countries on international rivers and lakes, many nations have negotiated about use of such water bodies.

During the past five decades, international organisations like United Nations Agencies, the World Bank and Regional Development Bank played a very small role in facilitating agreement on international river basins. The Indus treaty was signed by India and Pakistan in 19 September, 1960 (Biswas, 1992). After the negotiations between two countries on the sharing of Indus water, the subsequent agreement between four provinces of Pakistan on the allocation of river water took place.

The entire negotiating process between the two countries ran successfully for short period. In 1976 World Bank President Robert Mac Namera, discussed the issued of sharing of the Gangas' water between India and Pakistan (then including Bangladesh), But this matter did not make any progress for many reasons (Abas, 1984).

Role of International Organisations in Settling Water Disputes

Role of two other International Organisational programmes can be cited here in managing the river waters. They are the

United Nations Environment Programme (UNEP) on Zambsi River, and the United Nations Development Programme (UNDP) on the Mekong River Basin. The Zambsi Basin covers eight countries such as Angola, Botswana, Matawi, Mozambique, Namibia, Tanzania, Zambia, and Zimbabwe. UNEP arranged a conference on the environmental management of the common Zambsi River System in Harare, Zimbabwe, in May, 1987. The primary objective was to approve the draft Zambsi Action Plan (ZACPLAN) in close consultation with most of the countries concerned. The five co-basin countries Botswana, Mozambique, Tanzania, Zambia and Zimbabwe signed an agreement on the action for the environmentally sound management of the common Zambsi River System (David 1998). Real progress of implementation of the plan had taken more time span (Nakayama 1997).

The UNDP played a pivotal role in the agreement was signed on the lower Mekong by Cambodia, Laos, Thailand and Vietnam in 1995. China, the most powerful country in the upstream of the river was not a signatory to the agreement and not a member of the new Mekong River Commission (Nakayama, 1997). This may have some negative implications for the future development of the Mekong. Second, the most difficult part of any international agreement is the actual water allocation between the various co-basin countries. The Mekong agreement doesn't take any specific allocation of water between the countries. It gives slogan like "Reasonable and Equitable Distribution" and "Prevention and Cessation of harmful effects" on which some countries and objective experts may not agree. The mode for conflicts between countries on this issue in the future is likely to be high (Biswas et. al. 1999).

India represents diverse climatic, climatic, topographical and hydrological features. The total annual precipitation over the entire country is estimated to be 400 million ha-m, (4 billion m3) of water. Nag and Kathpalia (1975) estimated that of the total precipitation, about 59% lost by evaporation and transpiration, 12% percolates into the ground and remaining 1.15 x 10 12 m3 flows into the river systems. There are 14 major river basins in India, having a total annual discharge of 1.406 billion m3 (85%). The medium rivers account for 0.127 billion m3 (8%) water discharge. Above 0.2 x 10 12m3 of water is estimated to be flowing into India from outside and thus, the total surface flow is estimated to be 1.8 x 10 12 m3 (180 million ha-m), (Rao, 1975).

Barring a few major rivers like Brahmaputra, Ganga, Yamuna, Indus, Godavari, Krishna, Narmada and Cauvery, the rest of them are seasonal. These rivers during monsoon are in floods. River systems are interwoven with human civilization, this being particularly in India. In fact, river banks have been considered to be the cradle of major civilizations in the world. For instance, about the Ganga, Jawharlal Nehru wrote, "The story of the Ganga from her source to the sea, from old times to new, is the story of India's civilization and culture". The Ganges is the river of India, beloved of her people, round which are intertwined her racial memories, her hopes and fears, her songs of triumph, her victories and her defeats. She is a symbol of India's age old culture and civilization, ever changing, ever flowing and yet ever the same Ganges". Besides fulfilling the prime needs for life processes, rivers have been used for domestic, agricultural, fisheries, industrial, recreational aesthetic, navigational and power generation purposes.

Conclusion

Rivers are an integral part of the land. Rivers provide the societies with water for drinking and washing and with food, drugs and medicines, dyes and wood. Rivers act as a sink to carry away the wastes. It also serves as roadways for commerce, exploration and conquest. Both the developed and developing countries face the problem of pollution of the river because of industrial effluents, agricultural effluents and domestic sewerage. However, attempts have been made to clean up the polluted rivers in the world. In India most of the rivers have become toxic drains. The prime causes are urbanization, industrialization, agricultural run off etc., the reckless discharge and disposal of urban sewage into the rivers make it polluted.

Godavari is an important river of Andhra. It is a major east flowing river of the peninsular fiver system originates near Pharsiya village of Raipur district of Maharashtra state. The intense human activity in the basin area, produce solid waste and liquid effluents which tent to be concentrated in specific areas of the urban and industrial settlement. In the Godavari basin almost all these wastes are discharged untreated into the water course causing pollution in whole system. The present research work hovers around this research piece. We have picked up the house hold solid waste generation as a proxy variable for measuring the pollution of the river.

The level of development is not even in different areas of the state and poverty tends to be more intense in the less developed areas. Lack of basic minimum services like education, health, drinking water, nutrition, and housing is primarily responsible for backwardness of the areas.

25

Watershed Management: An Economic Analysis

P. Dhavamani and T. Vijaya Kumar

The concept of 'watershed' based integrated resources management planning gained great momentum both through the national and international organisations\Institution understanding the concept and techno-financial supports. The growth rates is quite fast, as a result there are quite a gap between the understanding and applications of the technologies and also between the institutional frameworks and the socio-economic environment to achieve sustainable benefit to the people.

The goal of integrated watershed development is rural poverty eradication thereby improving the quality of rural life and environments. The rural natural resource utilisations are often for beyond the carrying capacity of the natural resources base of the watershed of the region. This in turn causes the degradation of the natural resources, which is then gradually reflected in economy and quality of life in the area.

Land and water are the basic natural resources. Proper planning, utilization and management of these resources, has a tremendous impact towards the economic development of our country. The rural people may be considered as the third resource, as they are the real driving force for effective management and sustained use of these resources. Watershed management is a multidisciplinary activity in which several goals are to be achieved.

The watershed development project is operating under different schemes like National Development Programme for Rural Rural Areas, (NDPRA) National watershed Development programme (NWDP), Integrated Watershed Development IWDP) programme, Drough Prone Area Programme (DPAP), and Employment Assurance Scheme (EAS).

Virudhunagar District which is located on the southern western part of TamilNadu with an area of 4228 Km↑ is having an average annual rainfall of 792 mm. According to the TamilNadu water and Drainage Board Report of the 11 blocks of Virudhunagar district, Rajapalayam and Watrap blocks critically exploited (90-100%) the water sources and the Virudhunagar block is reported as safe regarding the exploitation of water source (70%).

To make an economic assessment of the programme, a major level study was undertaken relating to the sub watershed management project, in Meesalur block of the Virudhunagar.

With this above background the following objectives have been framed which are,

- to study the socio-economic conditions of the beneficiaries,
- to study the impact of the programme on land use, production, productivity and cropping pattern,
- to study the impact of the programme on income and employment of beneficiaries and
- to suggest appropriate policy measures to the sample area.

Land Holding Pattern

The land holding pattern is shown in Table 25.1. It reveals that nearly half of the total percentage i.e. 53.43% people are marginal farmers, 18.49% people are Small farmers and 29.07% people are large farmers. It is observed that in the study area most of the people come under the category of marginal farmer, large farmers and small farmers.

Out of the total population of 17.5% and 11.92% of landless labourers are completed both primary and middle education, following 45%, 27.52% and 12.76% of marginal farmers have completed primary, middle and secondary education. 35%, 44.03% and 31.91% of small farmers have completed primary, middle and secondary education. Under the large farmers 55.31%, 16.51%, 2.5% have completed small, middle and primary education. It shows that large farmers nearly 55.31 percent have secondary level of education and this reveals that all the farmers are literate. The education pattern is shown in Table 25.2.

Table 25.1: Land Holding Pattern of Beneficiaries

S. No.	Size groups landless (in ha.)	Total Area (in ha.)	No. of Households	Population
1.	Landless Labourers	---	12	48 (11.91)
2.	Marginal farmer (1-2)	130.4 (52.43)	33	132 (32.75)
3.	small farmer (2-3)	46.0 (18.49)	37	148 (36.72)
4.	large farmer (Above 3)	72.3 (29.07)	18	75 (18.61)
	Total:	248.7 (100%)	100	403 (100%)

(Figures in parenthesis indicate percentage to total)

Table 25.2: Educational Status of Beneficiary Households

S. No	Size groups Landless (in ha.)	Total Population	Primary	Middle	Secondary
1.	Landless Labourers	48	35 (17.5)	13 (11.92)	-----
2.	Marginal farmer	132	90 (45)	30 (27.52)	12 (12.76)
3.	Small farmer	148	70 (35)	48 (44.03)	30 (31.91
4.	Large farmer	75	5 (2.5)	18 (16.51)	52 (51.31)
	Total:	403 (100%)	200 (100%)	109 (99.99%)	94 (99.99%)

(Figures in parentheses indicate percentage to total. Underlines figure indicate percentage of literacy to the total population).

Land Use Pattern

The total cultivated area is increased from 80 hectares to 135 hectares. The details of land use pattern are shown in Table 25.3. As observed, 90.7 ha of non-cultivable land is decreased to 48.7 ha after use of watershed pattern. The village forest is decreased from 15.2 ha to 12.06 ha. It shows that after the completion of watershed project the cultivable land has increased and non-cultivable land has decreased.

Cropping Pattern of Beneficiaries' Household

The cropping intensive had increased from 56 to 87 (i.e. 56.2%) for pulzes varied from 12 to 20 (i.e. 14.54%) and maize varied from 12 to 28 (i.e. 29.10%). It reveals that due to the implementation of watershed all the cropping patterns have increased in the study area. The details are presented in Table 25.4.

Productivity of Crops

Both yield and yield rate of all the crops have gone up significantly. The data shown in Table 25.5 are that, the productivity of cotton had increased from 2.24 Q/ha to 5.22 Q/ha, pulzes have increased from 4.8 Q/ha to 8 Q/ha and maize have increased from increased from 4.8 Q/ha to 9.2 Q/ha. It is observed that all the crops have shown appreciable increasing in the productivity.

Income

The total annual income has increased from Rs. 5276 to Rs. 19075. The household income from agriculture has increased from Rs. 2837 to Rs. 7944 (i.e. 180%), from alied activities it has increased from Rs. 853 to Rs. 3854 (i.e. 351.8%) off farm it has increased from Rs. 627 to Rs. 3217 (i.e. 413%) and from forest it has increased from Rs. 959 to Rs. 4060 (i.e. 323.4%). It shows that the income of all households has increased greatly. The detailed analysis is shown in Table 25.6.

Table 25.3: Land Use Pattern of the Watershed

(in hectares)

S. No.	Items	Before		After	
		in ha.	Percentage to TGA	in ha.	Percentage to TGA
1.	Total geographical area (TGA)	248.7	100	248.7	100
2.	Village forest	38	15.27	30	12.06
3.	Village pasture	10	4	5	2
4.	Cultivable land	80	32.16	135	54.28
5.	Non cultivable land	90.7	36.46	48.7	19.58
6.	Pond	20	8.04	20	8.04
7.	Road & Paths	10	40	10	4

Table 25.4: Cropping Pattern of Beneficiary Household

(area in ha.)

S. No.	Name of Crops	Before the Project	After the project	Change
1.	Cotton	56	87	31 (56.2)
2.	Pulses	12	20	8 (14.54)
3.	Maize	12	28	16 (29.10)
	Total:	80	135	55 (68.75)

(Figures in parenthesis indicate percentage change).

Table 25.5: Change in Productive of Crops

S. No.	Crops	Yield rate Before the Project	Yield rate After the Project	Change	Percentage
1.	Cotton	224	522	298	133.1
2.	Pulses	48	80	32	66.67
3.	Maize	48	92	44	99.67

Table 25.6: Source Wise Income of Beneficiary Household

(Annual Income)

S. No.	Sources	Before the Project	After the Project	Percentage Change
1.	Agriculture	2837	7944	180.0
2.	Allied activities	853	3854	351.8
3.	Off farm	627	3217	413.0
4.	Forest	959	4060	323.4
	TOTAL	5276	19075	1268.2

Conclusion

The watershed management projects are the answers to the problem of frequent drought in the state. The departments of soil conservation, agriculture, foresting and animal husbandry are to work in close coordination for rational use of resources in drought areas. Wherever the projects are functioning the results are quite impressive and the beneficiaries are no doubt enjoying the benefits quickly. The watershed management is successful if all the resources optimally utilized.

References

1. Prakash Om, Sastry G. and Reddy Y.V.R., "Impact of Watershed Programme on Groundwater and Surface Water Development", Journal of Soil and Water Conservation, Vol. 3, No. 1&2, June 2004, pp. 1to 6.
2. Dharmarajan G., "Water Management" Kisan World, Vol. 30, No. 11, Nov. 2003, pp. 25-26.
3. Kalyanaraman. S., "National Waterways and Inter-linking Rivers of Bharat: A National Perspective", Kisan World Vol. 30. No. 1, Jan. 2003, pp. 32-35.
4. District Rural Development Agency, 2003-04 Report.

26

Tank Irrigation

M. V. Narasimha Sarma, G. B. Franklin and D. Kailasa Rao

Out of the five elements of the nature, water is the most important natural element supporting life on the earth. It stimulates the entire chain action and reaction in the life process. Water is consumed for basic human survival and development. Hence, tanks were variously managed largely following the principles of equity and justice in sharing these resources.

Tank irrigation is one of the important and oldest sources of irrigation in India. Rainwater-harvesting structures are popularly called as 'Tanks', which are small water reservoirs with earthen dams. Thus, tank irrigation is an age-old established practice in India, particularly in semi-arid zones of entire Southern India. Southern parts of India are noted for the intensity of tanks. There are about 127,000 tanks in the southern region consisting of Andhra Pradesh, Tamil Nadu and Karnataka states. Tank irrigation is also getting importance in other states. Tank irrigation is also getting importance in other states like Maharashtra, Gujarat, Rajasthan etc. However, over years, the area under tank irrigation has been declining and policy makers and planners are exploring the possibilities to revive the Tank Irrigation, as Tank Irrigation is the typical example of the water harvesting techniques, and are mostly managed by the local communities as common property resource. Budget constraints and poor community participation make the tank performance unsustainable. The immediate solution is to identify the appropriate investment strategies and make the local panchayats responsible for the operation and maintenance of the tanks. Resource mobilization by the local bodies is very essential.

Today, Andhra Pradesh has 82,500 such tanks irrigating more than 121 lakh acres directly.

Tanks have been an important source of water for irrigation purposes since ages. But in the last fifty years, there is a decline in tank irrigation especial in Andhra Pradesh. As it is traditional method, it has lot of importance because it facilitates irrigation and maintains the ground water level. As such the main focus of this paper is to whether the rural level institutions (Gram Panchayats) are taking it as one of an important activity which is essential for sustainable development of India. Besides this, the other objectives are:

1. To assess the activities taken by Gram Panchayats to preserve natural tanks.
2. To suggest suitable measures for preserving the natural tanks which are inevitable for agriculture development and environmental protection.

Tank Irrigation

A tank is a perfect example of a complete hydrological system in which inputs and outputs of material and energy can be readily identified. The geomorphologic conditions in semi arid upland are favored development of minor irrigation structures, particularly tank irrigation. Tank irrigation enabled the development appropriate situations which strengthened the social fabric in management of water resources. Restoration and rehabilitation of existing irrigational tanks is vital enough to restore the4 rural economy. Evolving appropriate methodology on restoration and management can lead into a sustainable development process. Today, the advantage is that most of the areas have existing structures and as such do not demand further capital investment.

Various studies on water management systems and subsequent interaction with growing communities provided valuable information on the deteriorating condition of rural economy. Though oldest in terms of structure and management, tank irrigation in India has fallen from a maximum of about 4.8 million ha in 1960-70, to less that 4 million ha in 1975-76. Out of a total 44-lakh hectares of irrigated land in Andhra Pradesh, 26 percent falls under tank irrigation. In some parts, it is 55 percent particularly in Telangana, Rayalaseema and upland areas of coastal region.

Four and half decades of social changes has had a definite impact on social structure and attitudes of people toward resource management. The education system has bypassed the traditional wisdom of resource management. There are several factors which caused the decline of tank irrigation in extent and reliability, especially in Andhra Pradesh. In the last forty years, focus, priority and investment shifted to major irrigation structures, and mega projects. Tank maintenance has been neglected.

The centralized management of the Government through Irrigation Department has decimated local management structure. Some tanks under local Panchayat bodies were not rehabilitated due to inadequate management resources. Farmer's participation has been reduced to mere tax or cess payers, which resulted in the erosion of sense of belonging among them towards their local resources. Successive governments have given extensive support to the development of individual irrigation sources through tube wells. Administratively, area under tank irrigation was rescheduled as under well irrigation. Tanks were also made redundant because of environmental degradation such as deforestation, overgrazing, soil erosion and siltation. In addition, changes in land use pattern particularly in the catchments zones of reservoirs, has aggravated soil erosion and subsequent siltation in tank beds. With the extension of rural agricultural community beyond the traditional sections, neo-farmers are yet to acquire proper agriculture and water management skills. With the growth of new agrarian society including small and marginal framers, and individual benefit schemes, the entire socio-political system underwent change resulting in a vacuum at the community leadership level.

In recent times, most of the tanks lost more than 50 percent of their water storage capacity either though siltation or damage to the bund, cumulatively, resulting in frequent flash floods.

Percolation mechanism was disturbed creating and overdraft of ground water resources. Water regulating devices were damaged due to erosion while water management committees failed to take proper care to harvest the available rainwater. Catchment area farmers' situation became more vulnerable than the command area farmers did. Shortage of water resources created conflicts among the small and marginal formers. In much of the area (almost 70%) only one crop is being raised, as is usually done under rain fed conditions. Agricultural labour, small and marginal farmers are hardest hit due to these conditions. More so, the victimized sections are women, who are left behind to struggle, while youth are faced with a directionless path.

Migration to nearby towns has been growing trend for the past one and half decade and is ever increasing. Census data for the decade 1980-90 reveals that in most of the district headquarters and towns, population growth has touched 45 percent which is attributed to the migration of these deprived sections from rural areas. Farmers, particularly small and marginal, have lost trust and faith in the system

However, in the past 10 years, several NGOs across the country have been striving to revive these traditional methods while taking cognizance of modern conditions. Even the government has taken up several projects across the country, independently and also has been implementing in collaboration with NGOs. Already several such localized management systems have been revived complete with physical and social mechanisms, in several places of India Notable among them are in Maharashtra, Rajasthan, Uttar Pradesh, Bihar, Karnataka and Andhra Pradesh. The state of Andhra Pradesh had declared 1993-94 as year of Minor Irrigation, recognizing the role of these mechanisms in the revival of environmental and ecological conditions in the villages.

Tank Irrigation System

The popular method of community-based maintenance system of tanks, existed historically, is disintegrated. Paucity of funds and meagre budgetary allocations in the past resulted in continued neglect of tank irrigation infrastructure in south India, which has equity and sustainability implications.

Tank water deficits occurs our 50% of the time period due to inadequate rainfall. Only 15% of the farms in the tank command own wells to provide supplemental source of water supply. Farms in tank commands in south India are predominantly small in size; 40% in less then 0.5 ha category, 60% in less than 1 ha size, and 80% in less than 2 ha size. Majority of the farms in the tank command being marginal holdings with tanks as the only source for irrigation and rural livelihood, deteriorating tank system has equity implications particularly in deficit rainfall situations. Currently, all 12351 minor irrigation sources taken together irrigate only 44% of the registered ayacut as against 82% in early 1950s. Loss in tank irrigated area has reached 1/4th of the net irrigated area in the state.

Similar evidences with tank irrigation systems are emerging in other major states. States of Andhra Pradesh, Tamil Nadu, Karnataka and Orissa, together accounting for 60% of the India's tank irrigated area have lost about 37% of the area irrigated by tanks during 1965-2000.

There is and urgent need for rehabilitating tank irrigation system infrastructure. Physical strengthening and improvements in the inflow, storage and distribution system are needed. Water users in tank commands need to be involved in planning and implementing the rehabilitation strategies. Tanks' performance as traditional water harvesting structures, conservation and recharging of ground water besides irrigation and several other ecological functions within the villages have to be restored and their maintenance sustained. In the light of the above, the main focus of this paper is to study the role of Gram Panchayats in the maintenance of tanks which are essential for the sustainable agriculture.

In the light of above, the main focus of the paper is to study the role of Gram Panchayats in the maintenance of tanks which plays a very important role for the sustainable agriculture.

This study is based on the opinion poll of Officials and Elected Representatives selected from 37 Gram Panchayats in 89 selected districts of Andhra Pradesh. Geographically, Andhra Pradesh is divided into three regions viz., Coastal Andhra, Rayalaseema and Telangana. Basing on the proportion of districts in these three regions, 3 districts were taken as sample from Andhra region, 2 districts from Rayalaseema region and 3 districts from Telangana region. Out of the sample districts, again 37 Gram Panchayats were selected by giving ample scope for notified and non-notified Gram Panchayats were selected for the study. Table 26.1 gives the sample districts and Gram Panchayats taken from different regions of Andhra Pradesh.

Statistical data has been collected through primary sources to know about the works done for maintaining the natural tanks in the states. In order to analyze the collected data simple statistical tools like percentages and chi-square test are also used.

Tanks Maintenance in Selected Villages

To know whether Gram Panchayats have taken up any kind of tank development, a query whether they ever took up any tank development was asked and the responses are presented in Table 26.2. The responses reveal that out of total respondents selected for study (246), 80.9 percent (199) responded negatively, where as 19.1 percent (47) responded positively. District-wise responses revels that majority of respondents i.e., 28 (70%) from Krishna district, 14 (82.4%) from Prkasam district, 36 (97.3%) from Srikakulam district, 27 (90.0%) from Anantapur district, 17 (56.7%) from Chittor district, 34 (91.2%) from Khammam district, 12 (57.1%) from Medak district and 31 (91.2%) from Mehboobnagar district expressed that they have not taken up Tank Development activities. The basic reason behind is that their financial position which did not allow then to take up the activities other than the routine functions of the Gram Panchayats.

In order to find our the opinion of officials and elected representatives about revenue sources for maintaining tanks in Gram Panchayats a query, whether the revenues sources are

Table 26.1: Sample Gram Panchayats of Different Districts in Andhra Pradesh

SI. No.	Region	District	Notified Grama Panchayatis	Non-Notified Grama Panchayatis
1.	Andhra	1.Krishna	1.Kanuru 2. Vuyyuru	1.Dosapadu 2. attubadipalem 3. Nibhanupudi
		2.Prakasm	1.anduvavaripalem 2. Mederametla	1.Gamallapalem 2. Maddipadu 3.Pellure
		3.Srikakulam	1.Narasannapet 2.Tekkali	1.Chapuram 2.Haripuram 3. Killipalem
2.	Rayalaseema	1.Anantapur	1.Gooty	1.Golla

		2.Chittoor	1.Putturu 2.Rachyapalyem	1.Basinikonda 2.Ellamandyam
3.	Telanganna	1.Khammam	1.Chunchupalli 2.Khanapuram	1.Sujatanagar 2.Vallabi 3.V.Venkataihpalem
		2.Medak	1.Esnapuram 2.Pothareddypalli	1.Pati 2.Kedavarapuveta 3.Gouraram
		3.Mahaboobanagar	1.Kothur 2.Shadnagar	1.Kandi 2.Prasanti nagar 3.Enugonda
	TOTAL	8	15	22

enough to take up the natural Tank maintenance was asked. The responses in the Table 26.2 reveals that 70.6 percent of respondents in the state (185 out of 262) said that the resources are not permitting to take up the activity, 14.1 percent did not respond (37) However, 15.3 percent (40) felt that there is scope for taking up the activities relating to tank maintenance.

On district wise breakup in Table 26.3 show that majority of respondents i.e., 63.4 percent (26) in Krishna district ,88,9 percent(16) in Prakasam district, 94.9 percent (37) from Srikakulam district, 87.1 percent(27)from Ananatapur district, 78.4 percent (29) from Khammam , 743 percent (26) from Mehboobnagar opined that their revenues are insufficient to take up this job. A majority of respondents i.e., 56.7 percent (17) from Chittor district felt that there is a scope to take up the tank maintenance activity. However, majority of respondents (13 out of 31) in Medak district did not respond to the question. These responses reveals that the revenues of Gram Panchayats are not enough to take up the tank maintenance activities because the revenues are not sufficient to carryout their routine activities

Suggestions

It is suggested that the Gram Panchayats would under take Tank Development activities such as removing salutation and strengthening of tank bunds so that the farming under the tank irrigation can be increased-will also fetch the revenue to Gram Panchayats by way of fish sales.

It is suggested that the tank maintenance should be also be included in activities under SGRY Programme.

As the tank area is reducing gradually due to various reasons, it may be suggested that the area should be preserved for tanks only and this area should not be given for plots or for any other purposes.

In order to sustain the under ground water it is suggested to convert the natural tanks in to percolation tank.

The most important step in the direction of finding solutions to issues of water and environmental conservation is to change

Table 26.2: District-Wise Responses of Officials and Elected Representatives to the Question Relating to Works Taken Up On Tank Development Activities

DISTRICT		Have you ever taken up Tank Development Activities?			Total
		No. Answer	Yes	No	
Krishna	Count	6	9	26	41
	% within District	14.6%	22.0%	63.4%	100.0%
	% within is the JGSY grant is sufficient to your village needs?	16.2%	22.5%	14.1%	15.6%

Prakasam	Count % within District % within is the JGSY grant is sufficient to your village needs?	1 5.6% 2.7%	1 5.6% 2.5%	16 88.9% 8.6%	18 100.o% 6.9%
Srikakulam	Count % within District % within is the JGSY grant is sufficient to your village needs?	2 5.1% 5.4%	-	37 94.9% 20.0%	39 100.0% 14.9%

Anantapur	Count	1	3	27	31
	% within District	3.2%	9.7%	87.1%	100.0%
	% within is the JGSY grant is sufficient to your village needs?	2.7%	7.5%	14.6%	11.5%
Chittoor	Count		17	13	30
	% within District	-	56.7%	43.3%	100.0%
	% within is the JGSY grant is sufficient to your village needs?		42.5%	7.0%	11.5%
Khammam	Count	5	3	29	37
	% within District	13.5%	8.1%	78.4%	100.0%
	% within is the JGSY grant is sufficient to your village needs?	13.5%	7.5%	15.7%	14.1%

Medak	Count	13	7	11	31
	% within District	41.9%	22.6%	35.5%	100.0%
	% within is the JGSY grant is sufficient to your village needs?	35.1%	17.5%	5.9%	11.8%
Mehboobnagar	Count	9	-	26	35
	% within District	25.7%		74.3%	100.0%
	% within is the JGSY grant is sufficient to your village needs?	24.3%		14.1%	13.4%

Total	Count % within District % within is the JGSY grant is sufficient to your village needs?	37 14.1% 100.0%	40 15.3% 100.0%	185 70.6 100.0%	262 100.0% 100.0%

*Chi-Square =95.150***,df=14*

Table 26.3: District-Wise Response of Officials and Elected Representatives on the Question About the Resources for Maintaining Irrigation Tanks

District		Do You think the Gram Panchayat revenues are sufficient to maintain the Tanks		
		Yes	No	Total
Krishna	Count	12	28	40
	% within District	30.0%	70.0%	100.0%
	% within is the JGSY grant is sufficient to your village needs?	25.5%	14.1%	16.3%
Prakasam	Count	3	14	17
	% within District	17.6%	82.4%	100.0
	% within is the JGSY grant is sufficient to your village needs?	6.4%	7.0%	6.9%
Srikakulam	Count	1	36	37

	% within District	2.7%	97.3%	100.0%
	% within is the JGSY grant is sufficient to your village needs?	2.1%	18.1%	15.0%
Anantapur	Count	3	27	30
	% within District	10.0%	90.0%	100.0%
	% within is the JGSY grant is sufficient to your village needs?	6.4%	13.6%	12.2%
Chittoor	Count	13	17	30
	% within District	43.3%	56.7%	100.0%
	% within is the JGSY grant is sufficient to your village needs?	27.7%	8.5%	12.2%
Khammam	Count	3	34	37
	% within District	8.1%	91.9%	100.0%

	% within is the JGSY grant is sufficient to your village needs?	6.4%	8.5%	15.0%
Medak	Count	9	12	21
	% within District	42.9%	57.1%	100.0%
	% within is the JGSY grant is sufficient to your village needs?	19.1%	6.0%	8.5%
Mahaboob Nagar	Count	3	31	34
	% within District	8.8%	91.2%	100.0%
	% within is the JGSY grant is sufficient to your village needs?	6.4%	15.6%	13.8%
Total	Count	47	199	246
	% within District	19.1%	80.9%	100.0%
	% within is the JGSY grant is sufficient to your village needs?	100.0%	100.0%	100.0%

people's attitudes and habits this includes each one of us. Conserve water because it is the right thing to do. As such it is suggested to form a group of water-conscious people and encourage friends and neighbors to be part of this group and promote water conservation through tanks.

27

Economics of Ground Water Management

G. Chandrasekar Rao and D. Krishnamoorthy

Ground water constitutes about 89 per cent of total fresh water resources in the planet. But in recent years in view of over exploitation of ground water, on the one hand, and scanty and erratic monsoons, there has been depletion of ground water to a great extent. Once upon a period, the towns and villages that used to be so marshy and wet for four to six months in a year have become so dry in these days. There are no sings of water stagnation even during the rainy season. The ground water level has been depleted to such an extent that it has become virtually impossible to restore the water table back. Even though there is a possibility of recharge of around water from the other areas, the process is very slow and it seems that it may take one year to replenish one meter. Koundouri (2004). In view of this management of ground water has become one of the most important issues in recent years. Added to it, there are also environmental problems such as aqua for mining, salt water intrusion, stream base flow reduction etc. For several reasons the efficient management of ground water resources through market mechanism has become very difficult. In recent years many economists have attempted to use many economic and econometric tools to analyse and solve the problems associated with the ground water management. In this paper and attempt is made to review the existing economic tools that are pressed into service to solve the problems associated with the ground water management and the difficulties involved in these tools.

Models for Ground Water Demand

Western countries are considered to be the forerunners in any aspect. In fixing price for ground water and in developing appropriate models explaining ground water demand, western countries particularly the United States is much ahead of eastern countries particularly India. Economics have developed broadly two types of models namely programming models and econometric models and have devised techniques for deriving willingness to pay and through 'Hedonic Valuation Technique and 'Contingency valuation technique'. A fuller understanding of these models and techniques would enable to fully appreciate the limitations of such models as well as problems involved in developing ground water pricing schemes.

Programming Models

Water being the public good, no observations are available on the wide range of prices needed for deriving demand for water and to estimate the elasticity coefficients. Accordingly, economists in recent years have leaned towards the use of 'shadow prices' derived from computer simulation techniques. For a given level of price, the economists estimate the profit maximizing level of output and the corresponding optimum level of demand for irrigation water. Gisser and Macado (1972) and Shunaway (1973) use linear programming approach to derive the demand functions. Others such as Howitt et al. (1980) Bernado et al, (1987) use positive non-linear programming which assumes that the cost of production is a quadratic function of acreage and incorporates the differential quality of land. These studies found very low classification In other words, the demand function was inelastic below the threshold price level. A major criticism of these models is that they ignore the impact of multiple applications of water for each crop.

Econometric Models

The econometric models use farm level microeconomic data sets to estimate the derived demand for ground water irrigation. These estimates rely on actual farmers' behaviors and are based on cross section data. Recent studies by Nieswiadomy (1988), Ogg and Gollehon (1989) provided empirical evidences on the price elasticity of demand for irrigation water. These studies have also brought out the effects pf water price on irrigation development, irrigation technology and irrigation technology demand Stabile et al. (1991). The general conclusion of these models is that farmers adapt rationally to water scarcity signals although estimated irrigation water demand curves are price inelastic. Moore et al. 19994b). The low price elasticity of demand for ground water irrigation might be attributed to the lack of data on crop level water use. These models may be efficient in explaining the short run behavior rather than the long run behavior of the farmers.

Hedonic Valuation Techniques

The quantity of ground water may affect the productivity of land as an input in agricultural production. The differences in prices and land rents determine the differences in the environmentally determined productivity differentials. Hence by using the data on land rent and land prices of properties, one can identify the contribution of each factor to the value of the traded good namely, land. This identifies an implicit or shadow price for quantity or even quality of ground water. The method commonly used in this process is known as 'hedonic technique. Guilloches (1971) first developed the principle of hedonic technique and later Rosen (1974) formalized it in a systematic manner. In recent years, King and Sinned (1988) attempted a study establishing a relationship between land prices and ground water access focusing on the quality of water. These studies emphasized valuing soil erosion and related effects on ground water use. The major finding of these studies is that value of ground water forms a significant proportion of 30% to 60% of land transaction prices. The principle of hedonic pricing of ground water assumes that there is perfectly completive marker for land and that both buyers and sellers are fully informed of the market conditions.

In recent years economists have developed the principle of Willingness to pay (WTP) to analyse the demand for common property resources including natural resources. This technique provides information about the control variables involved on the ground water use. It enables to derive and estimate the ground water demand if unction and problems involved in such an estimate. The price that the fully informed buyer pays for the land is the discounted value of the stream of future income flows. These assumptions seem to be unrealistic especially in developing countries.

The Contingency Valuation Technique

The ground water being of a nature of a public good, no value measures can be obtained from the choices that the farmers make in a market place. Under such a situation, a simulated market situation is created in which they are asked to express their willingness to pay for the existing or a potential environmental condition. This technique is known as contingency valuation method (CVM), being extensively used in environmental economics. It is just like asking the people directly how much they are willing to pay contingent on sue hypothetical change in the present state of safaris. Smith and Disgorges (1986) provide several applications of CVM to the measurement of water quality benefits. The main advantage of CVM is that it can potentially measure the economic benefits or damages consistent with the economic theory. Apart from the available goods and services, this method evaluates the proposed goods and services. However, in eliciting the information for the CVM, extreme care has to be taken in the preparation of questionnaire. The economic analysis of the data may also pose challenges.

Policy Instruments for Ground Water Management

Several policy measures can be pursued to effectively manage the ground water level. A tax on farmers, for instance, can restrain them from exploiting the ground water below certain desirable level. However, appropriate level of marginal tax rate has to be determined. A differential tax structure has to be created because of local differences in both monetary value of reserves and the vulnerability of the environment to changes in the ground water level. For instance, when tube wells are dug, taxes may be imposed depending on the deepness of the tube well dug. This is particularly relevant in Rayalaseema districts where farmers and households go up to 800 to 1000 feet.

Alternatively subsidies can be provided for ensuring a certain ground water level which is beyond the desirable level. But subsidies are not generally economically efficient and they can create distortions in the economy.

Another important instrument of ground water management is the introduction of markets for ground water. Tradable permits can be introduced and they can be traded in accordance with a set of rules and regulations. Though there are certain defects in this method, it helps to improve economic and technical efficiency.

Environment performance standards are to be introduced to the farmers to which they should comply with. There should be coercion from the public, along with providing technical assistance to persuade them.

Concluding Observations

Ground is a precious natural resource that the nature has given to human beings. This resource should be judiciously harnessed and utilized so that there will be sustainability. There are broadly four important economic models that prescribe tools for the efficient management of ground water. These models are Programming Models, econometric models, Hedonic Valuation Technique and contingency valuation method. There are many advantages and disadvantages in each method. Economists also suggest sacral policy measures such as taxes, subsidies etc., to effectively utilize the ground water level and to ensure sustainability. These policy measures are to be pursued at the earliest so that the further depletion of ground water level can be avoided particularly in the drought prone districts of Rayalaseema.

References

1. Koundouri, P. (2004), "Current Issues in the Economics of Ground Water Resources Management", Journal of Economic Surveys, Vol. 18., No.5, P. 704.
2. Gisser, M and Mercado, A. (1972), "Integration of the Agricultural Demand Functions for Water and the Hydrologic Model of the Pecos Bain", Water Resources Research, Vol. 8., No. 6, Pp. 1373-1384.
3. Shunaway, C. R. (1973), "Derive Demand for Irrigation Water: The California Aqueduct", South Western Journal of Agricultural Economics, Vol. 5, Pp.195-200; Howitt, R. E., Watson, W.D., and Adams, R. M. (1980), "A Revaluation of Price Elasticities for Irrigation Water", Water Resources Research, Vol. 16, Pp. 623-628.
4. Bernado, D.J., Whittlesey, N.K., Saxton, J.E., and Bassett, D.L. (1987), "An Irrigation Model for the Management of Limited Water Supplies", Western Journal of Agricultural Economics, Vol. 12, Pp.164-173.
5. Nieswiadomy, M. (1988), "Input Substitution in Irrigated Agriculture in the High Plains of Texas: 1970-80", Western Journal of Agricultural Economics, Vol. 13, Pp.70.
6. Ogg, C and Gollehon, N. (1989), "Western Irrigation Response to Pumping Costs: A Water Demand Analysis Using Climatic Regions", Water Resources Research, Vol. 25, Pp. 767-773.
7. Schaible, G. Kim, C and Whittlesy, N. (1991), "Water Conservation Potential from Irrigation Technology Transitions in the Pacific North West", Western Journal of Agricultural Economics, Vol. 16, Pp. 194-206.

28

Management of Rural Drinking Water

R. Kuruppa Swamy and C. Bhupathi

India is very rich in resources not only in human but also with natural resources. Even though, we are gifted with such rich resources, the nation is not in a position to utilize in an efficient and effective manner. The core resource which is like a lifeblood for our highly populated country, is drinking water. The future India is hanging in a big question mark of water sufficiency safe drinking water is necessary for a healthy life particularly in this polluted environment. An attempt has been made here to make an inner view in rural area about drinking water facilities with the following objectives.

a) To evaluate drinking water availability in India.
b) To analyze the status of rural drinking water scenario.
c) To examine the future requirement of drinking water.
d) To suggest remedial measures and appropriate technologies to overcome drinking water problems.

Declining Water Sources

The annual per capita availability of freshwater in 1951 was 5,177 cubic meters, which declined to 1,869 cubic meters in 2001. It is likely to fall further to 1,341 cubic meters in 2025 and in 2050, it will be 1,140 cubic meters. It is generally presumed that if per capital level falls to 1,000 cubic meters, it could seriously affect the health and economic activity of the entire country. At this level, water crisis will be seen in 25 percent of India's geographical area, affecting 21 percent of the total population. Already, 5.5 percent of the country's geographical area and 7.6

percent of the population are facing acute water storage, with availability less than 500 cubic meters.

Unrestricted exploitation of ground water has other manifestations. In West Bengal, almost 5,00,000 people are affected by arsenic through groundwater. Increased salinity in Gujarat, Haryana, Karnataka, Punjab, Rajas than and Tamil Nadu was well as high fluoride levels in peninsular India and western parts of the country affect nearly 14 million people. The solution lies in recharging of aquifers to stabilize the flow as well as arrest contamination. To check the depletion of groundwater aquifers, a regulatory mechanism needs to be created and rigorously implemented.

Rural Drinking Water Status

The National Water Policy (1987 and 2003) prioritizes mainly on meeting the drinking water needs. While the Global Water Supply and Sanitation Assessment Report – 2000 targets to reduce the proportion of people without having access to water supply to half by 2015 and provides access to water supply for all by 2005.The Indian Government has aimed at providing safe Water by 2004. Importance is given to non covered and quality affected habitations following which 'Partially Covered' habitations will be covered.

In India, the State Governments are responsible for providing drinking water facilities to rural areas. The Central Government provides financial assistance, policy guidance and technological support. Both the Central and State Governments have made huge investments through various programmes. The goal of providing adequate water has considerable been achieved in India. However, it does not commensurate with the huge investments made. Rs.320 billion has been invested on rural drinking water supply in the last 50 years, 86.9 percent of about 1.4 million rural habitations has been covered. 11.7 percent habitations are partially covered and 1.4 percent is yet to be covered. 15 percent are affected with quality problems like excess fluoride, arsenic, iron and nitrate contamination. 3.5 million hand pumps and 116 thousand pipe water supply schemes in different parts of the country has not been able to quench the thirst, particularly during the summer months. Added to this, service levels in this sector needs greater importance irrespective of the progress achieved.

Water Quality

Lack of reliable data, however, makes it difficult to appreciate the magnitude and impact of the crippling and incurable diseases like fluorosis and arsenical dermatitis. Fluoride contamination affects districts in 15 states and excess arsenic affects 8 districts of West Bengal. Fluoride levels are high in Andhra Pradesh, Gujarat, Haryana, Karnataka, Punjab, Rajasthan and Tamil Nadu. The number of Quality affected habitations with excess fluoride/ arsenic/ salinity/ iron etc., is about 1.54 lakh.

Towards following up the quality problems as cut lined, a large number of district water testing laboratories have been established in Panchayat Raj by the engineering department in different States under an elaborate action termed RGNDWM. In the present socio-economic condition, reaching the vast rural areas of the country with decentralized water quality- monitoring programme is an almost impossible task and the formidable problem is to bring water samples from the remote parts of the districts to the labs. Although samples may be collected and brought to the labs for examination, pooling them at one place for subsequent transportation is extremely difficult. Also, to collect and bring samples regularly for chemical/ bacteriological quality assessment has also been not easy because of storage problems.

Therefore, there is need for introducing simple bacteriological quality assessment tests such as the H2S Strip Test, which can be done by people themselves. Routing quality assessment (both chemical and bacteriological) can be done in the local field labs that may be established in school or PHCs.

Research studies in 144 countries by Esrey and Noodes (1992-93) show that interventions like Safe Disposal of Excreta; Household and personal hygiene, Quantity and Quality of water can make significant difference in the overall health and quality of life of people, especially that of children.

Recycling

The fourth path to a more secure water future lies in recycling. The dictum here is 'waste not, want not.' Terrace farming, practiced in many hillside communities throughout the world, may be the simplest example of effective water recycling and multiple uses. In terraced farming, water flowing from the higher terrain is not drained but is used to irrigate plants in the lower terrain.

Even wastewater or sewerage can be – and has been – processed and recycled for use. The reed-bed system, used in many countries, represents an eco-friendly way of treating polluted wastewater for reuse. Such diverse countries as Israel, Namibia, India, and Singapore practice recycling. Even when circumstances make it difficult to recycle wastewater, 'grey' water can be used to recharge groundwater, such practices help curb salinity levels, raise the water table in aquifers, and improve the ecological health of wetlands or sanctuaries.

Making Water Safe and Potable

Safe drinking water must be among the highest priorities for every nation on earth. Today contaminated water kills more people than cancer, AIDS, wars and accidents. It is vitally important that the water which human beings drink, be free from disease – causing germs and toxic chemicals that pose a threat to public health. Moreover, given that more than 80 percent of the world's population lives in developing countries, advanced technologies for making drinking water safe, should be developed.

Safe drinking water must be among the highest priorities for every nation on earth. Today contaminated water kills more people than cancer, AIDS, wars or accidents. It is vitally important that the water which human drink be free of disease-causing germs and toxic chemicals that pose a threat to public health. Moreover, given that more than 80 percent of the world's population lives in developing countries, technologies for making drinking water safe.

Successful Cases in India

The sprawling desert province of India Rajasthan offers one of the most successful efforts on harvesting and using water to meet community farming and family needs. We highlight it for two reasons. First, many areas in Central and West Asia have remarkably similar geo-climatic conditions to those in Saharan Africa, which makes the experience in Rajasthan both relevant and replicable. Second, which makes the experience showcases an example in which the 'technical solution of an urban engineer' – characterized by digging deeper borewells and using hand pumps – has been replaced by the 'commonsense' and 'rural wisdom' of local participants. Nongovernmental agencies recruited people from some 15 remote rural schools and 50 community centers located in dry or brackish water areas. After considerable interaction with and input from the villagers, more than 200 undergrounds tanks were constructed during the ensuing decade using local labourers and materials. The initiative, which employed 6,000 people, provided an additional 12 million litres of collected rainwater upon its completion. Maintenance problems, which plagued the piped-water and hand-pump system, are now few in number. These communal tanks and wells, moreover, serve as a meeting place for rural women who come there not only for water but for news, gossip and a guilt-free respite from their men and families. In eastern Rajasthan, a rain-fed land a nongovernmental organization, Tarun, Bharat Sangh, has helped local people build 4,500 check-dams and water-harvest facilities in 850 villages using local money and expertise. This effort has raised well levels 2 to 3 metres and turned seasonal rivulets and tributaries into perennial sources of water for some 100,000 people. In 2000, project leader Rajendra Singh, won the Ramon Magsaysay Award for his efforts.

Appropriate Technologies for Home Use

In isolated rural communities in developing countries and during emergencies, there should be access to rapid but reliable methods of purification that supply small volumes of water (10 to 1,000 litres). The systems should rely as much as possible on local labour and material. Use of alum, permanganate and chlorine tablets for quick purification is easy and practicable at the domestic level. A well-known and safe method practiced at homes in South Asia involves a mud-pot filtering system.

The top pot contains pre-washed gravel and sand through which raw water passes. The water exists through a hole in the bottom of the pot into a second pot kept below. The mouth of the second pot is covered with cloth filter while a crushed coal bed lies on a pad below, removing many toxins and germs from the water. Clean water exists through a hole in the bottom of the second pot and then is collected below in a third earthenware pot. The collection rate is slow, but it can be done overnight at a home so that clean, cool drinking water is available throughout the day. This method needs no electric power, filters or chemicals. As a result, maintenance costs are minimal, requiring only funds for the charcoal, gravel and sand that must e replaced every few days.

The Solar Classification Method

The solar disinfection method (or SODIS) is an easy, small-scale and cost effective technique for providing safe water at homes or in small communities. Water is filtered to remove the solids and particulate matter. The water is then moved into a throw-way, colorless and transparent bottle where it is kept in the sun for irradiation. To maximize the effectiveness of the process, the bottle should lie on the ground and its surface should be blackened to better absorb the light and generate heat. The combination of solar radiation and heat inactivates pathogens. The treated water can now be stored in a cool mud pot for drinking. This method has been successfully tested in Bolivia, Burkina Faso, China, Colombia, Indonesia, Thailand and Togo.6 In places where electric supply is available, filter cartridges (with or without irradiation) can be used either on stored or flow-through water supplies.

Various Schemes

In recent years, there have been two important developments in the implementation of rural water supply programmes in India; one, promotion of people's participation in implementation and maintenance of water supply sources and; two, decentralization process leading to involvement of many local organizations at the district level in manners.

Year	Programme
1954	Water Supply and Sanitation
1972 – 73	Accelerated Rural Water Supply Programme
1974 – 75	Minimum Needs Programme (ARWSP was withdrawn)
1977 – 78	ARWSP was reintroduced
1986	National Drinking Water Mission (NDWM)
1991	NDWM was renamed as Rajiv Gandhi Drinking Water Mission
1999	Sector Reforms Programme
2002	Swjaladhara

The Government of India has extended the sector reform package to all the districts in the country through a national programme of drinking water programme called 'Sawjaladhara' in 2003.

People's Participation

Field research has shown that stake holders are involved in Operation and Maintenance (O&M) only when they pay for it: when they are certain that they will control the funds, which are collected from O&M, and the water supply would be dependable. However, except in a few projects beneficiaries have not been made aware of the technology aspects or given the choice between different technologies and the right to know the details of expenditure on the project including user costs.

Conclusion

By effectively implementing the above-mentioned suggestions, we can reduce the drinking water scarcity is going to arise in near future. The government policy should be framed on such way of encouraging private participations in providing safe drinking water for every Indian, without providing safe drinking, we cannot ensure a healthy India. The prime objective should be preserving the existing water resources and rainwater harvesting along with planning of numerous trees throughout our home soil.

29

Issues in Interlinking of Rivers

B. Saranga Pani

The proposal of interlinking of rivers has been presented as a major initiative and the only answer to country's present and future needs. However several distinguished personalities including former civil servants, three former Secretaries of Ministry of Water Resource Management, noted environmentalists and hydrologists have expressed serious doubts about the necessity and feasibility of the interlinking of rivers.

Given the variability in the endowment of water resources in the country, transfer of water from the 'surplus' to the 'deficit' regions through interlinking of rivers seems very plausible and the proposal appealed to the common man. But it is interesting to examine the questions like why the project was proposed and how did it emerge and whether it is necessary and beneficial. The present paper is a modest attempt in that direction. The paper is divided into four parts. The introductory part presents the background. The second part critically examines the proposal. The third part presents some important issues relating to the peninsular component. The conclusions are presented in the fourth part.

Background

Dr. K.L.Rao mooted the idea of linking of Ganga with Cauvery in 1972. The proposal appealed to the general public and acquired an enduring life. However the proposal was examined and found impractical because of the huge financial costs involved and the very large energy requirements. In 1980 Captain D.Dastur put forwarded a scheme of linking peninsular rivers by a garland canal and also the Himalayan Rivers by another canal.

He further proposed to connect the Himalayan and Peninsular Components with two pipe lines one through Delhi and other through Patna. This proposal has also been found impractical on technical and financial grounds.

Subsequently the Government of India established a National Water Development Agency in 1982 to work out basin wise surpluses and deficits and to study possibilities of storage, links and transfers of water resources in between the basins. It was initially entrusted with the work of the peninsular component. The Himalayan component was entrusted to NWDA much later in 1991. The NWDA has identified 36 links based on topo-sheet studies-17 of them under the peninsular component and 19 under the Himalayan component.

The National Commission for Integrated Water Resources Development plan examined these proposals and in its report in September 1999 felt that there was no imperative necessity for massive water transfers. It was of the opinion that the assessed needs could be met from full development and efficient utilization of intra-basin resources except in the case of Cauvery and Vaigai basins. The commission was of the view that limited water transfer from Godavari at Itchampalli and Polavaram towards south would take care of the deficit in Cauvery and Vaigai basins. In this context it also felt that though surplus was available in Mahanadi, the transfer from that river would require much longer link and in any case was not required for the immediate future. It did not discuss the proposed Himalayan links in detail because the data are classified has confidential, but did observe that the costs involved and the environmental problems would be enormous; that the further expansion of irrigation in the desert areas of Rajasthan would need examination from all angels; that the Himalayan component would require more detailed study and that the actual implementation was unlikely to be undertaken in the immediate coming decades (lyer: 315-316).

The Government of India was not seriously thinking of any river linking project would be clear from the absence of any reference to it in the Ninth Plan; the Prime Minister's failure to mention any such initiative in his address to the National Water Resource Council on 1st April 2002; the Tenth Plan which has laid special emphasis on water is also silent on river linking. The non-project has suddenly become most important undertaking of the Government as a result of direction of the Supreme Court.

The Supreme Court order in this case was one of the last to be issued before the retirement of Chief Justice Kirpal. Justice Kirpal was reported to have said after his retirement that the Supreme Court pronouncement in this case was not really in the nature of an order. This is surprising to know. The PIL was about the linking of rivers; the SC asked the Government of India about the possibility; that Government made a cautious submission; the SC then asked the Government to accelerate the project. That sounds very much like a direction and it has been so taken by the Government. A Task Force has been constituted by the NDA Government not to examine the soundness and viability of the project but to workout the modalities of its implementation. The taskforce has been shelved after the new Government came to power at the centre.

The inter-basin transfer is not something new. Already there are several such inter-basin transfers. For example Kurnool – Cuddapah Canal (1863-1970) transfers water from Tungabhadra basin to Pennar basin. Similarly Periyar – Vaigai (1895) canal transfer water from Periyar basin to Vaigai basin. Rajasthan Canal (1958) transfers water from Beas – Sutlej to Rajasthan, which is outside the Indus System. Sarada Sahayak, Parambikulum-Aliyar, Beas – Sutlej Link, Ramaganga – Ganga Link, Teluguganga, Sutlej Yamuna link, Sardar Sarovar Canal, Nagarjunasagar RBC, Tungabhadra HLC and Sriramsagar's Kakatiya Canal all transfer water from one basin to the other. All the above inter-basin transfers have two common features. They are relatively short. They are confined to a single State, at least they were when executed (Reddy: 5-6).

Proposal at a Critical Glance

The river linking aims at bringing down spatial and temporal inequalities in the availability of water resource within the country and proposes to introduce a controlled water management system. However it violates the basic ecological principle the no component in nature is in excess and every drop of rain water place a vital role in the eco-system.

The proposal of interlinking of rivers is a simplistic supply side solution. This has been based on the existing paradigm of water management. According to this paradigm some river basins or sub-basins have to be identified as surplus ones from which water may be transferred to some others defined as deficit water basins. There has been a gradual shift in the paradigm of water management from the supply side to the demand side and to a holistic and trans-disciplinary approach to water management all over the world. (Bandyopadhyay and Perveen: 5309).

In order to assess the 'Surplus' in a river basin a simple exercise in arithmetic hydrology has been employed that externalized the whole set of ecosystem services provided by water in a river basin. From an eco-hydrological viewpoint, the same floodwater is seen as a source of free minerals for the enrichment of land, free recharge of ground water resources, a free medium for the transportation of fish and conservation of biological diversity.

The diversion of water has significant impacts on physical and chemical composition of the sediment of land, river morphology, aquatic bio diversity and the configuration of the delta etc. These impacts have serious economic and livelihood implications and these should from an integral part of benefit cost analysis of the proposal.

Interlinking is supposed to increase the irrigation potential by 35 million hectares and to provide food security to the growing millions. But Food security does not however depend on the proposed expansion of irrigation potential solely. There are several cost effective ways to achieve sustaining food security. China has only half of the arable land per capita. Yet it is not thinking in terms on increasing the volume of water in agriculture. Its emphasis is on increasing the water use efficiency in existing irrigation areas. China produces 13 percent more food grains per capita than India. According to the noted agricultural scientist Prof. M.S.Swaminathan 'the inefficient and negligent use of water in agriculture is one of the most serious barriers to sustainable expansion of agricultural production. Public policy regarding the cost of water supplied by major irrigation projects and low cost or free distribution of power for pumping underground water aggravate the problem...Water consumption can be reduced radically, by us much as five-to-ten fold, at the same time significantly increasing crop yields' (Swaminathan: 93).

Interlinking meets the large demands of water in the already irrigated areas. But whether such large demands should unquestionably be accepted and met through supply side solutions such as large dams or interlinking of rivers is a very important question to be examined carefully from various angles. In the context of prevailing low efficiency of water conveyance in canal system and water use in irrigation tracts, provision of more water will lead to its inefficient use and there will be no motivation for efficient and economic use of water. Is this desirable?

Interlinking of rivers is supposed to solve the problem of recurring floods and droughts. No scientific and technical data have been provided to support this claim. The transfer of water from one river basin to another river basin is no answer at all to the needs of un-served areas by rivers. The proposal is about transferring water from 'surplus' river basins to 'deficit' river basins but not about transferring water from river basins to river less areas i.e., to the uplands and dry lands. That is not the nature of the project. Hence it is no solution to the recurring droughts. The river linking proposes to take water to a small part of arid and drought prone areas and even after river linking, large parts of drought prone areas have to meet their needs through local water conservation.

Nine major dams have to be constructed with 19 canals to connect the Himalayan rivers while 27 dams and 30 link canals have to be executed to connect the peninsular rivers. There is adequate knowledge now of what all this entails: changes in river morphology and water quality, large scale submergence of forests and agricultural land, displacement of millions of people and the related problems of resettlement and rehabilitation, reduction of downstream flows, diminution of ground water recharging, reduction of fresh water outflows into the sea and their impact on aquatic life, riparian communities and their livelihoods etc. These are observed in many projects and will need to be studied carefully in the case of each of the proposed links. (lyer in River Linking: A Millennium Folly:16).

River linking is not necessary for meeting domestic water requirements. Domestic water requirements are small in terms of quantity when compared for irrigation requirements. According to the experts, domestic water requirements can be met if the precipitation available with respective water sheds or sub-basins are harvested and conserved properly. Thus local water conservation is a better option for this purpose.

The supply of domestic water needs is coastal India may soon become more economic through emerging technologies like water desalination. The costs of desalination technology are coming down. However, large inland urban areas like New Delhi and industrial towns may still need water through intra-basin transfers.

The estimated cost of the project is Rs. 5,60,000 crores. This amount is twice the revenues that the Central Government in a year currently earns or is about 10 times of the total expenditure incurred for the expansion of irrigation during the plan period. If we take into consideration the usual cost escalation, the ultimate cost of the project would exceed the GDP of the country and finding resources for the project may be very difficult.

The proposal envisages hydel power generation of 34000 MW additionally. Most of the links are in fact going to require huge amounts of power for construction and to lift water across natural barriers. The Ministry of Environment and Forests estimated that the proposal would need at least 35000 MW to lift water. It is thus unlikely that the proposal would entail any net generation of power.

The Peninsular Component

The Himalayan component is Himalayan in magnitude and is yet to be fully conceptualized. The peninsular component envisages the construction of three major reservoirs at Itchampalli and Polavaram on Godavari and at Manibhadra on Mahanadi. Table 29.1 shows the areas submerged by these three projects.

On grounds of submergence of large forest area, Itchampalli project has been rejected in the past. The dams submerge more people and more area in Maharashtra and Chattisgarh than in Andhra Pradesh.

On similar grounds a dam at Tikrapura on Mahanadi was not accepted. It is estimated that Manibhadra on Mahanadi submerges more area than Tikrapura. Polavaram dam also submerges large areas both in Orissa and Andhra Pradesh. It is not known how environmental clearance is going to be given for these three major projects.

Orissa and Andhra Pradesh have claimed that there is no surplus water in Mahanadi and Godavari respectively. How then it is possible to transfer water through Krishna, Pennar and Cauvery basins? The National Water Development Agency proposes to link Ganga to Mahanadi to over come the objections of the state of Orissa. Since there are doubts about prolonged surplus flows in Ganga, Bramhaputra is proposed to be linked to Ganga. But this requires constructions of large dams on Ganga and Bramhaputra. A large dam has to be constructed in Nepal and Bangladesh are required are required to transfer Ganga water to Mahanadi. How the Government of India proposes to tackle this issue is not known so far.

Peninsular component results in considerable loss in Hydel Power Generation in existing and future projects. The proposal results in loss of Hydel Generation at Itchampalli (900 MW) and Polavaram (720MW) since the entire Godavari surplus is

Table 29.1

Dam	Total areas are merged (ha)	Forest area submerged (ha)	Cultivated area submerged (ha)	No. of Villages affected	No. of people displaced
Manibhadra	63,003	9,828	32,621	218	79,000
Itchampalli	92,555	21,734	37,782	229	91,280
Polavaram	47,043	6,070	40,973	250	1,09,087
TOTAL	2,02,601	37,632	1,11,376	697	2,79,367

Note: The numbers in the above table are from project reports prepared in early 80s. The displaced people would now easily be 1½ time higher.

transferred either by lifting or by gravitation. Nagarjuna Sagar dam powerhouse (480 MW) and Srisailam Right Bank Power House (690 MW) will have little practice value. Once Polavaram is linked to Prakasam Barrage no water flows through Nagarjuna Sagar Dam Power House. The proposed Almatti – Pennar link also will effect power generation at Almatti, Jurala and Srisailam. Is this loss of power acceptable to Andhra Pradesh?

According to the experts inter-basin transfers on their own do not have any impact on floods. Detailed cost estimates of the peninsular component are not available. No insurmountable technological problems in inter-basins transfers are involved. India has sufficient expertise. But economic viability and need for such transfers has to be established clearly. According to the National Commission for Integrated Water Resource Development Plan, the shortages in Krishna, Pennar and Cauvery basins are really marginal and are not such that cannot be met by good intra-basin management. Thus, the need for long distance water transfer has to be categorically established. The National Water Development Agency failed to prepare a single acceptable detailed project report in its 20 years of existence. It work is largely confined to feasible studies. There is a long way to go before inter-basin transfers gain a modicum of acceptability.

Conclusion

Interlinking of river is still not a project, since none of the 30 links on 37 rivers is fully studied as yet, nor have any of the concerned, responsible ministries sanctioned the same. No study, pre-feasibility or feasibility study by the Task Force in ILR is made public till date, in spit of promises made at various for a by the officials and politicians. It is being pushed unscientifically. It is a project that would harm the river ecosystems enormously without providing a solution to the flood problem, as claimed. Linking of rivers is not the only solution to India's problems, as alternative, least destructive ways of harnessing water resources exist. In these circumstances the idea of interlinking of rivers has to examined from different angles. In examining the idea, an interdisciplinary approach with all environmental, ecological, economical, technical and human concerns has to be applied. The task of Environmental Impact Assessment should be entrusted to a truly Independent and professional organization. Projects which ensure least displacement and minimum environmental effect must only be selected. In order to ensure equity in the distribution of benefits, primacy should be given to the affected people conferring on them first rights towards the benefits of the project. While assessing the human concerns we have to adopt ' the risks and rights approach' as suggested by the World Commission on Dams. The interlinking of river must not create millions of development and environmental refugees.

With any major project, the state has to resolve four distinct types of conflicts. These are:

a) Compensation for resettlement and rehabilitation of the displaced.
b) Compensation for environmental damages from the displaced.
c) Sharing the benefits and costs of the projects among the states.
d) Cooperative management of the project in international river basins.

The capacity of the state based on past experience seems to be limited in resolving these conflicts. According to Singh who chaired the working group on inter-basin transfer of water of Ministry of Water Resources "there really seems to be no convincing argument or vital national interest, which can justify this mammoth undertaking (interlinking), in its entirety". One must not entirely rely on the supply sides solutions which either impinge in demands by others or cause serious damage to the nature. We have to realize that each new source of water is more expensive to develop than the previous one. Hence demand side management must become a new paradigm for the management of scarce water resource.

References

1. Bandyopadhyay. J and Perveen Sharma (2004), "Interlinking of River Waters in India - Assessing the Justifications", EPW, December 11.
2. Hangovan. M (2004), "Interlinking of Rivers in India", Mimeo.
3. Iyer Ramaswamy, R (2003), "Water–Perspectives, Issues, Concerns", Sage Publications, New Delhi.
4. Medha Patkar (2004), "River Linking: A Millennium Folly?" National Alliance of People's Movement.
5. Reddy.M.S. (2002), "Inter-Basin Water Transfer National Water Grid - The Reality", Dildar Hussain Memorial Lecture, The Institutions of Engineers, Hyderabad, Mimeo.
6. Singh, B (2003), "A Big Dream of Little Logic", The Hindustan Times, New Delhi, March 9.
7. Swaminadhan, M.S. (1999), "A Century of Hopes: Harmony with Nature and Freedom from Hunger", East West Books, Madras.
8. Venkataramana, P (2004), "Interlinking of Rivers: Are we Failing It?" Mimeo.

30

Watershed and the Development of Agriculture in Drought-Prone Areas

A. Ranga Reddy

Drought is a creeping disaster, which brings large scale starvation, mal-nutrition, shortage of food grains and jungle of unemployment. 63 per cent of cultivated are in India comes under the category of rainfed and contributes about 40 per cent of total output.

In these areas by introduction of productive programmes Government has made a significant drop in the poverty ration in the country from 55 percent in 1973 to 36 per cent in 1993 – 94 the absolute number f poor have, however, remained constant at around 320 million over the years. An acceleration in poverty alleviation is imperative to break this link between poverty and environment. Depletion of environment particularly in the tribal areas is largely attributable to the increasing biotic pressure on the fragile eco-system in the absence of adequate investments and appropriate practices to augment and conserve the land and water resources. Overtime tree coverage has been depleted, soil erosion has increase, ground water level has gone down and consequently the severity of drought has increased leading to ecological degeneration. A fairly comfortable level of water available per person in the early stages of development, however a significant decline has been noticed in the share of water availability over the years.

The per capita water has reduced from about 5277 m3 in the year 1955 to the present level in 1970 m3 in the year 19983. This shows that there s an urgent need for conserving and generating water resources at rural level, to meet farm ad family needs for the root cause of famine, Nobel laureate welfare economist Amartya

Sen identifies wide-spread failure of entitlement on the part of substantial section of the population as the main cause of famines. The present paper highlights the causes of drought, symptoms of droughts and impact of watershed over agriculture and allied areas.

Substantial areas of India periodically experienced droughts leading to considerable loss of agricultural production, livestock, besides causing misery to people inhabiting these areas. 54 districts in the country together with parts of another 18 districts contiguous to them were identified as drought prone

The Drought Prone Area Programme started in 1970-71 as Rural works programme, covering 12 percent of the country's population and nearly one-fifth of the area in the country labour intensive schemes such as medium and minor irrigation, road construction, soil conservation and afforestation were taken up under this programme. The main thrust of the programmes continued to be income generating and infrastructure oriented. Very lately Micro – watershed was considered to be the most scientific basis for optimum utilisation of available resources and maintaining ecological and environmental balance.

Causes of Droughts

It is widely believed that drought conditions in the country are increasing and ecological degradation is taking place unabated especially in drought prone and desert areas. The main reasons for this degradation is large scale denudation of forest cover leaving the land vulnerable to soil to wind and water erosion. Population growth and poverty on one hand and the pressure of raising demand from affluence and urbanization on the other have been exerting powerful pressure on the eco-system in the dry land areas. Ground water is being used at a faster rate than at which it is being re-charged. Further breakdown of traditional institutions for managing common property resources and the failure of new institutions to fill the vacuum have also been responsible for the mismanagement of natural resources. About 80 percent of India's cultivated lands id being slowly reduced to unproductive parched terrain due to wing and water erosion·

Sporadic Rainfall

There is an inter-relationship between rainfall and greenery, lesser the rainfall, lesser the greenery in any area. If rainfall is below 750 mm in any area, it is considered as drought prone area. In India, as rainfall is erratic and sporadic drought is found in one area or the other, some prolonged droughts leading to famines. The annual rainfall is an indicator to ascertain whether a particular region is drought prone or not.

Table 30.1 reveals that any geographical areas located in low rainfall zones both in North, South India. Rajasthan, Sourastra and Rayalaseema have a long history f droughts and famines because of low annual rainfall ranging from 311 mm to 738mm.

Falling Forest Area

Forests are considered as renewable and contribute substantially to the economic development and ecological balance. However the forest wealth is dwindling due to over exploitation, over grazing, unsustainable practices.

This decrease in forest wealth area is resulting in soil erosion, silting of irrigation dams. National forest policy 1988 stipulated a target of 33.0 per cent of geographical area. Decrease in rainfall and increase in earth's temperature etc., aggravating the situation in drought prone areas. Table 30.2 presents a bird's eye view of it.

Table 30.2 indicates that dense forest cover is on the decline in the country. This declining impact is felt in the climate conditions in the country. India experienced an unprecedented heat wave conditions for many days with maximum temperature produced further moisture stress in drought prone areas.

Growing Dark Areas

There is immediate need to arrest the extending drought prone areas in the country and this could be done only by conserving and judicial utilisation of water resources in these areas.

Table 30.1: Annual Rainfall

S.No.	Sub – Division	Normal 2		1994	1995	1996
		A	B	(a)	(a)	(a)
1.	Plains of West U.P	**859**	**947**	**753**	**781**	**1097**
2.	Haryana, Delhi, Chandigarh	575	761	891	949	953
3.	Rajasthan, West	311	393	398	381	447
4.	Rajasthan, East	658	705	889	775	886
5.	Sourastra, Kutch, Diu	552	584	776	352	502
6.	Marathwada	818	819	563	730	885
7.	Rayalaseema	686	738	683	920	1277
8.	North Interior Karnataka	704	872	845	756	766

Source: Central Statistical Office: Statistical Pocket Book, India 1997, pp. 254 - 75

A. Based on both India Meteorological Dept. observatory and state rain gauge date available during the period 1901 to 1970.

B. Based on India Meteorological Dept. observatory data available during the period 1901 to 1970.

Table 30.2: Forest Cover Estimates, 1981 – 97

Period	Total Forest Cover (Million .Ha)	Per cent of Geographic area	Per cent of area under	
			Dense forest	Open forest
1981 – 83	64.08	19.5	-	-
1985 – 87	63.88	19.4	59.1	40.2
1987 – 89	63.94	19.5	60.2	39.1
1989 – 91	63.94	19.5	60.2	39.1
1991 – 93	63.89	19.4	60.2	39.0
1993 – 95	63.34	19.3	58.0	41.3
1996 – 97	63.34	19.3	58.0	42.0

Forest cover is the sum of dense forest, open forest, plus mangroves forest (not shown).

Source: Government of India, Economic Survey 1998-99, p.157.

Further, the ground water potential should be periodically re-assessed by experts and its exploitation should be regulated with reference to recharge possibilities and consideration of social equality. The table provides a macro-picture of ground water exploitation among the Indian States.

Table 30.3 projects that the states and their level of ground water exploitation by farmers and reaching the point of dark areas. In Andhra Pradesh, certain areas of Karimnagar (7), Chittoor (3), Anantapur (3), Nalgonda (3) and Nizamabad (3) were found as dark areas. The number in brackets speaks number of Mandals in that District. Further over-exploited ground water Mandals are – Tirupati (Rural) in Chittoor District, Vempalli in Kadapa, Midajal in Mehboobnagar, Dugaondi in Warangal, Undrajavaram in West Godavari. Among all States, Punjab and Haryana were found to be over exploiting their ground water followed by Rajasthan and Tamilnadu.

Table 30.3: Categorisation of Block/Mandals/Taluks/Watersheds in India on the basis of Over Exploitation of Groundwater: 1998-99

S. No	States	No. of Districts	No. of Mandals/ Blocks/ Taluk/Watersheds	No. of Blocks/Mandals/Taluk/Watershed			
				No.	Percent	No.	Percent
1.	Andhra Pradesh	23	1104	6	0.54	24	2.17
2.	Bihar	42	585	-	-	1	0.17
3.	Gujarat	19	184	12	6.52	14	7.61
4.	Haryana	16	108	45	41.67		5.56
5.	Karnataka	19	175	6	3.43	12	6.86
6.	Kerala	14	154	-	-	1	0.65
7.	Madhya Pradesh	45	459	-	-	3	0.65
8.	Maharastra	30	1503	-	-	34	2.26
9.	Punjab	12	118	62	52.54	8	6.78

10.	Rajasthan	30	23	45	19.07	11	4.66
11.	Tamilnadu	21	384	54	14.06	43	11.20
12.	Uttar Pradesh	63	895	19	2.12	22	2.46

Source: Government of India, Ministry of Water Resources, Annual Report, 1998-99, p.74.

The fifty years experience in free India shows that every drop of water has to be conserved and distributed carefully to the productive areas like micro-watersheds, water harvests, check dams and drips. The other dimension of fragile natural resources was poverty, which is eating fabric of India.

Perpetuation of Poverty

In rural India, Poverty is the root cause for degradation and destruction of shrubs, herbs, mini forests, grazing lands, either for fuel, fibre, fodder and food. The wasteful use of excessive water, energy wood, brick, has further aggravated the situation. Many fertile areas are encroached by urban agglomerations. The following table gives a macro-picture of poverty levels both rural and urban among States.

Table 30.4 shows that rural ad urban poverty was drastically decreased in the states like Andhra Pradesh, Kerala, Punjab, Haryana, Tamilnadu and West Bengal, whereas other states were found to be waiting in the respect and in absolute population terms is still a major problem not only to the masses facing poverty but also to the environment and its resources.

Watershed: Concept and Objectives

An area drained by a river is thus the largest watershed, while micro-watersheds are those that are drained by rivulets or streams. Contour bunding planned around such watersheds help conserve water and soil, optimizing the use of water resources available in an area in the most economical way and make conventional irrigation systems based on large dams quite redundant. Linking agricultural intensification with soil and moisture conservation and institutional development has the potential to dramatically improve the managerial status of rainfall areas every where. It provides the necessary inter-ecological linkages and is a logical unit for sustainable use of land and water. It also has the advantage of biophysical, social and economic inputs, which if optimally managed, lead to diversified high agricultural

Table 30.4: Urban and Rural Poverty at State Level

S. No.	State	Rural (Percent)		Urban (Percent)	
		late 1950s	Early 1990s	late1950s	Early 1990s
1.	Andhra Pradesh	65.14	35.89	48.03	30.59
2.	Assam	39.92	49.33	15.53	11.95
3.	Bihar	64.52	63.20	60.26	42.39
4.	Jammu & Kashmir	37.53	31.20	33.09	14.01
5.	Karnataka	54.08	46.88	53.19	34.09
6.	Kerala	69.18	33.01	54.21	30.62
7.	Madhya Pradesh	56.68	49.79	47.63	38.17
8.	Maharastra	65.93	50.50	43.47	34.47
9.	Orissa	60.86	34.66	58.05	43.31
10.	Punjab & Haryana	31.24	20.64	36.51	13.64
11.	Rajasthan	46.36	45.79	45.18	29.50
12.	Tamilnadu	69.65	41.80	46.60	31.87

13.	Uttar Pradesh	47.38	41.72	59.44	39.35
14.	West Bengal	50.33	31.51	28.34	23.79

Note: Late 1950s refers to the average over 1957-58 to 1959-60;
Early 1990s to the average over 1990-91 to 1993-94.

Source: Gaurav Datt (1998), Poverty in India and Indian States - An Update, India Journal of Labour Economics, Vol. 41, No. 42.

production, control environmental degradation and for the recharge of ground water.

Aiming at holistic and sustainable development of vast rainfed areas an ensuring long-term food security, bridging regional disparity and employment opportunities for the rural poor, a National watershed Development project for Rainfed Areas (NWDPRA) was implemented during the Eighth plan (1992-97). The major components under the project include: treatment of arable and non-arable and land and drainage lines. For the Ninth Plan, NWDPRA has been restructured to include community oriented and participatory approach, higher degree of flexibility in choice of technology and resource allocation. It is linked with bankable programmes. During Ninth Plan it is targeted to treat 5 million hectares rainfed areas as against 4.3 million hectares covered during Eighth Plan.

The watershed management other objective was to conserve rain water and top soils with peoples participation. Animal husbandry, agro-forestry, horticulture, fisheries development, sericulture, agro-processing etc., are some of the diverse activities covered it. 2,621 Blocks have been identified in which a micro watershed of 500 to 5,000 hectares have been taken up for treatment. In all 2,554 micro watersheds with an area of 453.84 lakh hectare have been

According to M.S. Swaminathan watershed policy are to be linked with technology missions of pluses, oil seeds, and cotton, Further, he added that policy vacuum for sustainable use of natural resources, land use policy and precision faming

Paradigm of Watershed Development

Watershed development programme should be implemented with the cooperation and participation of beneficiaries. This can be ensured by having a watershed development team (WDT). The general body should consist of all adult members of watershed area. However, for operational convenience the WDT shall consist of 10 members of whom at least 5 shall be women. The representation to SCs and STs in the WDT shall be in proportion to their strength in the general body. It is also necessary to provide administrative and other support to the watershed team. The team shall be assisted by 2 persons comprising a village level extension officer drawn from Agricultural Development and another, preferably a matriculate educated village youth selected by the beneficiaries of micro-watershed with about 500 ha. Constitution of watershed team shall take effect six months previous to the commencement of the year. The functionaries shall undergo a multi-disciplinary training during the first three months and the rest of three months in survey and preparation of plan for implementation. It should be mandatory to make accounts public through the general body of the WDT.

It is decided to entrust 25 per cent of watersheds to the voluntary organisations (VOs) for implementation.

The main thrust in the Programme should be resource regeneration/conservation for sustainable development. The programmes have all the ingredients on resource inventory and management. Financial norms per hectare should be fixed so that the proportionate funding is allowed depending on the project. Rice, sugarcane and heavy duty crops should be strictly prohibited in these watershed areas. The ground water, in case of extreme drought should be only used for existing orchards, if any, and be fully diverted as drinking water. No heavy machinery that displaces labour should be used for desilting etc. It should be the policy of the WDT to maintain the structures created under the programme by handing over such assets to them. The pricing of electricity should be rationalised with a view to discourage over drawl of ground water.

Managerial Handicaps

Most of schemes taken up are of ad hoc nature and without due consideration of cost benefit ratios. There is an appropriate multi-disciplinary agency at the district, block and the watershed level to prepare integrated plans which could be taken up for implementation. Maintenance of the assets created has suffered, especially in respect of water harvesting structures. In several places beneficiaries were not motivated to assume responsibility for maintenance after the works are substantial. Moreover the concerned Departments do not have adequate provision for maintenance in their budgets.

Location Specific Crafts

Conservation of natural resources has to be made providing profitable by providing necessary infrastructure, technologies and institutional back up. Further, the socio-economic policies including pricing of inputs which reduce pressure on natural resources, augment such resources by arresting their depletion are going to be critical for protecting the environment. Policies in the non-agricultural sector in such areas will have a close bearing on the protection of the environment by reducing biotic pressure. Establishment of wool processing ad tanneries and ecologically vulnerable areas can raise the employment and income for local people and thus reduce nomadism and irrigation which will have favourable impact on environment. Development of crafts and other income earning opportunities will have the similar effect of reducing nomadisom. All this would require the development of infrastructure and research in the evolution of location specific technologies based on indigenous innovations including the tapping of solar and wind energy abundantly available in such areas.

Watershed Development in Andhra Pradesh

Under Vijayanagara rulers, the tanks and minor irrigation projects were popular and made a dent in farming. They are nor new to this concept, in the villages of Andhra Pradesh State. The state has made a four-year (1995 – 96 to 1998 – 99) watershed development plan. It has invested more than Rs. 3,000 crores in 4,239 watershed projects, covering 2.1 million hectares of land. Anna Hazare, a person behind Ralegau Siddu's success services was seriously taken. It is observed that earlier water table was at depth of 18 – 20 meters. Now they are at six meters, as in Anantapur District, Rainfall Deficiency 15 to 25 per cent, reduction in cropped area of 50 percent, normal reduction of crop yield f 50 per cent, dry spells and impact crop damage were the parameters of monitoring drought in the state. in short term remedy, employment schemes, health education and supply of medicine, re-scheduling loans, contingency agricultural action plan, supply of fodder and feed, transportation of potable water and morale building by filed visits and in long term. Watershed Development protecting forests, wasteland development complete irrigation projects, strengthening rural water supply infra linking rivers, were considered for complete removal of droughts on earth.

Evaluation

There is a severe criticism over it operation functioning that politicians and bureaucrats, have formed fictitious NGO's just to grab the projects is missing. Some influential people are taking contracts to develop watersheds. A whole set of non-governmental organisations are a part of the politician-bureaucrat nexus. In 1997, Chittoor District has shifted the DPAP funds of Rs. 2.25 crores to share capital of A.P. Dairy Development Corporation which is against the norms of DPAP. In 1997, 17 watersheds and in October, 25 watersheds were stopped in Kurnool District for lending capital. Andhra Pradesh is also one of the states that is not using the aerial photography and remote sensing methods in catching the advanced drought prone areas. Factionalism has also added fuel to fire in this area.

Conclusion

In overall, watershed of micro-nature at farm level and macro level at village were observed as a healthy remedy for chronic drought prone areas. It should be implemented as holistic approach by bringing farmers, bureaucrats politicians and Non – Governmental organisations at one point, inspite of umpteen hurdles. This is considered a low cost-high benefit scheme, which is to be propagated at grass root level farmers, especially marginal, small and tenant farmers, who are the lion-share holders of the farming society. Location specific crafts among farmers and non – farmers are to be encouraged, providing adequate infrastructure facilities to every village. Water, soil, fertility, green grass, grazing of lands have to be rejuvenated in every area and farming in particular.

References

1. Government of India: Ninth Five Year Plan, 1997-2002, New Delhi.
2. Government of India: Economic Survey, 1998- 99, p.13.
3. Government of India: Annual Report, 1998-99, Ministry of Water Resources, New Delhi, p.8.
4. Kartar Singh: Sustainable Development: Some Reflections, Indian Journal of Agricultural Economics, January- March, 1999, p.20.
5. The Hindu: Survey of the Environment, 1996, p.223.
6. Planning Commission: Report of the Technical Committee on Drought Prone Areas Programme, (Chairman: C.H.Hanumantha Rao), Government of India, New Delhi, 1994.
7. The Hindu: Survey of Environment 1996, p.223.
8. Government of India: Economic Survey, 1998-99, p.12.
9. Government of India: India 1998, p.310.
10. M.S.Swaminathan: Link Watershed Policy to Tech. Missions, The Economic Times, January 13, 2000.
11. S.M.Virmani: Watershed Management for Sustainable Farming, The Hindu, Survey of Indian Agriculture 1999, p.303.
12. The Hindu: Interface-Focus-Drought, Govt. of Andhra Pradesh, January 17, 2000, p.8.
13. Correspondent: Cyber Babu of Hyderabad, Down to Earth, Feb.15, 1999.
14. Manish Tiwari: Changing Colours, Down to Earth, June 15, 1999.
15. Telugu Newspaper: Distorted Development on Drought, Vaarttha, Dec.20, 1999.

31

Water Management Policies for Sustainable Development

M. Thyagaraju

Introduction

The emerging challenge to water management in the twenty-first century is how to achieve sustainable development in the face of continued expansion of population and economic activity and the pervasive problems of poverty and environmental degradation. In the arid and semi-arid regions of the developing world, water is already extremely scarce, but even in the sub-humid and humid zones, competition for readily - an available supply is strong and rapidly increasing. The time has passed when abundant supplies of water were readily available for development at low economic, social, and environmental cost. Now we are entering the period of the "maturing water economy", with increasing competition for access to fix supplies, a growing risk of water pollution, and sharply higher economic, social, and environmental cost of development. The shift is from a supply orientation to emphasis on demand management. These trends necessitate a new look at water policy, especially in developing countries.

No matter how effective existing water policies may have been in guiding water resources management over the past decades, they are not suitable for meeting the challenges of the maturing water economy of the future. Yet, the last comprehensive look at water policy for developing countries a recent resurgence of interest in the subject has included a study of water resources policy and management in addition, the world bank is currently undertaking in depth study of water resources programmes and policies in developing countries to provide a factual basis for revising bank policies, strategies, and programmes on water resources management. Finally, a United Nations Inter-secretariat group for water resources has been preparing a comprehensive report on a proposed water strategy for the next decade.

It present a framework for water policy for sustainable development, and shows how water policy is linked to policies in other sectors, including public finance, agriculture, energy, industry and commerce, health, human settlements, transport, and the environment. The intent is to identity the essential elements of a national water policy, while giving only incidental attention to what the content of that policy should be. This attempt may provide some insights to those concerned with formulating new or revised water policies for sustainable development.

Proposed Framework for Water Resources Policy

The term policy is used here to mean a general rule or guideline for decisions or actions in specific case. For example, a typical water resources allocation policy would be one that gives priority to domestic water uses in the event of a water shortage. Case-by-case decisions on water allocation would then be guided by this policy. Water policies may show up in various forms, constitutions, laws, administrative regulations, long-range plans and programmes, and budgets. Rarely are such policies neatly codified so that they can be readily identified. Therefore, formulation of the specific elements of a water policy is an essential prerequisite to an assessment of its adequacy and completeness. To this end, a framework for policy analysis is presented here, based on the interrelationship of the three systems.

The first of these, the natural water resources system, entails the hydrologic cycle, with its components of precipitation, evaporation, surface runoff, and groundwater flows, as well as the broader 'hydrologic continuum', defined by Leopold to include the soil, biota, and atmosphere as well as water. In the aggregate, this system is the water and water-related natural resources endowment (or 'supply') available for human uses.

The second is the human activity system which is composed of the many human activities that affect, or are affected by, the natural water resources system. At one extreme, as in the Nile Valley, people have extensively modified the natural system by constructing storage reservoirs, diversion works, and canals to meet their irrigation needs. At the other extreme, as in Bangladesh, those inhabiting the floodplains of major streams such as the Ganges and Brahmaputra rivers are at the mercy of natural forces. Between these extremes are works such as stream recession irrigation in West Africa. In the aggregate, these human activities comprise the 'demand' side for water uses such as irrigation, domestic water supply, waste disposal, navigation, hydroelectric power, fisheries, and recreation, and for reduction in damages from flooding, water pollution, and drought.

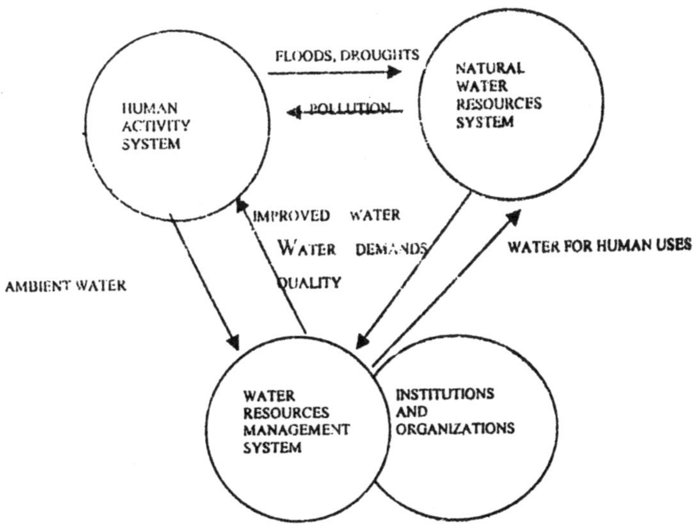

Proposed Framework for Water Resources Policy

Finally, the water resources management system embodies the activities and relationships in the public and private sectors concerned with harmonizing the supply and demand sides so as to achieve the objectives of the society. In this context, demand includes both uses for water such as for irrigation and domestic needs, and adverse impacts such as pollution arising from human activities, while supply also includes adverse impacts, such as natural floods and droughts, imposed by the water resources system on human activities. An essential support to the water resources management system is the institutional and organizational framework for management.

In the sections that follow, we will identify those elements of a national water policy that are relevant to each system. An effective water resources policy includes specific elements, which (a) preserve the integrity of the natural water resources system, and (b) provide water and water-related services to people in an economically efficient, equitable, environmentally sound, and sustainable manner.

Natural Water Resources System

Maintaining the integrity of the hydrologic continuum, as proposed by Leopold, is essential to the sustainable use of the natural water resources system. Policies concerned with achieving a scientific understanding of the hydrologic continuum and the use of such understanding in water resources assessment and planning, are relevant. Examples include:

1. Establishing and maintaining an effective national hydrologic data system; Coordinating this system with other specialized public and private data systems; establishing open access to these data bank systems; participating in a national geographic information system combining data series on land, water, and other resources; and promoting the highest scientific standards in all of these activities.
2. Sustained support for research on the natural water resources system and its linkages with other natural resources and the human activity system.

3. Adopting appropriate spatial units for water resources assessment and planning, such as the river basin or groundwater aquifer, so as to incorporate major land-water-ecosystem interactions.
4. Adopting conjunctive management of quantity and quality of surface water and groundwater to maintain the integrity of the hydrologic system and achieve efficient use of these water resources.
5. Managing water resources for multiple purposes in order to capture complementary and to reduce competition and identify trade-offs among uses in the natural water resources systems.
6. Integrating environmental impact assessment into water planning, including the effects of development on aquatic and terrestrial ecosystems, on humans and on the built environment.

Human Activity System

Polices of special relevance to the human activity system are those concerned with

a. Specific water demands for human activities, such as irrigation water for agriculture, potable water for domestic use, and water for industry, electric power generation, waste disposal, navigation, fisheries, and recreation;
b. Human adjustments to water-based natural hazards such as floods and droughts; and
c. Human-caused degradation of natural systems, such as pollution, sedimentation, and salinization. In general, these policies are concerned with influencing human activities so as to reduce adverse impacts on the natural water resources system and minimize economic and social losses natural hazards.

Demand for Water Services

1. Adopting demand management as an integral part of water management, including formulating and evaluating demand reduction methods and strategies as complements to and substitutes for supply augmentation projects, in order to bring projected demands for and supplies of water into balance.

2. Using prices as a tool for demand management, including volumetric pricing of supply or wastewater on the basis of marginal supply or disposal costs, along with increasing block rates. Where appropriate, seasonal pricing and temporary drought surcharges should be imposed.
3. Implementing efficient technical measures for curtailing urban water use and transmission losses in the supply system. This includes changes in plumbing codes to require water-saving plumbing fixtures, programmes of leak detection and control, and sustained operation and maintenance.
4. Opting for recycling and other technical means to reduce withdrawal rates for water for industry, especially for cooling.
5. Using technical means for controlling irrigation water use, including drip irrigation, sprinkler irrigation, land leveling, canal lining, along with institutional means such as modifying water rights systems to encourage efficient use of irrigation water.
6. Utilizing lower-grade water for certain domestic, commercial, industrial and agricultural purposes. The use of brackish water and treated wastewater for non-potable purposes often involves installation of dual water supply systems.

Human Adjustments to Floods and Droughts

1. Controlling human occupancy of flood-prone lands to minimize flood risks. This involves effective enforcement of regulations encouraging compatible land uses, such as recreational, agricultural, and some commercial uses, while restricting non-compatible uses.
2. Adopting a loss-minimization strategy for flood management, including flood-proofing structures and adopting flood insurance, flood warning systems, and evacuation and restoration plans.
3. Basing redevelopment programmes following flood disasters on risk-minimization land-use controls and management strategies. Public investments, and subsidies and controls on private investment for redevelopment, would be in accordance with such essential human adjustments.

4. Planning for human adjustments to drought based on specific rules for reducing water withdrawals to achieve efficient and equitable sharing of limited water resources, through pooling of available supplies, allocation to uses of the greatest social value, with appropriate compensation to losers.

Reduction of Pollution from Human Activities

1. Reducing generation of pollution at the source, through changes in production processes, by-product recovery, and wastewater reuse, making use of technical advice, regulation and enforcement, pricing policy, and tax incentives.
2. Adopting a polluter-pays policy, including the levy of effluent charges adequate to achieve desired reduction of pollutants, and earmarked to finance the clean-up costs of residual pollution.
3. Installing basic sanitation facilities in rural and low-income urban areas, including community involvement in planning and installing and maintaining low-cost facilities meeting minimum standards.
4. Reducing water pollution from agricultural, grazing, and forestry activities by lowering sedimentation from soil erosion, cutting down discharges of pesticides and fertilizers, and reducing the saline content of irrigation return flow. Tools that may be used are subsidies (where appropriate), removal, of perverse subsidies, changes in property rights, and tighter regulation of forestry activities, and enforceable stipulations on types and methods of application of agricultural chemicals.

Water Resources Management System

Policies relevant to water resources management are those that guide the planning and implementation of public and private programmes and strategies for harmonizing the supply of and demand for water to meet the efficiency, equity and sustainability objective s of society. Examples of such policies are:

1. Establishing unified national objective and priorities for water resources management, including setting guidelines for resolving the inevitable conflicts between national economic growth and

self-sufficiency, regional development, equitable income distribution and social impacts, environmental quality, and sustainability of the resource base.

2. Developing constructive international agreements on water management, which entails equitable sharing of benefits and costs of development /management of international river basins, and clear definition of rights and responsibilities of affected nations.

3. Guiding national investments in water resources development by means of capital investment budgets and programmes, national cost-sharing, international or bilateral grants and/or loans, cost-sharing by provincial, local, and private agencies, and private investment.

4. Adopting project formulation and evaluation criteria involving benefit-cost analysis, risk-assessment analysis, and multiple objective (including environmental impact) analysis to be used for project and program feasibility studies and monitoring and evaluation of performance.

5. Establishing a better balance between development the creation of new projects, such as dams and irrigation systems and management focusing on more efficient use of existing facilities.

6. Planning for involuntary resettlement from development projects, such as storage reservoirs, so as minimize economic and social dislocation, promote development opportunities, and mitigate adverse effects in an equitable manner.

7. Adopting workable approaches to deal with water conflicts that emphasize negotiation and mediation rather than confrontation.

8. Formulating procedures for allocation of water and waste assimilation capacity that take account of interdependency of water uses and the role of pricing policy. Alternative approaches via water markets with clear property rights versus allocation via planning; or some combination of these two.

9. Establishing standards on centralization versus decentralization of water planning and implementation; for example, reliance on a highly centralized national irrigation or power agency versus regional or local agencies.

10. Promoting public involvement /local participation in project planning and implementation, especially for irrigation, upstream watershed management, and rural and urban water supply and sanitation projects.
11. Providing for adequate funding of project operation and maintenance, example from user charges, especially for projects to be turned over to local water users for operation and maintenance.
12. Planning for effective monitoring and ex-post evaluation of projects.

Institutions and Organizations

Policies concerning national institutions and organizations provide an essential basis for effective water resources management. These policies are ordinarily incorporated in national legislation and the organizational structure of government.

1. Establishing a national water code, which may involve private ownership of surface water and ground water rights (riparian or prior appropriation), full government ownership, with rights to use (including limitations) granted by government, or mixed public-private rights to water use which recognize water as a collective good. The code should include a water rights system, which recognizes the hydrological realities of surface water - groundwater and return flow linkages, and the stochastic nature of precipitation and stream flows.
2. Formulating an approach to organization for water resources management, including integration of activities of different agencies at the planning and implementation stages, spatial integration by river basin, water resources demand region, or political jurisdiction, and division of responsibilities for water resources management among national, provincial, local public, and private sectors. The activities involve water allocation, regulation of use and abuse, development, preservation, and operation of water supply and treatment facilities.

Policy Overlaps

The preceding discussion on the major elements of a national water policy was without reference to the specific locus of these elements in the national governmental structure. In face, water resources management is typically divided among a number of governmental sectors. This means that water policies are not the exclusive domain of a water resources sector but overlap with other sectoral policies, as illustrated in figure. For example, in many countries, the ministry of agriculture has purview over irrigation, and many policies concerning this extremely important water use are established by this agency. Similarly, other water uses such as hydroelectric power and navigation is the policy domain of ministries of energy and transport. Urban and rural water supply and sanitation are often the concerns of the ministries of health and human settlements, while environmental agencies establish policies for water quality and preservation of natural aquatic ecosystems, and forestry agencies are often involved in watershed management activities, which have major repercussions on water resources. In addition, national macro-economic policies on finance and trade can have important impacts on water resources management.

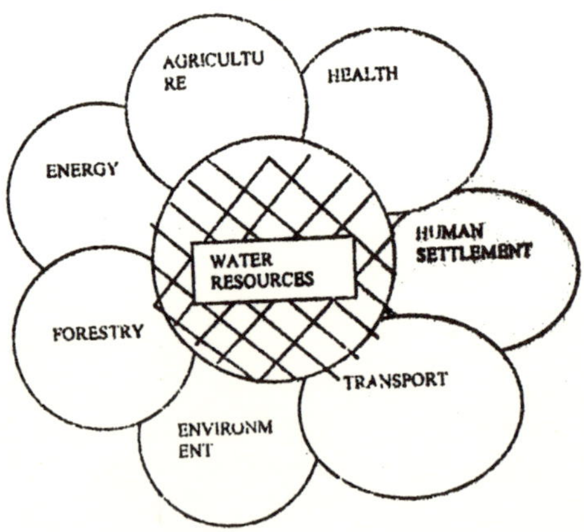

Policy Overlaps: Water Resources and Other National Sectors

The feature of policy overlap in water resources has been analyzing the links between water and other sectors of the economy, including those in agriculture, industry, transport, energy and health. In conceptual framework an overall national water policy entails

a. Policies covering the water resources, sector as a whole.

b. Policies relating to specific sub-sectors of water resources, such as potable water and irrigation, and

c. Policies concerned with other sectors (e.g. energy) that affect water resources.

In India, the sources of water may be classified as surface and sub-soil water. The major surface sources of water include rivers, dams, tanks, lakes etc., and sub-soil water sources include open dug wells, sallow tube wells, deep tube wells etc. It is interesting to mention about various rivers in India, which are very important sources of water at surface level. Rivers in India may be classified as (1) Himalayan Rivers, (ii) Peninsular Rivers, (iii) Coastal Rivers and (iv) rivers of the inland drainage basin. The Himalayan Rivers are perennial as they are generally snow-fed and have reasonable flow throughout the year. During the monsoon the Himalayas receive very heavy rainfall and rivers discharge the maximum quantity of water causing frequent floods. The peninsular rivers are generally rain fed and therefore fluctuate in volume. A large number of the streams are non-perennial. The coastal streams, especially on the west coast are short in length and have limited catchments areas. Most of them are flashy and non-perennial. The streams of the inland drainage basin western Rajasthan are few and far between. Most of them are of an ephemeral Character. They drain towards the individual basins or salt lakes like the Sambhar or are lost in the sands having no out let to the sea. The luni is the only river of this category that drains in to the Rann of Kach.

A basic tenant of India philosophy is that the external world of man, the world of materials and things are made up to five elements and man should restrain himself from interfering with these endowments. The five elements are earth, water air space and fire. It is too well known that man is not yet in a mood to respect this insight.

The environmental questions and the recognition of ecological demands, is a light in the right direction and sooner than later we may begin to see nature, that which is external to man and the one that is within him, in a friendlier manner.

The idea of sustainable use of water and its development, stems from this thought process. We submit that such a perception should govern all our activities and more so the ones recognized as earth, water, air space and fire.

Table 31.1 explains the annual requirement of fresh water for India in future. Conjunctive use of surface and groundwater is very essential to meet the growing future demand for water in India. Moreover, in future there will be grant pressure on surface water. Hence, sustainable development of water mostly depends on environment friendly management of surface water sources In India.

That contemporary water management experts advocate this idea of sustainable water management should not be difficult for Indians either to accept it or adopt it. To begin with sub-soil water exploitation schemes qualify most for sustainable development strategies. One has to emphasize the reversibility of relation ship between crop and sub-soil water. It is water availability that determines the choice of the crop and in the event of a conflict it is the crop that is changed and not the water resource or its supply augmentation.

Conclusion

Based on the framework presented here, the important elements of a water resources policy can be developed on a comprehensive and consistent basis for any specific use. Though our focus is national policies, the approach can be applied also to local, provincial, and international levels.

Table 31.1: Annual Requirement of Fresh Water in India

S.No	Different use s of water	2000 AD		2025 AD	
		Surface water	Ground water	Surface water	Ground water
1	Irrigation	420.00	210.00	510.00	260.00
2	Other uses	80.00	40.00	190.00	90.00
I	Domestic & Livestock*	32.85		46.00	
II	Industries*	30.00		120.00	
III	Thermal Power*	3.30		4.00	
IV	Miscellaneous*	53.85		110.00	

*Appropriate from both sources where applicable.
Sources: Central Water Commission.

References

1. Ali, M., Radosevich, G.E and Khan A.A (eds) 1987, "Water Resources Policy for Asia", A.A Balkema, Rotterdam.
2. Biswas, A.K. (ed) 1978, United Nations Water Conference - Summary and Main Documents, Pergamon Press, Oxford.
3. Leopold, L.B, 1990, "Ethos, Equity and the Water Resource', Environment, Vol. 32, No. 2, March, pp. 17-20; 37-42.
4. Munasinghe, M.1990, "Water Supply Policies and Issues in Developing Countries", Natural Resources Forum, Vol. 14, No.1, February, pp.33-48.
5. UNEP (United Nations Environment Programme), 1989, "Sustainable Water Development and Management", International Journal of Water Resources Development, Vol. 5, No. 4, December, pp. 225-51.